Turning Points

IN WORLD HISTORY

The Rise of the Soviet Union

Thomas Streissguth, *Book Editor*

Daniel Leone, *President*
Bonnie Szumski, *Publisher*
Scott Barbour, *Managing Editor*

Greenhaven Press, Inc., San Diego, California

Every effort has been made to trace the owners of copyrighted material. The articles in this volume may have been edited for content, length, and/or reading level. The titles have been changed to enhance the editorial purpose.

No part of this book may be reproduced or used in any form or by any means, electrical, mechanical, or otherwise, including, but not limited to, photocopy, recording, or any information storage and retrieval system, without prior written permission from the publisher.

Library of Congress Cataloging-in-Publication Data

The rise of the Soviet Union / Thomas Streissguth, book editor.
    p. cm. — (Turning points in world history)
    Includes bibliographical references and index.
    ISBN 0-7377-0928-6 (pbk. : alk. paper)—
ISBN 0-7377-0929-4 (lib. bdg. : alk. paper)
    1. Soviet Union—History. I. Streissguth, Thomas, 1958–
II. Turning points in world history (Greenhaven Press)

DK266 .R55 2002
947.084—dc21   2001040866

Cover photo: Novosti/Corbis
Library of Congress, 98

Printed in the U.S.A.

Contents

nally composed of four republics, the union would eventually include sixteen states under the control of the central government in Moscow.

Chapter 3: Building Socialism

though the Bolsheviks eventually put an end to the NEP, the economic recovery that resulted from it may have saved their regime from destruction.

Chapter 4: The Soviet Union and the World

Foreword

Certain past events stand out as pivotal, as having effects and outcomes that change the course of history. These events are often referred to as turning points. Historian Louis L. Snyder provides this useful definition:

> A turning point in history is an event, happening, or stage which thrusts the course of historical development into a different direction. By definition a turning point is a great event, but it is even more—a great event with the explosive impact of altering the trend of man's life on the planet.

History's turning points have taken many forms. Some were single, brief, and shattering events with immediate and obvious impact. The invasion of Britain by William the Conqueror in 1066, for example, swiftly transformed that land's political and social institutions and paved the way for the rise of the modern English nation. By contrast, other single events were deemed of minor significance when they occurred, only later recognized as turning points. The assassination of a little-known European nobleman, Archduke Franz Ferdinand, on June 28, 1914, in the Bosnian town of Sarajevo was such an event; only after it touched off a chain reaction of political-military crises that escalated into the global conflict known as World War I did the murder's true significance become evident.

Other crucial turning points occurred not in terms of a few hours, days, months, or even years, but instead as evolutionary developments spanning decades or even centuries. One of the most pivotal turning points in human history, for instance—the development of agriculture, which replaced nomadic hunter-gatherer societies with more permanent settlements—occurred over the course of many generations. Still other great turning points were neither events nor developments, but rather revolutionary new inventions and innovations that significantly altered social customs and ideas, military tactics, home life, the spread of knowledge, and the human condition in general. The developments of writing, gunpowder, the printing press, antibiotics, the electric light, atomic energy, television, and the computer, the last two of which have recently ushered in the world-altering information age, represent only some of these innovative turning points.

Each anthology in the Greenhaven Turning Points in World History series presents a group of essays chosen for their accessibility. The anthology's structure also enhances this accessibility. First, an introductory essay provides a general overview of the principal events and figures involved, placing the topic in its historical context. The essays that follow explore various aspects in more detail, some targeting political trends and consequences, others social, literary, cultural, and/or technological ramifications, and still others pivotal leaders and other influential figures. To aid the reader in choosing the material of immediate interest or need, each essay is introduced by a concise summary of the contributing writer's main themes and insights.

In addition, each volume contains extensive research tools, including a collection of excerpts from primary source documents pertaining to the historical events and figures under discussion. In the anthology on the French Revolution, for example, readers can examine the works of Rousseau, Voltaire, and other writers and thinkers whose championing of human rights helped fuel the French people's growing desire for liberty; the French *Declaration of the Rights of Man and Citizen*, presented to King Louis XVI by the French National Assembly on October 2, 1789; and eyewitness accounts of the attack on the royal palace and the horrors of the Reign of Terror. To guide students interested in pursuing further research on the subject, each volume features an extensive bibliography, which for easy access has been divided into separate sections by topic. Finally, a comprehensive index allows readers to scan and locate content efficiently. Each of the anthologies in the Greenhaven Turning Points in World History series provides students with a complete, detailed, and enlightening examination of a crucial historical watershed.

Introduction

Since the reign of the sixteenth-century monarch Ivan the Terrible, the Russian Empire ruled by the principle of divine right. The czars (emperors) of this vast state governed as they wished. The state punished dissent by torture, imprisonment, exile, and execution, and gave no voice to the Russian people in creating the laws and institutions that governed them. The roots of Russian absolutism lay in the country's long history of isolation and invasion: The adoption of the Eastern rites of Christianity in the tenth century divided Russian culture from that of Western Europe for nearly one thousand years, and the Mongol invasion of the thirteenth century had given the country over to the rule of harsh Tatar lords, who ruled by using Russian princes as their principal tools of collecting tribute and denouncing their enemies. The princes of Moscow eventually helped drive out the Tatars and then claimed the right to rule the entire Russian nation as "czar" (Caesar). In their governments, they largely followed the harsh methods of their former Tatar overlords.

Resistance to Russia's autocracy came sporadically. A "Decembrist Revolt" of army officers occurred in 1825 but accomplished very little. In 1861, Russia's serfs were freed, an event that led to the founding of revolutionary parties inspired by the writings of Western Europeans such as Karl Marx. The underground Russian socialist movement of the late nineteenth century established the Social Revolutionary Party, dedicated to the seizure of estates and the redistribution of the land to the peasants. The socialist parties gained followers from among young students and the small class of Russian intellectuals, but when Czar Alexander II was assassinated in 1881, the harsh reaction drove these scattered revolutionary groups underground.

One of these socialists, Vladimir Ilyich Ulyanov, known as Lenin, was banished to Siberia for his subversive activities.

Lenin's term of exile did not soften his determination to see the czar and the imperial government destroyed. After winning his freedom, Lenin moved to St. Petersburg, the Russian capital, where he worked part-time as a lawyer and full-time as a revolutionary. In 1900, Lenin moved out of the country to exile in Western Europe, where he dedicated his time to overthrowing the new czar, Nicholas II, and establishing a Communist state, a utopian nation of the future that would be dedicated to economic justice by and for the workers. Lenin believed he had found his blueprint for revolution in the works of Marx and Friedrich Engels and their book *The Communist Manifesto.*

Lenin wrote and worked tirelessly for the Russian Social Democratic Party, developing his own version of Marxist theory and adapting it as he saw fit to conditions within Russia. Lenin believed in the revolutionary elite, a vanguard of dedicated professionals who would lead the revolution and instruct the masses of workers and peasants in the goal of socialism. The elite would need to select precisely the right moment to overthrow the czar and, with the help of the masses, establish the subsequent socialist government, which was one step on the road to the ultimate goal of communism—the utopia of perfect equality and justice that would make organized government itself a thing of the past. At a meeting of the Social Democratic Party in 1903, Lenin established this revolutionary elite by splitting from a more moderate wing of the party and forming his own "Bolshevik" (majority) faction, which called for absolute obedience to Lenin's own ideas and a future one-party government.

Humiliation and Revolt

Russia's ambitions as a world power were buttressed by its reputation for military prowess, which it had won by the defeat of Napoléon and the French army in 1812. In the nineteenth century, the Russian Empire was the largest state in history, stretching south to the Black Sea and east to the deserts of Mongolia and the Pacific Ocean. But in the Far East, Russian ambition and military might encountered the empire of Japan, whose rulers sought control of the Pacific coastal islands and Manchuria, a vast region of mountain and desert lying between Russian Siberia and the empire of China.

The rivalry sparked war in 1904, a conflict that went badly for Russia. The czar's armies were soundly defeated in Manchuria, and the Russian fleet was annihilated by the Japanese at the Battle of Tsushima. Defeat in the Russo-Japanese War represented a complete humiliation for the czar and his officers, revealing that the Russian military had been completely unprepared for war against an enemy considered inferior in every way. The incompetence and corruption of the czar's government angered Russians, who had made hard sacrifices to support the war effort.

In 1905, in the aftermath of this defeat, a spontaneous revolution broke out in Russian cities. There were mutinies in the army and hundreds of strikes and demonstrations in Russian factories and streets. The uprising was put down by brute force, and its leaders were jailed or exiled. As disorganized and leaderless as the 1905 revolution turned out to be, however, it still had an important effect on the Russian socialists. As Orlando Figes, a historian of the Russian Revolution, points out,

> In the long run the Bolsheviks were the real victors of the 1905 Revolution. . . . It was only after 1905 that the rival wings of the Social Democratic movement emerged as two distinctive parties, each with its own political culture, system of ethics, philosophy and methods. Lenin's tactical shifts made all the difference. The basic tenets of the Bolshevik political philosophy had already been formed by 1903, but it was only after 1905, as Lenin digested the practical lessons of the failed revolution, that its unique strategic features began to emerge. Hence Lenin's reference, fifteen years later, to the 1905 Revolution as a "dress rehearsal" for the Bolshevik seizure of power.[1]

The czar realized that, to avoid future trouble, his government would have to make some concessions to those demanding a representative government. An assembly known as the Duma, which had once been an advisory council to the czar, was again allowed to meet. Hopeful Russians believed that this might be the first step on the road to representative government and that the country might achieve a peaceful transition to a figurehead monarchy and an elected assembly.

World War I

In the summer of 1914, trouble among the Balkan nations of Central Europe sparked a declaration of war, followed by four years of fighting by the great powers of Europe. Russia found itself drawn into World War I through a military alliance it had signed with Great Britain and France, nations that had ranged themselves against Germany and Austria-Hungary. On the war's distant eastern fronts, Russian armies found themselves outmaneuvered and outgunned by the Germans and stalemated against Austria. The war quickly developed into a futile slaughter of poorly trained, poorly clothed, and poorly fed Russian soldiers, and the string of defeats brought rising discontent on the home front. The corruption of the czarist government again came to light, highlighted by the military failures, and popular hatred for the imperial family focused on the foreign-born empress Alexandra and her companion, the sinister Siberian peasant and faith healer Rasputin.

In early 1917, food rationing in Russsian cities brought strikes and violent demonstrations. Although the government called out the troops, many Russian soldiers were unwilling to confront the demonstrators, and soon a mass revolt was taking place in Russia's main cities. In the renamed capital of Petrograd, revolutionary leaders founded a soviet (council) of elected deputies representing the city's workers and soldiers. The Petrograd Soviet formed a shadow government that gradually undermined the authority of the czar as well as the Russian Duma.

To the ministers and the czar, the situation appeared hopeless. Persuaded by his military leaders and prominent members of the Duma, Nicholas decided to abdicate in favor of his brother, Grand Duke Michael. When Michael refused the crown, the Russian monarchy came to an abrupt end. The national government was left in the hands of the Duma, with the Petrograd Soviet working alongside it, issuing directives, setting up committees, and calling on demonstrators to fight the soviet's enemies in the streets of the capital. When the Duma established a provisional government and attempted to quell the ongoing riots, the soviet responded with Order No. 1, demanding that Russian soldiers disobey their officers and form councils among themselves to carry out further demonstrations and organize mutinies.

The Return of Lenin

Sensing that the time for the Bolshevik revolution was fast approaching, Lenin prepared for his return to Russia. The German government, which saw him as the key to weakening Russia and forcing it out of the war, offered him money and transportation. In a sealed train, Lenin was transported across Germany to Finland and across the Russian border to Petrograd, where he arrived to the enthusiastic cheers of Bolshevik supporters in April 1917.

Lenin's iron will and mesmerizing speeches, and the Bolshevik insistence on Russia's withdrawal from the war, gained the party more followers in Petrograd. Slogans such as "Bread, Land, and Peace" fit the Russian mood perfectly, exhausted as the nation was by the bloodshed, food shortages, and general misery brought by the war. The rest of the nation shifted toward the Social Revolutionaries, and in May, after further demonstrations, a Social Revoutionary leader named Aleksandr Kerensky joined the provisional government as its war minister.

Challenged by the Petrograd Soviet, the provisional government's tenuous hold on the country deteriorated in July, when an offensive at the front failed. This time, the Bolsheviks were in position to take advantage of the discontent, and Bolshevik agitation sparked further riots in July. Lenin demanded a transfer of power to the local soviets, but he was forced to flee when the demonstrations fizzled out. Kerensky became the country's prime minister. Realizing that the Bolsheviks represented the most serious threat to the provisional government, Kerensky issued orders for Lenin's immediate arrest. The mission was foiled by Lenin's escape across the border to Finland.

The Bolsheviks won further support when General Lavr Kornilov marched his army on Petrograd in September to put down the unrest. Kornilov was stopped by armed workers and by mutiny within his ranks; instead of stopping the Bolsheviks, he had only won them further popular support. The Petrograd Soviet—particularly its Bolshevik members—played an important role in this victory for the ongoing revolution, and gained more followers in the city at the expense of the provisional government and the Duma. While the members of the Duma dithered and delayed the meeting of the Constituent Assembly, a Moscow Soviet was founded, placed in the hands of the Bolsheviks, and a Red Guard of Bolshevik fighters prepared under the leadership of Leon Trotsky.

Lenin knew that the weakening provisional government needed only a firm shove, applied at the precise moment, to fall into historical oblivion. On the night of November 6, 1917, that moment came. Lenin returned to Petrograd, and Red Guards began seizing telegraph and telephone stations, railway stations, government offices, and strategic crossroads. The Winter Palace, the headquarters of the Duma, was also attacked by Bolshevik soldiers, who occupied the building and arrested government ministers. This "October" Revolution (according to the old Russian calendar) left the Bolsheviks firmly in control, but they still faced resistance from other revolutionary factions as well as a counterrevolution from the White forces under Kornilov and other generals still loyal to the czar and the monarchy.

The Civil War

The Bolsheviks had their most difficult task ahead: The consolidation of power over a huge and chaotic nation where communication was poor and where—outside of most urban areas—Bolshevik opponents held control. Realizing that some concessions had to be made, Lenin agreed to hold elections to the Constituent Assembly. The Bolsheviks won 175 out of 707 seats, and about one-fourth of the popular vote, while the Social Revolutionaries held an absolute majority of 370. The assembly convened for the first time on

January 18, 1918, but as Lenin realized, such a representative body posed a dangerous challenge to Bolshevik power. When members returned to the assembly chamber after the first session, they found their way barred by troops loyal to the Bolsheviks, after which the Bolshevik-led Soviet of People's Commissars declared the assembly dissolved.

In effect, the Bolsheviks declared all revolutionary parties but their own illegal. Russia had fulfilled the Bolshevik dream of a one-party state. Renaming themselves the Communist Party, the Bolsheviks fought a long campaign to rid themselves of rivals and dissenters by jailing, exiling, or shooting Mensheviks, Social Revolutionaries, and anyone else considered a potential opponent of the Bolsheviks or a supporter of the old regime. A terror campaign managed by the Bolsheviks' new secret police force, known by the acronym Cheka, deployed a vast network of informers and operatives to stamp out and destroy all suspected counter-revolutionaries.

The Bolsheviks still had a vast country to conquer; they held only Petrograd, Moscow, and other western Russian cities, while the White (anti-Communist) armies held most of the countryside, Siberia, and southern Russia. In the meantime, Germany was advancing eastward, and the nations once subject to the Russian czar, including Finland, Poland, and the Baltic republics, declared their independence. The governments of Britain, France, and the United States, seeing the Bolshevik revolution as a threat to their own governments, landed troops at several Russian ports in support of the scattered White armies. To avoid a humiliating military defeat by Germany, Lenin decided to come to terms with the German government. In 1918 he agreed to the Treaty of Brest-Litovsk, in which Russia gave up a large swath of its western territory in exchange for a cease-fire.

The Bolsheviks had plenty of internal enemies to fight. But with Trotsky's tireless and stern leadership, the Red Army managed to beat off the White armies and keep their grip on the principal cities of western Russia. The Whites, meanwhile, could not manage to cooperate and coordinate their campaign. Nor could the Whites manage to gain enough popular support to erode the power of the Bolsheviks within Russia's cities. By the end of 1920, the last White army had fled Russia, and the Red Army could declare victory and an end to the civil war.

War Communism and the New Economic Policy

To fight this war, Lenin and the Bolsheviks had decreed policies of food requisitioning, the seizure of industries, and forced conscription into the Red Army. These policies of "war communism" put people throughout Russia in a desperate situation. Starvation, epidemics, and violent crime became the daily lot of millions of Russian civilians. Orlando Figes describes these conditions:

> By 1921 the whole population was living in patched-up clothes and shoes, cooking with broken kitchen utensils, drinking from cracked cups. Everyone needed something new. People set up stalls in the streets to sell or exchange their basic household goods, much as they do today in most of Russia's cities; flea-markets boomed; while "bagging" [bartering goods for food] to and from the countryside once again became a mass phenomenon.[2]

As Lenin realized, the dire state of postrevolutionary Russia seriously threatened Bolshevik control. There was widespread hostility to the Reds despite their defeat of the White armies, and famine was weakening their power base in the cities of western Russia. Industrial production was so low that the urban areas did not have sufficient goods to acquire food from the countryside. The forced requisitioning of food was unpopular in the countryside, and peasants were not even producing surplus food for market, as private markets had been banned by the Bolsheviks in 1920.

To solve these problems, Lenin decided to support a New Economic Policy in March 1921. Small businesses were allowed to operate privately, in contradiction to the socialist practice of public ownership of all production. A tax was placed on farmers, to be paid in goods; anything they produced over the taxed amount, they could sell on their own. The state also established semi-independent trusts to operate heavy industries, which were allowed to buy raw materials and sell finished goods on their own without the directives of central planning agencies. A new class of "Nepmen" came into being: middlemen who bought and sold privately, supplying consumer goods to the people and arranging the marketing of goods for businesses. The state returned enterprises that employed fewer than twenty workers to their former owners.

The New Economic Policy restored the Russian economy and also stabilized prices. Industrial production gradually improved, harvests increased, and the country managed to raise enough money to import needed machinery. But the plan also threatened Bolshevik control of Russia, and the more successful it became, the greater the opposition to it was among the highest echelons of the party. Fearing a loss of control and the end of their revolution, the Bolshevik government ended the privileges and the NEP experiment.

The Revolutionary Elite

Lenin prized party discipline above all. Each member of his Communist Party was supposed to carry out agreed-on policies and directives without question. Lenin put in place a clear chain of command, from the cells formed in individual businesses, schools, and other public organizations, up through city and regional committees, and then to the Congress of Soviets, which met each year to make important decisions on policy and the proper direction of the revolution. At the top, Communist leaders—all in thrall to Lenin—jockeyed for position and influence on the Central Committee of the Congress and the Politburo, the group of executive leaders who ran the party and made the most important appointments to party positions.

Instead of a state owned and operated by the workers, Russia saw the rise to power of a revolutionary elite, people who ruled with unquestioned authority in the style of the czars of old. The state banned any and all opposition journals and newspapers, made political activity among non-Bolsheviks illegal, and began a campaign against the Russian Orthodox Church. Church property was confiscated and turned over for the use of the party, and Orthodox priests were jailed. As a result, the church largely went underground. The millennia-old faith of the Russians in the Eastern Orthodox Church was replaced by a new faith in the doctrines of Lenin, Marx, and revolutionary socialism as it was interpreted and carried out at the highest levels. The new dogma of class warfare, pitting virtuous Russian workers against the vilified bourgeoisie, was disseminated by an obedient press and educational system, forming a new catechism for the Russian people.

A new "Soviet man" was in the making. The state used its power to identify its chosen enemies and to remold every citizen into the image of the revolutionary proletarian. Robert Service describes the process as follows:

> The authorities emphasized the need not only for literacy and numeracy but also for punctuality, conscientiousness at work and personal hygiene. The desirability of individual self-improvement was stressed; but so, too, was the goal of getting citizens to subordinate their personal interests to those of the general good as defined by the party. A transformation in social attitudes was deemed crucial. This would involve breaking people's adherence to the way they thought and acted not only in public life but also within the intimacy of the family.[3]

The Union of Soviet Socialist Republics, as it was christened by the constitution of 1922, resembled a vast military barracks, where every minute of the individual's life was strictly regulated and closely monitored. Willing or not, every citizen of the new state found himself or herself participating in the ongoing revolution, while the authorities suspiciously examined their work and their attitude for a lack of zeal in the common cause.

The Rise of Stalin

Exhausted by the years of endless work for the party and his revolution, Lenin suffered a series of strokes in the early 1920s that left him unable to write or speak. While the leader's health declined, his followers maneuvered to gain leadership of the Politburo and the Central Committee. One of the most skilled maneuverers was Joseph Stalin, a loyal Bolshevik from the region of Georgia who had served the party as a writer, recruiter, bank robber, and expert on Russia's ethnic nationalities.

Stalin saw Lenin's illness as an opportunity to consolidate his power in the highest party organizations. He had one serious hurdle to overcome: Lenin's own opinion of him. Before his death in January 1924, Lenin had written a "testament" in which he criticized Stalin for his "crudeness" and declared him unfit for party leadership. When the testament was read out at a meeting in April, just after Lenin's death, Stalin freely admitted his faults. His humble pose won support among several of the members present, including Lev Kamenev and Grigory Zinovyev, who turned aside a motion to expel Stalin from the party and with whom he formed a high-level triumvirate.

Stalin gradually strengthened his power by setting his opponents against each other and undermining them one by one. Kamenev, Zinovyev, and Trotsky were discredited and eventually fell from grace in the party and among the public. To further consolidate his hold on the country, Stalin began a campaign of collectivization in the late 1920s. Private farmers were driven onto collective farms, and Communist authority was enforced at gunpoint in the countryside. The collectivization drive was prepared by a "famine" announced by the government that, in fact, did not exist. The famine was blamed on wealthy farmers known as kulaks, who were accused of hoarding their food in order to get a higher price.

By 1929, the collectivization drive was in full swing, with the Communist Party doing its utmost to eliminate the kulaks as a social class. The result was a bitter struggle in the countryside between middle-class and poor peasants, egged on by local Communist cadres and backed up by the Red Army. Millions of deaths by violence and famine occurred over the next several years; many Russian peasants destroyed their equipment and slaughtered their animals rather than see their property fall into the hands of the local soviets.

The kolkhoz, or collective farm, gradually replaced the private farming estate, with much of its equipment and livestock expropriated from the kulaks. But because the most productive farmers had been either killed or sent to labor camps, and because so much equipment had been destroyed, Russian agriculture suffered a long-lasting downturn, aggravated by inefficiencies in the state-controlled distribution of seed, fertilizer, and harvested crops. Millions of farmers in Russia and Ukraine died of hunger in one of the world's most productive grain-growing regions, while Russia exported food in order to buy machinery for a crash program of industrialization. By the late 1930s, nearly every acre of Russian farmland was under collective management.

Catching Up with the West

Stalin's major goal was an industrialization program that would make the Soviet Union the equal of the Western industrial powers. To this end, the Soviet economy was put under the control of a Five-Year Plan, which ran from 1928 through 1932. The plan was created by a state planning commission known as Gosplan, which controlled a network of smaller planning ministries for each industrial sector. The plan emphasized the manufacture of basic industrial goods such as cement, steel, and chemicals, and the development of natural resources such as timber and coal. Immense steel plants were built in the Ural Mountains region, and coal mines were built in the Donets Basin of Ukraine. Hydropower stations on the southern rivers delivered electricity to new plants under construction in Ukraine, central Russia, and southern Siberia. Each Soviet republic had its targeted production for each commodity, and each enterprise had its stated production goal. Down to the individual worker, the plan and the goal defined and controlled all and held the force of law, the infringement of which could be deemed a criminal offense.

The emphasis on heavy industry, however, led Soviet manufacturers to neglect consumer goods. Furthermore, a basic flaw in the Soviet system soon became apparent to the ordinary Soviet worker: Goods were shoddy, made by workers concerned not with quality but with meeting production targets. The Soviet economy also proved extremely wasteful;

planners responsible for the distribution of goods shipped them throughout the vast nation with little or no regard for their demand in any particular locale. As a result, chronic shortages of some consumer goods developed in certain areas. The regime held prices low, without regard to the cost of materials or production. But chronic inefficiency caused constant shortages, and consumers could not buy goods at any prices.

The workers' state promised by the Bolsheviks proved a cruel disappointment to Soviet workers. While they labored long hours to meet their targets, they found their standard of living gradually falling as the pace of industrialization increased. Workers had little recourse because trade unions were under the control of Communist Party officials and served the party's interests. Any form of protest was considered an action against the state, since according to Communist philosophy, what was good for the government was good for the workers. The state which could do no wrong, made the strikes, sit-downs, slowdowns, and other forms of workers' protests that plagued capitalist countries illegal.

Stalin's industrialization campaign was carried out with the help of party propaganda, which exhorted workers to work harder and longer. The Stakhanovite campaign of 1935 used a Ukrainian miner, Stakhanov, as an example of enthusiastic work production; exceeding work goals was expected of all workers, and those who met these expectations were rewarded with benefits denied to ordinary workers, such as vacations, medals, mention in party newspapers and, occasionally, permission to travel abroad. Meanwhile, the ordinary worker who simply produced his fair share saw his wages hold steady while the government imposed strict control over his movements.

By the 1930s, Stalin's power had become absolute. His statements and decisions were not questioned by anyone; in the press and in Soviet publications, he was completely identified with the Soviet system and with the USSR as a state. The Soviet ideology had become a religion, and the doctrines of Lenin and Stalin were passed down as holy scripture. As David Satter, in his book *Age of Delirium*, puts it,

The Soviet Union was something new. It was the first state in history to be based explicitly on atheism, and it compensated for the missing absolute by endowing itself with the attributes of God. . . . What became important was not what was true but what could be made to appear to be true as the structure of factual reality was replaced with organized falsification so that real life might, if only after the fact, appear to conform to the Soviet ideology.[4]

Stalin saw many enemies among the people he led and within the party he professed to love. Despite his complete control over the huge nation, Stalin was a paranoid individual with a deep suspicion of those around him, especially those who had gained any authority or popularity of their own. Trotsky, his main enemy, had been driven into exile in 1929. Following his banishing of Trotsky, whom he held up as a traitor and enemy of the state, Stalin concentrated on former Mensheviks, Social Revolutionaries, and other members of the Bolshevik Party considered too moderate. The accusations of counterrevolution, sabotage, and Trotskyite opposition were leveled at longtime party members, including Kamenev and Zinovyev, the two men who had done the most to assure Stalin's rise to power. A network of informants was developed at the highest levels of the Communist Party, and opposition was snuffed out through show trials, imprisonment, confessions extracted through torture, and swift executions.

The Great Purge

Stalin saw one of his greatest threats in Sergei Kirov, a popular party leader in Leningrad who might have aspired to Stalin's role as a national party leader. On December 1, 1934, Kirov was assassinated at the Smolny Institute in Leningrad. After showing great emotion and sorrow in the wake of Kirov's death, Stalin used the murder as the justification for a bloody campaign against all remaining enemies, real or imagined, both within the party and among ordinary Soviet citizens.

The Great Purge that followed reached its height in 1936–1937 when every level of Soviet society was subjected to a terrifying campaign of intimidation. Ordinary citizens were arrested on the denunciations of their fellow workers, neighbors, or even family members. Friends and coworkers might be arrested as well, accused of criminal associations. At a spectacular show trial in 1938, Nikolai Bukharin and twenty other important party officials were accused of conspiring to expose Soviet secrets and return the USSR to a capitalist system. All were found guilty, and most were immediately executed. In many cases, however, authorities did not even bother with a trial.

In 1937, the purge extended to the military as well, which Stalin saw as a dire threat to his authority. Marshal Mikhayl Tukhachevsky, a hero of the Russian Civil War, was the most prominent victim executed as part of the Red Army purge, but the majority of high officers of the Red Army were either imprisoned or executed as well. Stalin mounted this attack on his own officers on the eve of another world war, which he surely saw was coming. Robert C. Tucker, in *Stalin in Power*, provides one possible explanation for the military purge:

> Those in the high command who looked to Tukhachevsky as their leader . . . belonged to the Bolshevik Civil War generation. . . . They were loyal Soviet soldiers but, especially in Tukhachevsky's case, men of independent mind and character who defended their viewpoints in high councils. Apart from the fact that three of [the high command] were Jews, this cohort of Bolshevik military professionals was strongly anti-Nazi in spite of its respect for German military prowess, and Stalin knew that it could not easily stomach the kind of accord with Hitler that he contemplated. . . . Finally, the Tukhachevsky command along with the military establishment that looked to it for leadership was, by its very existence, an obstacle to the totally autocratic new state that Stalin was forging.[5]

Stalin's purge of the military took place at a time when war again threatened Europe. The rise of the Nazi Party in Germany brought about the rapid buildup of Germany's army and navy, in defiance of the World War I treaties that had severely restricted the size of the German military. In the interest of weakening Soviet Russia, the Gestapo, the state police established by the Nazis, sought to cast suspicion on the most capable Red Army leaders. Cooperating fully with Stalin's NKVD, the Soviet police organization that was carrying out the arrests and executions, the Gestapo supplied confessions and incriminating evidence, which were presented at the trials of these leaders. As a result, the Nazis had the satisfaction of seeing Russia's army decapitated just as Germany was preparing for a war of conquest that would directly threaten the Soviet borders.

In the meantime, at Stalin's behest, the USSR wrote another constitution in 1936. This document declared the federation of eleven Soviet republics. Several "autonomous" republics and regions were also created as homelands for ethnic minorities within Russia itself. Control was concentrated in federal ministries in Moscow, although the separate republics were given some independence in the matters of culture, language, and education. A Supreme Soviet was formed to pass laws, but in effect this two-house legislature would serve as a rubber stamp for the edicts passed on to it by a smaller executive committee, the Presidium. Although elections were held, all candidates ran unopposed, and all were members of the Communist Party, which had a structure and organization that mirrored that of the constitutional government.

The real power within the Soviet Union had always lain with the party, and it was within the party that the average Soviet citizen had his or her only chance to rise to a position of influence. From an early age, students were indoctrinated in the history and functions of the party and given the revolutionary icon of Lenin to study and worship. The Komsomol, or Communist Youth League, accepted members from the age of nine and served as a preparation ground for future party functionaries. By the time of higher education, the student had learned one lesson particularly well: Advancement and opportunity came only with party membership, and following the official party line was essential to one's career and future.

Soviet culture followed the demands and needs of a pervasive and monolithic state. The party laid down strict guidelines for writers; banned art viewed as decadent, individualistic, or counterrevolutionary; closely monitored the work of scientists; and directed all creative activity to the glorification of the state and the Bolshevik revolution. Political dissent was completely stifled, as the government put forward dictates and slogans with the sole purpose of enhancing productivity and loyalty among the people. Lacking any means of dissent or creative opposition, the Soviet Union stagnated, its inefficient economy grinding down to a crawl and its people growing cynical, desperate, and finally resigned.

The Great Patriotic War

Realizing that Hitler's Germany—and possibly Japan—would eventually pose a serious threat to his nation, and that France and Great Britain would probably not be of much help in the coming war, Stalin attempted to hold off the inevitable by signing the German-Soviet Pact of August 1939. The two nations agreed to ten years of friendship and cooperation, and in a secret treaty protocol agreed to carve up Poland between them at the expected outbreak of war in Central Europe. The Soviet Union also received Germany's permission to occupy the Baltic republics of Latvia, Estonia, and Lithuania. In September, the Nazis duly invaded western Poland, completely unopposed by the Western European Allies, and World War II began.

The treaty with Germany bought the Soviet Union less time than Stalin might have hoped. After his conquest of Western Europe in 1940 and 1941, Hitler turned to the east. On June 21, 1941, Germany invaded its ertswhile ally, and the unprepared Soviet forces were thrown back hundreds of miles from the frontier; the Soviet air force was completely destroyed on the ground. As his armies reeled from the Nazi blitzkrieg, Stalin went into a state of shock, from which he did not recover for weeks. In the meantime, his advisers and ministers desperately tried to rally the Red Army, while millions of citizens fled eastward before the German advance. The villages and towns of western Russia and Ukraine were devastated by German planes, tanks, and infantry; the Baltic republics fell like dominoes as disorganized remnants of the Red Army retreated toward Leningrad. By the winter of

1942, the German army had reached the suburbs of both Leningrad and Moscow and was driving on the Volga River and the important industrial city of Stalingrad.

That bitterly cold winter, however, proved to be the turning point of World War II. German armies were stopped just west of Moscow and surrounded and defeated at Stalingrad. Although the Germans began a siege of Leningrad, and the majority of the city's population eventually perished from bombs, artillery, or starvation, this tactic failed in the end. On Stalin's orders, Soviet industrial plants were disassembled and moved to the east; workers were brought from Siberian labor camps and put on killing shifts to produce the needed military hardware.

Stalin's new allies—the United States, Britain, and France—found themselves occupied with their own all-out war with Germany in Western Europe. But the United States did provide assistance to the Soviet Union in the form of the Lend-Lease Program, in which essential ships, tanks, and artillery pieces were lent to Stalin's armies. Defeated by weather and by space, the German army was finally thrown back in 1944; late in the year, the Red Army drove into occupied Poland and then moved on to Germany itself. In the spring of 1945, the Red Army finally reached the German capital of Berlin. The war in Europe ended with Hitler's suicide on April 30, 1945, and Germany's surrender one week later.

In February 1945, with victory in sight, the Allies had met at Yalta, on the Crimea peninsula, to decide the future of Europe. Determined to establish the United Nations, an international diplomatic organization, and to get the Soviet Union involved in the war with Japan, U.S. president Franklin Roosevelt made important concessions at the conference, including the right of the Soviet Union to establish for itself a sphere of influence in Central Europe. The Allied powers allowed Stalin future control of Mongolia, naval bases at the Manchurian city known as Port Arthur, and the possession of territory along the Soviet Pacific coast that Japan had held since the end of the Russo-Japanese War in 1905.

As part of the agreement signed at Yalta, the Soviet Union did finally declare war on Japan, but not until August 8,

1945, two days after the destruction of the Japanese city of Hiroshima by a U.S. atomic bomb. Japan formally surrendered on September 2.

End of an Alliance

The end of the war also brought the end of the alliance between the Soviet Union and the Western powers. The Red Army, in its drive through Central Europe, had remained unopposed in Poland, Czechoslovakia, Hungary, Romania, and Bulgaria, and saw to it that, after the war, Communists friendly to the Soviet government held power in these once-independent nations. The Soviet Union saw this as a protective measure, intending to set up a buffer zone of friendly governments that would prevent another surprise like the German invasion of June 1941. As described by Prime Minister Winston Churchill of Great Britain, an "iron curtain" fell in Europe, dividing the nations allied with the United States from those in the Soviet sphere of influence. Germany itself was divided into four zones of control, each occupied by one of the Allies. Berlin, lying in the Soviet zone, was divided among the Allies; the Soviets occupied the eastern sector of that city.

As Europe slowly rebuilt from World War II, a cold war developed between the United States and the Soviet Union, the two world superpowers. The former allies competed for trade, military dominance, and allies among the nations of the world emerging from their old status as European colonies. In the foreground of the war were the respective leaders of the two countries, speaking out against the injustices in each other's nations. Sharing public consciousness were two growing arsenals of nuclear weapons, which threatened to engulf the world in yet another and more devastating world war.

The Communist Party had always seen itself locked in a struggle, with either class enemies within the nation or hostile invaders from without. In part, this sentiment had its roots deep in Russian history, and in the invasions that the nation had suffered from both east and west. From the Soviet government's viewpoint, the military and economic power of the United States after World War II posed a direct threat to the survival of the Soviet Union. These suspicions seemed confirmed by the abrupt end of the Lend-Lease Program, during a time when the Soviet Union was just starting to recover from the devastating impact of the war, which had left more than 20 million Soviet citizens dead. Soviet suspicions were reinforced by the military alliances of the postwar world, such as the North Atlantic Treaty Organization (NATO), which set up a powerful bloc of U.S.-allied nations in Western Europe, and the U.S.-created Marshall Plan, which extended aid to Europe and created a cordon of states friendly to the United States along the front lines of the U.S.-Soviet confrontation.

The death of Stalin in March 1953 left the Soviet Union with a vacuum at the topmost levels of the Communist Party. After so many years of totalitarian rule under Stalin, the Soviet government had no clear method for choosing a successor. A power struggle developed at the top among Georgi Malenkov, Vyacheslav Molotov, Nikita Khrushchev, and Lavrenti Beria. These four men had been favored by Stalin with appointments to top posts in the Soviet government. Leaders of a system deemed to be scientific and historically inevitable, they entered into Byzantine alliances, rivalries, and machinations whose outcome was far from clear for many years.

Historian Fred Coleman, writing in 1996, sees the death of Stalin as a far-reaching event that still affects Russian society:

> Stalin's death opened a power struggle in Russia that continues to this day. The great dictator held all political, economic, and military decision-making in his hands. With his death, on March 5, 1953, all his formidable power was up for grabs. Ambitious potential successors have maneuvered ever since to secure as much of that authority as possible for themselves. The result has been a permanent battle for the top leadership, with no holds barred. No elections, no constitutional guarantees, have yet made a difference in any of the worst political crises in Moscow since the Stalin era. Ultimately, only the effective use of brute force has been decisive. No other aspect of the Stalinist legacy is more ominous for the future.[6]

The post-Stalin infighting reached a climax with the arrest and execution of Lavrenti Beria in the fall of 1953. From this event emerged two powerful figures: Georgi Malenkov, titular head of state and of the party, and Nikita Khrushchev, appointed first secretary of the Central Committee. By 1958, Khrushchev's maneuvering of his own allies into important party positions enabled him to take undisputed control of the party and the nation. Although he had defeated several important rivals, he had also allowed them to live: a breakthrough that represented a very different style of leadership for the Soviet Union.

As time passed, Khrushchev distanced himself from Stalinist policies, and in a "secret speech" at the Twentieth Party Congress in February 1956 he touched off an ideological crisis by directly criticizing Stalin's purges and his "cult of personality." The excesses of the Stalinist age—the show trials, labor camps, forced collectivization, and summary executions—were laid bare for party members to examine, discuss, and criticize. A process of "destalinization" began in Communist parties around the world, which scrambled to keep up with the revolutionary changes taking place in Soviet ideology. To the despair of conservatives now referred to as "Stalinists," Khrushchev also decreed a cultural thaw for Soviet citizens. Previously banned writers were allowed to publish their books, and the forbidden subjects of political repression and labor camps saw the light of day for the first time in Soviet books and newspapers. The landmark event of the cultural thaw was the publication in 1962 of Aleksandr Solzhenitsyn's *One Day in the Life of Ivan Denisovich*, a depiction of the brutal life in a Siberian labor camp.

With his "secret speech" at the Twentieth Party Congress, Khrushchev unleashed a long and agonizing change within the Soviet Communist Party. But he intended much more: a sweeping reform of the Soviet economy through innovation in industry and agriculture. Planners were instructed to emphasize production of consumer goods over heavy industry; an ambitious program to grow corn in the arid plains of Central Asia was implemented; and the Soviet government allowed cultural and scientific exchanges with the West. Khrushchev also decreed a split between industrial and agricultural planning ministries in each republic and region, a direct blow to the power of entrenched Soviet bureaucrats.

Meanwhile, even as the cold war was reaching its height, Khrushchev was showing a friendlier face to the West. Following Lenin's original line—which was still the constant measure of integrity within the Soviet government—he also vowed that some day the Communist nations would surpass and "bury" the United States and its allies, which he believed would soon be discarding their outdated capitalist economies and multiparty political systems.

Stagnation and Confrontation

Khrushchev still saw the Soviet Union as a world power, as the leader in an international fight against Western decadence and imperialism. In Khrushchev's view, it was the Soviet Union's obligation to aid and abet revolutionary movements around the world, with the Communist ideology provided the guiding light for nations emerging from colonial exploitation. Soviet diplomats struck alliances with Egypt, Burma, India, and Afghanistan, all countries once under the control of Great Britain. Khrushchev also gave full support to the Cuban revolutionary Fidel Castro, who seized control of his island nation from a corrupt, U.S.-backed regime in 1959. The Soviet Union exchanged its grain and arms for Cuban sugar, and Castro was promised the full support of the Soviet military in any confrontation with the United States, which lay just ninety miles from Cuba's northern shore.

The Soviet-Cuban alliance brought the most frightening confrontation of the cold war in the fall of 1962, when a U.S. high-altitude spy plane spotted Soviet nuclear missiles on Cuban soil. Cuban Missile Crisis had begun, with the United States imposing a naval blockade on Cuba, and Khrushchev threatening direct action by his military to break it. Eventually, through a series of letters and secret communications, the superpowers narrowly avoided a nuclear confrontation. While the Soviet Union agreed to withdraw its missiles from Cuba, the United States agreed to disassemble nuclear weapons installed in Turkey, a NATO ally bordering the Soviet Union.

Within the Soviet Union, Khrushchev's peers saw the missile crisis as a defeat for Soviet prestige. Khrushchev's popularity declined, not only because of this event but also because of this event but also from the failure of reforms he had introduced in industry and agriculture. Inefficiency, low production, poor quality, and shortages continued to plague the economy, while Soviet defense spending grew increasingly burdensome. Eventually, Khrushchev's energy and stubbornness led to his downfall. Shaken up by his reform of the party and by his economic initiatives, his colleagues on the Presidium turned against him. A majority of Central Committee members aligned with his opponents and voted in favor of a resolution condemning, in part, Khrushchev's own "cult of personality." On October 14, 1964, he was quietly forced to resign all of his official posts. The government assigned him a modest dacha (villa) near Moscow, where he lived on a government pension, never to return to the Soviet government or to the service of the Communist Party. As one who had emerged from a bitter party struggle with his life and his freedom, however, Khrushchev was a symbol of the progress the Soviet Union had made since the days of Joseph Stalin.

Under the collective leadership of the first secretary of the Communist Party, Leonid Brezhnev, Soviet prime minister Alexei Kosygin, and Soviet president Nikolai Podgorny, the Communist Party and the Soviet Union returned to business as usual. The new regional ministries Khrushchev had created were abolished, and power was again concentrated in the central government in Moscow. Under Brezhnev, who emerged as the "first among equals," party bureaucrats and officials lived in comfort and privilege. They were allowed their own schools, shops, and vacation retreats; their children followed in their footsteps within the Soviet ministries and committees, and their class of *nomenklatura* formed a hereditary Soviet aristocracy.

Brezhnev led the fight against political reform outside the Soviet Union as well. Since the end of World War II, the Soviet-allied countries of Central Europe had formed a loyal front against the suspected ambitions of NATO and the United States. Under Soviet direction, the Communist governments of this region had signed the Warsaw Pact in 1955, which unified the various military commands under Soviet control. But these nations also had a history of democratic freedom that could not be completely overcome by treaties and directives from Moscow. In the spring of 1968, Czechoslovakia, under Communist Party first secretary Alexander Dubcek, began experimenting with a free press and open debate regarding socialism and economic policy. On August 20, Soviet tanks rolled into Prague, the Czech capital, and the campaign dubbed "communism with a human face" abruptly ended. The invasion of Czechoslovakia vividly illustrated the "Brezhnev Doctrine" to Communist governments in the rest of Europe and around the world: No deviations from one-party rule and the party line as determined by the Soviet government would be tolerated.

Despite its economic problems and the dissent that was growing in Central Europe, the Soviet Union remained a superpower. The Soviet space program, a leading symbol of progress and technology, was matching and in some areas surpassing that of the United States. The enormous Soviet nuclear arsenal was persuading U.S. leaders to come to the negotiating table in an effort to equalize the military chessboard. The newly independent nations of Asia and Africa were turning to Communist ideology for guidance and to the Soviet Union for arms and economic aid. With its enormous stretches of land and natural resources, the Soviet Union to many seemed the country of the future.

Yet in many ways the Soviet Union was still operating as it had in the 1920s. Gosplan was still drawing up its Five-Year Plans, and the central government still had control over the allocation of natural resources. Collectivization did not encourage new investment in agricultural equipment; the annual Soviet grain harvests continued to decline, and the country still had to import grain from the United States. Workers grew apathetic, and bureaucratic managers of state enterprises grew corrupt. Survival meant making deals outside the law and the plan, and a black market in machinery, raw materials, and consumer goods grew several times faster than the official, legal economy. Education, health care, infrastructure, and social services went into decline. The rigidity of the centrally planned economy proved ill suited to an era of rapid change and open global trade, which rewarded innovation and adaptability above all. While the standard of living within the Soviet Union stagnated, Brezhnev and the party promised that better times and true communism were just around the corner—just as the Western countries were enjoying sharp rises in their economic production, living standards, and health and education levels.

The Soviet Union's problems, both at home and abroad, multiplied. The policy of more open public debate, initiated by Nikita Khrushchev at the Twentieth Party Congress, was turning into a dangerous tide of dissent and criticism. As production fell and the economy continued to slide, the member republics increasingly went their own way, with leaders in the Baltics and in Central Asia coming under pressure from their own citizens to defy Moscow's directives, ignore the Five-Year Plans, and deviate from the official party lines. In 1979, the Soviet army invaded the Central Asian nation of Afghanistan to settle a civil war among several political and regional factions. Although it was intended as a quick intervention, the Afghan invasion turned into a full-scale war, with Soviet forces fighting ineffectively against well-armed and tenacious guerrillas operating in the rugged Afghan mountains.

In the midst of the Afghan debacle, Leonid Brezhnev died, on November 10, 1982. Brezhnev's successor, former KGB chief Yuri Andropov, could do little to stop the country's disintegration. Andropov's campaign to root out corruption and bring a stop to absenteeism and alcoholism—which he blamed for the nation's economic troubles—failed, cut short by his death on February 9, 1984. Andropov's successor, Konstantin Chernenko—already terminally ill when he took power that spring—proved similarly unable to arrest the Soviet Union's decline.

Gorbachev

Mikhail Gorbachev succeeded Chernenko on the latter's death in early 1985. A young and loyal party official from

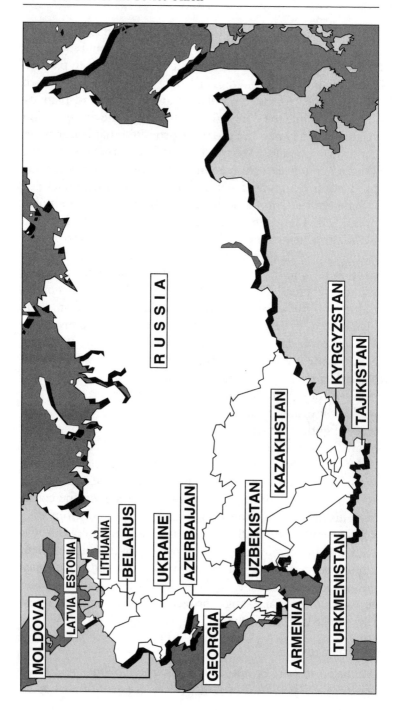

Stavropol, in southern Russia, Gorbachev attacked the Soviet Union's many problems with zeal and optimism. He quickly attached two bywords to his remaking of the Soviet system: glasnost (openness), which would permit criticism of the system and its shortcomings, and perestroika (restructuring), which would allow larger family farming plots and private business cooperatives but keep large enterprises and natural resources in the hands of the state. Gorbachev promised a free press, closer relations with the West, and an end to corruption accompanied by accountability for Soviet officials and the *nomenklatura*. He also brought the popular Boris Yeltsin to Moscow to clean up the capital's inefficient and corrupt party organization.

The "revolution from above" was the most ambitious reform program yet undertaken, but Gorbachev never looked on Soviet central planning or communism itself as institutions in need of reform. Instead, his intent was to renew and fulfill the workers' utopia once promised by Lenin but never realized by Lenin's successors. As Fred Coleman writes,

> Communist leaders kept their system going long after it should have been pronounced clinically dead. They did so partly to maintain their privileged positions and partly in the hope that somehow the system could be reformed, improved, and ultimately saved. . . . Soviet officials believed their system was worth saving, if only they could figure out how. To some the answer was reform. To others the answer was to resist all reform.[7]

Unfortunately for Gorbachev, the forces that would tear the Soviet Union apart had been gaining strength for many years and could not be stopped by his well-meaning, half-hearted measures. As the economy failed to respond to perestroika, furious debates broke out between "moderate" and "conservative" elements within the Communist Party, each contesting control of the Soviet republics and the autonomous regions. Gorbachev's decision to allow open elections to the national legislature hastened the process of political disintegration, as did the ousting of the energetic and popular party boss Boris Yeltsin from his posts in November 1987. Yeltsin quickly became the focal point of opposition to the failed perestroika campaign, to the privileges of Communist Party officials, and to Gorbachev himself.

In response to opposition, Gorbachev passed a sweeping reform of the highest echelons of Soviet government, remaking the executive branch in the constitutional images of the United States and nations of Western Europe. The Soviet Union established the offices of president and vice president and adopted a cabinet of ministers who would report to the president. A new constitutional article passed in 1990 ended the monopoly of the Communist Party in favor of a multiparty state. In direct opposition to the old Bolshevik ideal of government by a disciplined revolutionary elite, this measure was designed to bring about more democratic politics, but instead it accelerated the sharp decline of Gorbachev's authority and popularity. In the meantime, the more radical reformers were leaving the party altogether, following Boris Yeltsin in establishing a totally independent Russian parliament. Independence movements were gaining strength in other Soviet republics as well, while the authority of the national government and the Communist Party was slipping. Demonstrations in the republic of Georgia and in the Baltics led to bloody confrontations; meanwhile, Communist governments were falling in Central Europe. Eventually, Gorbachev ordered the withdrawal of Soviet troops from Europe; the Warsaw Pact, which had been established in 1955 in response to the formation of NATO, promptly collapsed.

The result of Gorbachev's reforms appeared to be the complete opposite of his intention to revive the Communist state and the centrally planned economy. Seeing their power and privileges sliding away, the leaders of the Soviet army, the KGB, and the party itself turned against Gorbachev. In August 1991, on the eve of the signing of a new union treaty that would have given the Soviet republics more independence, Vice President Gennady Yenayev and KGB head Vladimir Kryuchkov staged a coup in Moscow, declaring that Gorbachev had resigned for reasons of poor health. While Gorbachev was being held under house arrest, Boris Yeltsin organized resistance to the coup from the front steps of the

Russian parliament building in Moscow. When opponents gathered on the streets of Moscow and within the Soviet military, the coup collapsed and its leaders were arrested.

The coup attempt had failed, and instead of reviving Soviet power it now brought about the state's rapid disintegration. One by one, the Soviet republics, including Russia, declared their independence from the Soviet government. On December 8, 1991, Russia, Ukraine, and Belarus declared the founding of the Commonwealth of Independent States, a new state that eight other former republics would join. On December 25, Gorbachev resigned, and by the end of the year the Soviet Union had ceased to exist. Russia took over the Soviet Union's seat in the United Nations, and Russian diplomats replaced the Soviet officials in embassies around the world. Although the decline had taken place over many years, the final collapse happened with stunning swiftness.

The workers' utopia dreamed of and promised by Lenin turned out to be a failure. Although his revolution was probably the single most important event of the twentieth century, by the end of that century it had been completely swept away. Russia and the former Soviet republics continue to struggle with faltering economies, corruption, declining health standards, and sharply stratified societies, legacies of the revolution that was supposed to bring their people to a bright, happy, and egalitarian future.

Notes

1. Orlando Figes, *A People's Tragedy: A History of the Russian Revolution*. New York: Viking, 1997, p. 210.

2. Figes, *A People's Tragedy*, p. 770.

3. Robert Service, *A History of Twentieth-Century Russia*. Cambridge, MA: Harvard University Press, 1998, p. 143.

4. David Satter, *Age of Delirium: The Decline and Fall of the Soviet Union*. New York: Alfred A. Knopf, p. xv.

5. Robert C. Tucker, *Stalin in Power: The Revolution from Above, 1928–1941*. New York: W.W. Norton, p. 379.

6. Fred Coleman, *The Decline and Fall of the Soviet Empire: Forty Years That Shook the World from Stalin to Yeltsin*. New York: St. Martin's, 1996, p. 31.

7. Coleman, *The Decline and Fall of the Soviet Empire*, p. 47.

Chapter 1

The Revolution and Its Aftermath

The Course of the Russian Revolution

J.N. Westwood

Protests against the czarist political and economic system in Russia had been occurring since the mid-nineteenth century. However, these protests increased significantly in the early twentieth century. A 1905 uprising led to some democratic reforms but left the czar firmly in control. In March 1917, bread shortages led to rioting that dislodged the government of the czar, which was replaced by a provisional government. On November 7, the provisional government was overthrown by a group of soldiers, sailors, and workers led by the Bolsheviks, whose leader was Vladimir Ilyich Lenin. This revolution (which is commonly referred to as the "October Revolution" because it occurred on October 25 in the old Russian calendar) inaugurated an era of Socialist control of Russia that would form the foundation of the Soviet Union for decades to come. In the following selection, J.N. Westwood summarizes the events that brought Lenin and his Bolsheviks to power. Westwood is the author of *Russia, 1917–1964*, from which this excerpt was taken.

Vladimir Ilyitch Ulyanov was born in 1870. His father was a school inspector of moderately liberal views. When Vladimir Ilyitch was 17 his elder brother was executed for plotting a murder attempt on the Tsar, and he himself was expelled from Kazan University. He soon became a leading St. Petersburg Marxist and was duly imprisoned and then sentenced to a quite comfortable exile in Siberia. In exile he married a fellow-revolutionary, Krupskaya, and in 1900 he

Excerpted from *Russia: 1917–1964*, by J.N. Westwood (New York: Harper & Row). Copyright © 1966 by J.N. Westwood. Reprinted by permission of Chrysalis Books.

joined the Russian émigrés, spending most of his time up to 1917 in England and Switzerland, where he organised his supporters, and played the leading part in producing the illegal newspaper *Iskra*, which was smuggled into Russia together with copies of other revolutionary books and pamphlets. In 1901 he adopted his final pseudonym, Lenin, derived from the River Lena in Siberia.

Lenin was energetic, single-minded, and strong-willed. He also had a useful unscrupulousness in dealing with those who opposed him. This was not because he was ruthless and dishonest by nature, but because he was so certain of his own rightness that any means of assuring the victory of his ideas seemed justified, and in any case he had rejected much of conventional morality. (This ruthlessness subsequently became a hallmark of successful Communist leaders, including some who possessed few other qualities to excuse it.)

What Lenin brought to the Russian Marxists was a modification of doctrine to make Marxism more suitable for Russian conditions, and the concept of a select and professionalised party, single-minded and able, if necessary, to act decisively without the support of public opinion. He incorporated into Marxist doctrine the possibility of one social class making not one, but two, revolutions. This concept at once enabled Marxists to expect a workers' revolution in their own lifetime. It also gave a place to Russia's dominant social class, the peasantry; for in the first—bourgeois—revolution envisaged by Lenin the bourgeois attack on the monarchy was to be stimulated and largely executed by the proletariat acting in alliance with the peasants. In the second revolution the proletariat would overthrow the bourgeoisie, again with the help of the peasantry.

Lenin realised that neither the workers nor the peasants were really interested in Marxism or in revolution; they simply wanted to improve their own material situation. Lenin's devoted elite party would therefore become the 'vanguard of the working class' and would strive to teach the workers that their true interest lay in revolution, not just in wage increases and better working conditions.

The party which Lenin created was highly professionalised, with its officials receiving a salary from party funds. There was inflexible discipline and unquestioned obedience to the centre: that is, to Lenin. At a congress of the Russian Social Democratic Party held in London in 1902 Lenin caused a split and the movement divided into two factions, Lenin's 'Bolshevik' Party and the 'Menshevik' Party, whose adherents would not accept Lenin's unscrupulousness and his demand for tight control over members. The next two years witnessed constant squabbles between the two factions, especially among the émigrés, and this was one reason why the Marxists were ineffective during the 1905 Revolution [an uprising of peasants, students, and workers]. In this competition the Mensheviks had more support (especially among the workers) but this was balanced by the greater decisiveness of the Bolsheviks.

The pre-war decade was a lean time for the revolutionaries. With their leaders abroad and engaged in pamphlet quarrels, and various reforms and improvements taking place inside Russia, it seemed that peaceful and constitutional evolution promised more than revolution. Support for the Marxists, and especially for the Bolshevik wing, further diminished in the first years of the First World War, when a genuine if misguided patriotism inspired all parties—except, that is, Lenin's, who openly hoped for a Russian defeat which would pave the way for revolution.

The Russian Revolution

After some successes it soon became clear that Russia had again embarked on a war for which she was ill-prepared. The soldiers lacked munitions, equipment and clothing, and the railways were failing. Readiness to throw into battle masses of poorly trained and poorly equipped infantry was of little avail, and by the third winter of the war Russians of all classes saw the need for a change of government. The upper classes were repelled by the intrigues at St. Petersburg (now renamed Petrograd, which sounded less Teutonic). In the Tsar's absence, the Empress under the influence of Rasputin—a politically ignorant holy man—interfered in government and planted incompetent favourites in key positions. The townspeople were hard-hit by rising prices and by transport break-downs which caused food shortages. The peasants were the main suppliers both of infantry and horses and were beginning to realise that both were being uselessly sacrificed.

In December 1916 Prince Yusupov and his associates filled Rasputin with cyanide and bullets and dumped the body in the River Neva; so strong was approval of this deed that the assassins were merely exiled to their country estates. In March 1917 bread rationing was introduced in the capital, and badly organised. There were strikes and then street demonstrations, followed by riots and bigger strikes and demonstrations. Many of the garrison troops who were ordered to suppress the disturbances showed sympathy towards the demonstrators, and some joined in. A few officials and ministers were roughly handled, prisoners were released, and the courts burned. In all there were about a thousand serious casualties in March in Petrograd, but little blood was shed elsewhere.

Meanwhile, the few revolutionary leaders still in Petrograd organised a council ('soviet') of workers' and soldiers' representatives, elected by factories and by regiments. This Soviet held its sessions next to the Duma [the principal legislative assembly]. Then, in mid-March, Nicholas was persuaded by his generals and the Duma leaders to abdicate. The Grand Duke Michael, whom he appointed as his successor, refused the title: Russia was without a Tsar.

What was left to fill the power vacuum was the Soviet of Workers and Soldiers, which had an executive representing various left-wing parties and factions (including the Bolsheviks), and the Duma, which formed a Provisional Government composed of liberal and conservative leaders (and one Social Revolutionary). The Duma suspected that the Soviet was deliberately fostering violence and chaos, while the Soviet feared that the Duma (which after all was a legal and properly-elected body) would use troops to suppress it. Both the Duma and the Soviet were afraid that monarchist army officers would mobilise forces to restore the old regime. Largely to forestall this the Soviet issued its famous Order No. 1, which called on soldiers to ignore their officers and elect their own regimental committees.

The Soviet and the Duma agreed to maintain Provisional Government consisting chiefly of Duma members and to arrange countrywide elections for a Constituent Assembly, which would decide how the new Russia should be ruled. Meanwhile the German government, anxious to promote chaos in Russia so that it would be forced out of the war, arranged the shipment of about 30 revolutionary émigrés (including Lenin and other Bolsheviks) from Switzerland to Petrograd.

The Bolshevik Revolution

Lenin arrived in Petrograd in mid-April and immediately criticised the local Bolsheviks for co-operating so willingly with the other left-wing groups in the Soviet. He declared that the Provisional Government should receive no support, that the land should be given to the peasants and that the war against Germany should stop. Although many Bolsheviks at first opposed him they changed their minds when they realised that slogans like 'All land to the Peasants' and 'No More War' were gaining support for the Party. In May, anti-government demonstrations were staged, resulting in six left-wing ministers joining the Provisional Government and [Aleksandr] Kerensky, a Social Revolutionary and a member of the Soviet, becoming Minister of War.

Kerensky, partly in response to western pleas, partly to create a wave of patriotism which would carry the Government forward, launched a big offensive in July which after initial advances degenerated into a retreat. This defeat, together with Bolshevik agitation, set off further demonstrations and the slogan 'All Power to the Soviets' was put forward. Revolutionary sailors from the Kronstadt naval base were brought to the capital by the Bolsheviks, who hoped to unseat the Government.

But this first attempt to dislodge the Provisional Government failed to win enough popular support and, when it was reported that the Bolsheviks had received money from the German government, opinion in the streets turned against them. Lenin was forced into hiding in Finland. Kerensky be-

came Prime Minister and the remaining Bolsheviks con-
tented themselves with propaganda work, especially in the
army, and with the creation of their own illegal armed force.
This was the Red Guard, consisting of factory workers
equipped with rifles purloined from the army.

In September a combination of mistrust and misunder-
standing caused the Commander-in-Chief, [Lavr Georgevich]
Kornilov, to march against Petrograd. His advance fizzled
out, defeated more by the Petrograd Soviet than by Kerensky; Kornilov's soldiers, confronted by armed workers from
the capital and influenced by Bolshevik agitation in their
ranks, refused to fight. The Bolshevik members of the Soviet
had a leading part in these events and could henceforth
claim to have 'saved the Revolution'. [Leon] Trotsky, a former Menshevik turned Bolshevik, and a brilliant orator and
organiser, was released from prison; Bolsheviks began to
muster majorities in the Petrograd Soviet and the subsequently formed Moscow Soviet.

At the same time those who wished to see the restoration
of law and order lost confidence in the Provisional Government. Under its Prime Minister, the liberal [Pavel] Mi-
lyukov, it had certainly achieved some needed reforms—
freedom of the press, equal rights for Jews, abolition of the
death penalty, real autonomy for Poland and Finland—but it
could only act with the acquiescence of the Soviet. It had responsibility but lacked authority. A politically mature middle
class on which it might have leaned had never developed
under tsarist autocracy. The weakness induced by the two-
headed leadership (with the Soviet constantly gaining public
support at the expense of the government and Duma) was
paralleled by the growing ineffectiveness of the Social Revolutionaries, who were numerically strong in both the Soviet
and the Duma. They were split into various factions and
moreover were hampered by their desire, or need, to coa-
lesce with the liberal Cadet Party. The latter opposed determined action (including at one stage determined action
against the Bolsheviks) and succeeded in postponing the
convening of the promised Constituent Assembly. The Provisional Government lost much support among the peasants

by postponing land reform so that it might be discussed by the Constituent Assembly. Also, its continuation of the war hampered its action in other fields and was an enormous burden; but peace with Germany was possible only at a very high territorial price which few Russians would accept.

In October the Petrograd Soviet appointed a 'Military Revolutionary Committee' to prevent another Kornilov-type threat, and under the leadership of Trotsky the Bolshevik members of this soon dominated its proceedings. Trotsky succeeded in obtaining rifles for thousands more of the Red Guard, agitators continued their work, street demonstrations were organised. By this time the Provisional Government could muster few reliable forces; the old and unpopular police force had been disbanded and most army units were paralysed by Bolshevik agitation. On 6 November Lenin appeared in disguise at the Bolshevik headquarters and that night the Red Guards occupied key points in the capital—railway stations, telephone exchanges, banks, printing presses. Kerensky slipped out of the Winter Palace, where his ministers were conferring, to seek loyal troops. In his absence the Palace was occupied by Red Guards and sailors, and the ministers were arrested. Kerensky was unable to assemble a reliable army to restore the situation; at one point he only escaped capture by disguising himself as a sailor. He took no further part in events, settling down to a long and comparatively quiet life in the USA.

In Petrograd the Bolshevik takeover had been almost bloodless, but in Moscow and some other towns there was protracted fighting as the Bolsheviks took power with their armed workers, soldiers and sailors. And except in a few solidly 'Red' localities, like Kronstadt, there was a possibility of counter-insurrection. Moreover, having used the support of other left-wing parties, the Bolsheviks were faced with the possibility of a coalition government, a prospect which Lenin did not relish. At the Congress of Soviets, which met immediately after the Bolshevik coup and contained representatives of workers' and peasants' soviets from many Russian towns, the Bolsheviks and their temporary ally, the Left Social Revolutionary Party, had a majority. But they were faced with strong opposition from orthodox Social Revolutionaries and Mensheviks. However, taking advantage of a protest walk-out by their opponents, they passed resolutions establishing the Congress as the supreme ruling body, appointing a Council of People's Commissars (all Bolsheviks) to be a ruling cabinet, confiscating the landowners' estates, and proposing an end to the war with Germany.

Thus the Bolsheviks—even though they lacked the support of a majority of Russians—were in power.

Lenin's Betrayal of Russia

Dmitri Volkogonov

His status as a decorated and loyal Soviet general allowed
Dmitri Volkogonov nearly unlimited access to his nation's
top-secret historical archives. In the years of glasnost, or
"openness," begun in the late 1980s, Volkogonov and other
writers found themselves free to research, describe, analyze,
and criticize the actions of their past leaders. Volkogonov's
biographies of Lenin, Trotsky, and Stalin rank among the
most detailed and fascinating history books ever written. By
showing the human side of these leaders, treated in the past
by Russian writers as near-perfect and unapproachable icons,
Volkogonov reveals cruelty, incompetence, paranoia, and a
remarkable lust for power as the most telling results of the
Communist utopia. He summarized his works in his final
book, *Autopsy for an Empire*, in which he reviewed the lives of
the seven men who had led the Soviet Union after the revolution of October 1917. In the following passage, Volkogonov argues that Lenin betrayed Russia during World War
I by accepting money from Germany and supporting the
Germans in their effort to overthrow the czar and defeat the
Russian army. In subsequent years, according to this author,
Lenin and the leaders that followed him continued to betray
the Russian people by manipulating public opinion, imposing dictatorial regimes, and unleashing civil war.

It was the third year of the First World War. Millions of soldiers were dying in the trenches, bombarded and gassed,
hanging in grey tatters on the barbed wire. The war had
crossed its 'equator'. Few doubted that Germany and its allies would be defeated in the end, especially now that the

Reprinted and edited with the permission of The Free Press, a division of Simon &
Schuster, Inc., from *Autopsy for an Empire: The Seven Leaders Who Built the Soviet
Regime*, by Dmitri Volkogonov. Translated and edited by Harold Shukman. Copyright © 1998 by Novosti Publishers. English language translation copyright © 1998
by Harold Shukman.

United States had entered the war on the Allied side. Russia's position was bad, but not desperate. The front had been stabilized. However, socialist agitation was having a serious effect on army morale. Reinforcements were frequently arriving at only half strength. Mass desertion had begun. The last President of the Russian State Duma, Mikhail Rodzyanko, later recalled that in 1917 'desertion from the front amounted to one and a half million. About two million soldiers had been captured by the Germans'. . . The Bolshevik agitators were working on the natural reluctance of the peasants to fight.

Lenin, meanwhile, in peaceful Switzerland, was engaged in philosophical self-education, writing articles, going for walks in the company of his wife and his friend Inessa Armand, eagerly following the news from the front. He himself had never worn military uniform or squatted in a blood-soaked trench. He had never looked into the dreadful face of war. He realized that the combatants themselves were incapable of ending this ugly, savage war, and he also knew that the war held the key to his own future.

The desire to end the bloodshed was felt by some people in a position to exercise influence. As early as February 1915, King Gustav V of Sweden wrote to [Russian]Tsar Nicholas II: 'You understand, dear Nicky, how much the horrors of this frightful war upset me. And therefore it is quite natural that my thoughts are preoccupied in seeking the means that could put an end to the dreadful slaughter . . . I am prompted by my conscience to tell you that at any moment, sooner or later, whenever you find it convenient, I am willing to serve you in any way in this matter . . . What do you think of my offer to help?' Nothing came of this initiative.

Two years later, on 4 February 1917, the Bulgarian envoy to Berlin, Rizov, visited the Russian envoy to Norway, Gulkevich, and requested that a telegram be sent to Petrograd reporting 'Germany's desire to conclude a separate peace with Russia on highly favourable terms'. Petrograd replied to Gulkevich: 'Listen [to the proposal] and be sure to obtain a precise formulation of the terms.' It was all too late. February was pregnant with irreversible events.

A National Betrayal

From the beginning of the slaughter, Lenin was not, as might have been expected, in favour of its termination, but instead called for its 'socialization'. Writing to one of his agents, Alexander Shlyapnikov, on 7 October 1914, two months after the outbreak of fighting, he roundly condemned the campaign for peace. 'The "peace" slogan is not the right one. The proper slogan must be to turn national war into civil war.' Lenin had already created another plank of the Bolshevik platform on the conflict when Germany declared war on Russia on 1 August 1914. He immediately sat down to write his 'Theses on the War', later published in collected form under the title *War and Russian Social Democracy*. In it there appear lines that only a rigidly orthodox thinker like Lenin could have written. He described the attempt 'to slaughter the proletarians of all lands by setting the hired slaves of one nation against the hired slaves of another for the benefit of the bourgeoisie' as being 'the *only real* content and meaning of this war' (emphasis added).

The absurdity of this proposition is obvious, but the foundation stone of socialist propaganda had been laid. He went on to state that: 'From the point of view of the working class and the labouring masses of all the peoples of Russia, the lesser evil would be the defeat of the tsarist monarchy and its forces.' Lenin was calling for nothing less than the defeat of his own government, of his country (which was incidentally not an instigator of the war), and better still for turning the war into a revolution and a civil war. For all their professed internationalism, the position taken by Lenin and the Leninists did nothing to bring the ending of the slaughter any nearer. On the contrary, theirs was a policy of throwing still more fuel on the flames of war.

At the same time, Lenin's line on the war represented a blatant national betrayal derived from profound contempt for both Russia's state interests and those of her allies. He could not have made this clearer than when he stated that 'tsarism is a hundred times worse than kaiserism.' It was possibly this sentiment that led Lenin in time to the idea of a coincidence of interests between the Bolsheviks and Berlin.

The Tsar, his government and his armies were an obstacle to Germany's far-reaching plans for expansion, and also to Lenin's for seizing power in Russia. From the moment the war broke out, Germany and the Bolsheviks had a common enemy in tsarist Russia, and from this Lenin drew the conclusion that the Russian army must be made to disintegrate. 'Even where the war is being waged,' he declared, 'we must remain revolutionaries. Even in wartime we must preach class struggle.'

At the end of September 1914 the Russian newspaper *Russkoe Slovo* (Russian Word) published an appeal from writers, artists and actors condemning German aggression. Among the many illustrious signatories was Maxim Gorky, who for years had been an active supporter of Lenin's organization. Lenin wrote an open letter addressed to Gorky in which he condemned his 'chauvinistical sermonizing'. He remarked in passing that the world-famous operatic bass Fedor Chaliapin, who had also signed the appeal, 'should not be judged too harshly . . . He knows nothing about the proletarian cause: today he's a friend of the workers and tomorrow—the Black Hundreds [tsarist secret police].' For Lenin, everyone was divided strictly into those who adopted a class (Leninist) position and were therefore allies, and those in the 'chauvinistical' camp who were therefore sworn enemies. Even in his article 'On the National Pride of the Great Russians', which every Soviet citizen was supposed to have read as a profoundly 'patriotic' piece of writing, Lenin asserted that 'the Great Russians should not "defend the fatherland" other than by wishing for the defeat of tsarism in any war, as the lesser evil for nine-tenths of Great Russia.' The slogans of pacificism and the idea of 'paralysing the war' were mocked by Lenin as 'ways of making fools of the working class', and he thought the notion of a 'democratic peace' without revolution 'profoundly wrong'.

It was typical of Lenin that, while calling for 'decisive action' against the militarists and for 'unleashing class struggle in the army', it did not occur to him to set an example himself. During the 1916 socialist conference in Zimmerwald, Switzerland, he loudly insisted that the delegates return to their native countries and personally organize strike movements against their belligerent governments. The German Social Democrat Karl Ledebour responded: 'But they'll just put me on trial in a court martial.' Lenin persisted, however, at which Ledebour retorted: 'And will you be going back to Russia to organize strikes against the war? Or are you going to stay in Switzerland?' Lenin did not dignify such a 'provocative' question with a reply. . . .

Arrangements with Germany

The Russian government's failings in the war and its weakness at home led to the self-destruction of the autocracy on a wave of discontent. A historical mutation began in 1917 which would lead in a few years to the creation of a new civilization, a new culture, and new political and social institutions which had little in common with Russia's history. Had the democratic February [1917] revolution [which overthrew the tsar] managed to hold, most likely Russia today would be a great democratic state, rather than one that has disintegrated.

Stuck in Zurich, Lenin became increasingly agitated by the thought that the train of the Russian revolution might depart for the future without him. He was saved from that eventuality by secret and unofficial contacts that had been established between certain Leninists and individuals who had the trust of the German authorities. Among these were Alexander Helphand, known as Parvus, an émigré from Russia, German social democrat and successful businessman in Scandinavia and Germany. Parvus was the author of an audacious plan according to which Germany, in order to win the war, would assist the outbreak of revolution in Russia. In declaring that tsarism's defeat 'here and now' would be the best way out of the war, Lenin was publicly, repeatedly and precisely stating his position as a virtual ally of Germany in its fight against his own country and its people.

General Erich von Ludendorff, 'the military brain of the German nation' and First Quartermaster of the army, described the role played by Lenin in Berlin's plans with frankness and extreme cynicism: 'In helping Lenin travel to Russia our government accepted a special responsibility. The enterprise was justified from a military point of view. We had to bring Russia down.' This was also Lenin's aim.

Research into these matters was strictly forbidden in the Soviet Union, but in the West much direct and indirect evidence has been discovered which established beyond doubt that a firm link existed between the Bolsheviks and Berlin. In recent years, documents from Russian archives that had previously been inaccessible have revealed the financial connections between Lenin's agents and Germany. Despite repeated 'purges', the archives preserved 'book-keeping' telegrams, accounts and statements of the amounts made available to the Bolsheviks by a generous German government.

After a meeting between Lenin and Parvus in May 1915, a close association was formed between a small circle of Lenin's most trusted agents, of whom the most important was Jacob Stanislavovich Ganetsky (Fuerstenberg), and the German side, with Parvus as the link. Ganetsky and Parvus were the mainspring of an ingenious mechanism. With money made available to him by Count Ulrich von und zu Brockdorff-Rantzau, the German ambassador in Copenhagen, and other sources, Parvus established a so-called Institute for the Study of the Social Consequences of the War, where he employed a number of Russian social democrats. Meanwhile, using German funds, Ganetsky established a firm in Stockholm for purchasing pharmaceutical products, such as medicines and contraceptives, for shipment to Petrograd, where they were in great demand. The proceeds from these sales enabled Ganetsky's assistant, [Mechislav] Kozlovsky, to transmit large sums of money to accounts in different banks, usually to a woman called Yevgeniya Sumenson. Hundreds of thousands of roubles were thus made available to the Bolsheviks for purposes such as the printing and distribution of newspapers and leaflets, the purchase of arms, and salaries for a large number of 'professional revolutionaries'. Dozens of telegrams testify to the constant flow of funds between Berlin and the Bolsheviks via Ganetsky and Parvus, aided by several intermediaries who knew nothing of this covert support for Lenin's party. Lenin, the consummate conspirator, did not mark these documents with his own instructions or give direct financial orders himself. He stood in the wings, watching the machine work for him and exercising only verbal authority.

Vast Sums of Money

Despite some remaining gaps in the evidence, there is no doubt that the October [1917] coup was supported by German money. And it continued to flow after the Bolshevik seizure of power, as the Germans tried in every way to prevent the accession of an anti-Bolshevik regime that would make common cause with the Western Allies and revive Russia's war against Germany. Count Wilhelm Mirbach, the German ambassador in Moscow, sent a cipher telegram to Berlin on 3 June 1918, one month before he was assassinated: 'Due to strong Entente competition, 3,000,000 marks per month necessary. In event of early need for change in our political line, a higher sum must be reckoned with.' Two days later, the German Foreign Ministry informed the Treasury that Mirbach had spent large sums to counter Allied efforts in Russia to persuade the Bolsheviks to change their line and accept Allied demands. Since it was the German view that the new regime was hanging by a thread, Mirbach's efforts were regarded as of cardinal importance, and in order to sustain them a fund of 'at least 40 million marks' was required.

In 1921 the leading German Social Democrat Eduard Berstein published a sensational article in the socialist newspaper *Vorwärts* in which he wrote: 'Lenin and his comrades received vast sums of money from the Kaiser's government for their destructive agitation . . . From absolutely reliable sources I have now ascertained that the sum was very large, an almost unbelievable amount, certainly more than fifty million gold marks, a sum about the source of which Lenin and his comrades could be in no doubt. One result of all this was the Brest-Litovsk Treaty.'

Accepting Russia's Defeat

In effect, the Bolshevik leadership had been bought by the Germans, and it was therefore not surprising that Lenin should compel the Russian delegation to the peace talks in

March 1918 to accept the harsh terms dictated by Germany. The 'indecent peace' was the price Lenin had to pay to acquire and retain power. Having not long before declared that the Bolsheviks would never agree to a separate peace, Lenin in fact accepted a defeat—after preaching defeatism for three years—that never was. He accepted defeat from an enemy who was already on his knees before the Allies. He not only accepted defeat, he also agreed to give the Germans a million square kilometres of Russian territory and 245.5 tonnes of gold. In the autumn of 1918, with Germany facing imminent defeat, the curator of the Russian gold reserve, Novitsky, reported to Lenin that another ninety-five tonnes of gold was ready for shipment to Germany.

Having utterly rejected all social democratic principles, soon after returning from exile to Petrograd in April 1917 Lenin embarked on a course of violent seizure of power. He refused to meet the socialist Prime Minister Alexander Kerensky. His slogans, primitive and rabble-rousing, worked without fail. The Bolsheviks promised the war-weary, land-starved and hungry people peace, land and bread, and told them that to achieve this they must first stick their bayonets into the ground, abandon the trenches and go home, where they should seize their allotments. Promised by Lenin's agitators that they would never be sent to the front, the troops of the vast Petrograd garrison threw their support behind the Bolsheviks. The power of [Alexander] Kerensky's Provisional Government melted like ice in the spring thaw. Meanwhile the Bolshevik demagogues promised the gullible and ignorant peasants-in-uniform prosperity, peace, land, bread, hospitals, liberty. At the First All-Russian Congress of Peasants' Deputies in May 1917, Lenin described the idyllic life they would lead: 'This will be a Russia in which free labour will work on free land.' His listeners would not have to wait long to discover whether his predictions were accurate. . . .

November 7

On the night of 6 November, the Bolshevik Red Guards seized a number of key locations in Petrograd, including the main post office and telephone exchange, stormed the Winter Palace and arrested Provisional Government Ministers. Next day, Trotsky informed the Second Congress of Soviets that the Bolsheviks had seized power in the name of the Soviets of Workers' and Soldiers' Deputies, thus ushering in the new era of Soviet rule in Russia. In fact, it was the Bolshevik Party under Lenin and his successors that would govern the country for the next seventy years, even if they continued to uphold the fiction that they were doing so in the name of the Soviets. The clan of professional revolutionaries would henceforth simply pass the sceptre of power from one pair of hands to the next.

For seven decades much would be written about 'Lenin's theory of socialist revolution'. In fact, it was not a consistent, synthesized body of theory. Its salient features were: the maximum manipulation of public opinion; the frenzied cultivation of the image of the class enemy, whether the Tsar, the bourgeoisie, the Mensheviks or the liberals; the disintegration of the army and state machine by means of outright rabble-rousing; pushing the state and the regime towards chaos and dislocation; staging a coup at the precise moment when the government was most weakened and compromised; establishing a harsh dictatorship which took away 'bourgeois liberties and rights'; using terror as a means of keeping millions of people in check; unleashing civil war.

These are only some of the features of Lenin's technique. They were implemented by a disciplined, organized party led by professional revolutionaries like Lenin himself, people capable of issuing an order to reduce rations for those not working on transport and to increase it for those who were: 'Let thousands die, but the country will be saved.' Lenin's logic was that some should be killed so that others should live.

Lenin was able to determine the precise moment at which the government was totally paralysed and defenceless, when if the Bolsheviks did not seize the moment, others would. The American journalist John Reed, who became a hero of the revolution, recorded Lenin saying on 3 November: '6 November will be too soon to act; the eighth too late. We have to act on the seventh, the day the [Second] Congress [of Soviets] opens.'

Yet, until the last minute, Lenin did not believe deep down in the success of the operation. As Richard Pipes has written: 'Lenin did not dare to show himself in public until the cabinet (presumably including Kerensky, of whose escape he was unaware) fell into Bolshevik hands. He spent most of [7 November] bandaged, wigged, and bespectacled. After Dan and Skobelev, passing by, saw through his disguise, he retired to his hideaway, where he took catnaps on the floor, while Trotsky came and went to report the latest news.'

The dying regime managed to issue a distress signal on the radio and in *Rabochaya gazeta* (Labour Gazette) on 11 November 1917:

> To All, To All, To All! The Provisional Council of the Russian Republic, yielding to the force of bayonets, was compelled on [7 November] to disperse and to interrupt its work for the time being. With the words 'liberty and socialism' on their lips, the usurpers are committing violence and mayhem. They have arrested and imprisoned in tsarist casemates members of the Provisional Government, including the socialist ministers . . . Blood and anarchy threaten to overwhelm the revolution, to drown liberty and the republic. . . .

The Russian Revolution preserved the traditional popular link between mystique and practice. Lenin's dogmas became the mystique, and destruction became the practice. 'Everything was destroyed except the tradition, except the plan, the blueprint of hatred and the leader's indomitable will,' wrote E. Bogdanov, an émigré philosopher. 'The people's instincts did the rest; a spicy broth which would with microbiological speed multiply the bacteria of Bolshevism in Russia . . . The people spat on the liberty and democracy they were offered [in February 1917] and were content only with their new and harsher slavery.'

The Bolsheviks Take Power

John Reed

As a correspondent for several left-leaning journals in the United States, John Reed reported from the Mexican revolution, from the front lines of the radical labor movement in the United States, and from the World War I battlefields of northern Europe. In 1917, the revolutionary turmoil of Russia attracted him to St. Petersburg, where he witnessed firsthand the social and political chaos of post-czarist Russia. He set down his observations in a frenetic and admiring account, entitled *Ten Days That Shook the World*, which has become a well-worn handbook for students of Russian history.

Reed never claimed to be an impartial observer. An enthusiastic supporter of the Bolsheviks, he returned to the United States after the revolution to help found the American Communist Labor Party. Indicted for sedition in the United States, he returned to Russia as a party delegate in 1920, but within a year was dead from a typhus infection. As a close friend of Lenin and a supporter of Lenin's revolution, he was accorded full honors, his grave given the place of honor beneath the Kremlin wall.

This extract from *Ten Days That Shook the World* describes the struggles and triumphs of the Bolsheviks in the weeks following the overthrow of the Provisional Government in October 1917.

Having settled the question of power, the Bolsheviki turned their attention to problems of practical administration. First of all the city, the country, the Army must be fed. Bands of sailors and Red Guards scoured the warehouses, the railway terminals, even the barges in the canals, unearthing and con-

---

Excerpted from *Ten Days That Shook the World*, by John Reed (New York: Boni and Liveright, 1919).

fiscating thousands of *poods*[1] of food held by private speculators. Emissaries were sent to the provinces, where with the
assistance of the Land Committees they seized the store-
houses of the great grain-dealers. Expeditions of sailors,
heavily armed, were sent out in groups of five thousand, to
the South, to Siberia, with roving commissions to capture
cities still held by the [czarist] White Guards, establish order,
and *get food*. Passenger traffic on the Trans-Siberian Railroad
was suspended for two weeks, while thirteen trains, loaded
with bolts of cloth and bars of iron assembled by the
Factory-Shop Committees, were sent out eastward, each in
charge of a Commissar, to barter with the Siberian peasants
for grain and potatoes. . . .

[Czarist General Alexei] Kaledin being in possession of
the coal-mines of the Don, the fuel question became urgent.
Smolny[2] shut off all electric lights in theatres, shops and
restaurants, cut down the number of street cars, and confiscated the private stores of fire-wood held by the fuel-dealers.
. . . And when the factories of Petrograd were about to close
down for lack of coal, the sailors of the Baltic Fleet turned
over to the workers two hundred thousand *poods* from the
bunkers of battle-ships. . . .

Toward the end of November occurred the "wine-
pogroms"—looting of the wine-cellars—beginning with the
plundering of the Winter Palace vaults. For days there were
drunken soldiers on the streets. . . . In all this was evident the
hand of the counter-revolutionists, who distributed among
the regiments plans showing the location of the stores of
liquor. The Commissars of Smolny began by pleading and ar-
guing, which did not stop the growing disorder, followed by
pitched battles between soldiers and Red Guards. . . . Finally
the Military Revolutionary Committee sent out companies of
sailors with machine-guns, who fired mercilessly upon the ri-
oters, killing many; and by executive order the wine-cellars
were invaded by Committees with hatchets, who smashed the
bottles—or blew them up with dynamite. . . .

1. A *pood* is thirty-six pounds. 2. Seat of the Bolshevik-led government in St. Petersburg (Petrograd).

Companies of Red Guards, disciplined and well-paid, were on duty at the headquarters of the Ward Soviets day and night, replacing the old Militia. In all quarters of the city small elective Revolutionary Tribunals were set up by the workers and soldiers to deal with petty crime. . . .

The great hotels, where the speculators still did a thriving business, were surrounded by Red Guards, and the speculators thrown into jail. . . .

Alert and suspicious, the working-class of the city constituted itself a vast spy system, through the servants prying into bourgeois households, and reporting all information to the Military Revolutionary Committee, which struck with an iron hand, unceasing. In this way was discovered the Monarchist plot led by former Duma-member [Vladimir] Purishkevitch and a group of nobles and officers, who had planned an officers' uprising, and had written a letter inviting Kaledin to Petrograd. . . . In this way was unearthed the conspiracy of the Petrograd Cadets, who were sending money and recruits to Kaledin. . . .

Revolutionary Discipline

The restrictions on the Press were increased by a decree making advertisements a monopoly of the official Government newspaper. At this all the other papers suspended publication as a protest, or disobeyed the law and were closed. . . . Only three weeks later did they finally submit.

Still the strike of the Ministries[3] went on, still the sabotage of the old officials, the stoppage of normal economic life. Behind Smolny was only the will of the vast, unorganised popular masses; and with them the Council of People's Commissars dealt, directing revolutionary mass-action against its enemies. In eloquent proclamations, couched in simple words and spread over Russia, Lenin explained the Revolution, urged the people to take the power into their own hands, by force to break down the resistance of the propertied classes, by force to take over the institutions of

3. After the October revolution, the Bolsheviks were thwarted by strikes among bureaucrats and ministers opposed to the new Soviet government.

Government. Revolutionary order. Revolutionary discipline! Strict accounting and control! No strikes! No loafing!

On the 20th of November the Military Revolutionary Committee issued a warning:

> The rich classes oppose the power of the Soviets—the Government of workers, soldiers and peasants. Their sympathisers halt the work of the employees of the Government and the Duma, incite strikes in the banks, try to interrupt communication by the railways, the post and the telegraph. . . .

> We warn them that they are playing with fire. The country and the Army are threatened with famine. To fight against it, the regular functioning of all services is indispensable. The Workers' and Peasants' Government is taking every measure to assure the country and the Army all that is necessary. Opposition to these measures is a crime against the People. We warn the rich classes and their sympathisers that, if they do not cease their sabotage and their provocation in halting the transportation of food, they will be the first to suffer. They will be deprived of the right of receiving food. All the reserves which they possess will be requisitioned. The property of the principal criminals will be confiscated.

> We have done our duty in warning those who play with fire.

> We are convinced that in case decisive measures become necessary, we shall be solidly supported by all workers, soldiers, and peasants.

On the 22d of November the walls of the city were placarded with a sheet headed "EXTRAORDINARY COMMUNICATION":

> The Council of People's Commissars has received an urgent telegram from the Staff of the Northern Front. . . .

> "There must be no further delay; do not let the Army die of hunger; the armies of the Northern Front have not received a crust of bread now for several days, and in two or three days they will not have any more biscuits—which are being

doled out to them from reserve supplies until now never touched. . . . Already delegates from all parts of the Front are talking of a necessary removal of part of the Army to the rear, foreseeing that in a few days there will be headlong flight of the soldiers, dying from hunger, ravaged by the three years' war in the trenches, sick, insufficiently clothed, bare-footed, driven mad by superhuman misery."

The Military Revolutionary Committee brings this to the notice of the Petrograd garrison and the workers of Petrograd. The situation at the Front demands the most urgent and decisive measures. . . . Meanwhile the higher functionaries of the Government institutions, banks, railroads, post and telegraph, are on strike and impeding the work of the Government in supplying the Front with provisions. . . . Each hour of delay may cost the life of thousands of soldiers. The counter-revolutionary functionaries are the most dishonest criminals toward their hungry and dying brethren on the Front. . . .

The MILITARY REVOLUTIONARY COMMITTEE GIVES THESE CRIMINALS A LAST WARNING. In event of the least resistance or opposition on their part, the harshness of the measures which will be adopted against them will correspond to the seriousness of their crime. . . .

Opposition to the Revolution

The masses of workers and soldiers responded by a savage tremor of rage, which swept all Russia. In the capital the Government and bank employees got out hundreds of proclamations and appeals, protesting, defending themselves, such as this one:

TO THE ATTENTION OF ALL CITIZENS.
THE STATE BANK IS CLOSED!
WHY?

Because the violence exercised by the Bolsheviki against the State Bank has made it impossible for us to work. The first act of the People's Commissars was to DEMAND TEN MILLION RUBLES, and on November 27th THEY DEMANDED TWENTY-

FIVE MILLIONS, without any indication as to where this money was to go.

. . . We functionaries cannot take part in plundering the people's property. We stopped work.

CITIZENS! The money in the State Bank is yours, the people's money, acquired by your labour, your sweat and blood. CITIZENS! Save the people's property from robbery, and us from violence, and we shall immediately resume work.

EMPLOYEES OF THE STATE BANK.

From the Ministry of Supplies, the Ministry of Finance, from the Special Supply Committee, declarations that the Military Revolutionary Committee made it impossible for the employees to work, appeals to the population to support them against Smolny. . . . But the dominant worker and soldier did not believe them; it was firmly fixed in the popular mind that the employees were sabotaging, starving the Army, starving the people. . . . In the long bread lines, which as formerly stood in the iron winter streets, it was not *the Government* which was blamed, as it had been under [Aleksandr] Kerensky, but the *tchinovniki*, the sabotageurs; for the Government was *their* Government, *their* Soviets—and the functionaries of the Ministries were against it. . . .

At the centre of all this opposition was the Duma, and its militant organ, the Committee for Salvation, protesting against all the decrees of the Council of People's Commissars, voting again and again not to recognise the Soviet Government, openly cooperating with the new counter-revolutionary "Governments" set up at Moghilev. . . . On the 17th of November, for example, the Committee for Salvation addressed "all Municipal Governments, Zemstvos [rural village committees], and all democratic and revolutionary organisations of peasants, workers, soldiers and other citizens," in these words:

Do not recognise the Government of the Bolsheviki, and struggle against it.

Form local Committees for Salvation of Country and Revolution, who will unite all democratic forces, so as to aid the All-Russian Committee for Salvation in the tasks which it has set itself. . . .

Meanwhile the elections for the Constituent Assembly in Petrograd gave an enormous plurality to the Bolsheviki; so that even the Mensheviki Internationalists pointed out that the Duma ought to be re-elected, as it no longer represented the political composition of the Petrograd population. . . . At the same time floods of resolutions from workers' organisations, from military units, even from the peasants in the surrounding country, poured in upon the Duma, calling it "counter-revolutionary, Kornilovitz," and demanding that it resign. The last days of the Duma were stormy with the bitter demands of the Municipal workers for decent living wages, and the threat of strikes. . . .

On the 23d a formal decree of the Military Revolutionary Committee dissolved the Committee for Salvation. On the 29th, the Council of People's Commissars ordered the dissolution and re-election of the Petrograd City Duma:

> In view of the fact that the Central Duma of Petrograd, elected September 2d, . . . has definitely lost the right to represent the population of Petrograd, being in complete disaccord with its state of mind and its aspirations . . . and in view of the fact that the personnel of the Duma majority, although having lost all political following, continues to make use of its prerogatives to resist in a counter-revolutionary manner the will of the workers, soldiers and peasants, to sabotage and obstruct the normal work of the Government—the Council of People's Commissars considers it its duty to invite the population of the capital to pronounce judgment on the policy of the organ of Municipal autonomy.

> To this end the Council of People's Commissars resolves:

> (1) To dissolve the Municipal Duma; the dissolution to take effect November 30th, 1917.

> (2) All functionaries elected or appointed by the present

Duma shall remain at their posts and fulfil the duties confided to them, until their places shall be filled by representatives of the new Duma.

(3) All Municipal employees shall continue to fulfil their duties; those who leave the service of their own accord shall be considered discharged.

(4) The new elections for the Municipal Duma of Petrograd are fixed for December 9th, 1917. . . .

(5) The Municipal Duma of Petrograd shall meet December 11th, 1917, at two o'clock.

(6) Those who disobey this decree, as well as those who intentionally harm or destroy the property of the Municipality, shall be immediately arrested and brought before the Revolutionary Tribunals. . . .

The Duma met defiantly, passing resolutions to the effect that it would "defend its position to the last drop of its blood," and appealing desperately to the population to save their "own elected City Government." But the population remained indifferent or hostile. On the 31st Mayor [Grigory] Schreider and several members were arrested, interrogated, and released. That day and the next the Duma continued to meet, interrupted frequently by Red Guards and sailors, who politely requested the assembly to disperse. At the meeting of December 2d, an officer and some sailors entered the Nicolai Hall while a member was speaking, and ordered the members to leave, or force would be used. They did so, protesting to the last, but finally "ceding to violence."

The new Duma, which was elected ten days later, and for which the "Moderate" Socialists refused to vote, was almost entirely Bolshevik. . . .

There remained several centres of dangerous opposition, such as the "republics" of Ukraine and Finland, which were showing definitely anti-Soviet tendencies. Both at Helsingfors and at Kiev the Governments were gathering troops which could be depended upon, and entering upon campaigns of crushing Bolshevism, and of disarming and expelling Russian troops. The Ukrainean Rada had taken command of all southern Russia, and was furnishing Kaledin reinforcements and supplies. Both Finland and Ukraine were beginning secret negotiations with the Germans, and were promptly, recognised by the Allied Governments, which loaned them huge sums of money, joining with the propertied classes to create counter-revolutionary centres of attack upon Soviet Russia. In the end, when Bolshevism had conquered in both these countries, the defeated bourgeoisie called in the Germans to restore them to power. . . .

But the most formidable menace to the Soviet Government was internal and two-headed—the Kaledin movement, and the Staff at Moghilev, where General [Nikolai] Dukhonin had assumed command.

The ubiquitous [Lt. Col. Mikhail] Muraviov was appointed commander of the war against the Cossacks, and a Red Army was recruited from among the factory workers. Hundreds of propagandists were sent to the Don.[4] The Council of People's Commissars issued a proclamation to the Cossacks, explaining what the Soviet Government was, how the propertied classes, the *tchin ovniki*, landlords, bankers and their allies, the Cossack princes, land-owners and Generals, were trying to destroy the Revolution, and prevent the confiscation of their wealth by the people.

On November 27th a committee of Cossacks came to Smolny to see Trotzky and Lenin. They demanded if it were true that the Soviet Government did not intend to divide the Cossack lands among the peasants of Great Russia? "No," answered Trotzky. The Cossacks deliberated for a while. "Well," they asked, "does the Soviet Government intend to confiscate the estates of our great Cossack land-owners and divide them among the working Cossacks?" To this Lenin replied. "That," he said, "is for *you* to do. We shall support the working Cossacks in all their actions. . . . The best way to begin is to form Cossack Soviets; you will be given represen-

---

4. The Don River region of the Ukraine was the homeland of the Cossacks, free peasants and smallholders who fervently opposed the Bolsheviks.

tation in the *Tsay-ee-kah*,[5] and then it will be *your* Government, too. . . ."

The Cossacks departed, thinking hard. Two weeks later General Kaledin received a deputation from his troops. "Will you," they asked, "promise to divide the great estates of the Cossack landlords among the working Cossacks?"

"Only over my dead body," responded Kaledin. A month later, seeing his army melt away before his eyes, Kaledin blew out his brains. And the Cossack movement was no more. . . .

Tearing Down the Old

Immensely strengthened by the collapse of the last important stronghold of hostile military power in Russia [at Moghilev, on December 2, 1917], the Soviet Government began with confidence the organisation of the state. Many of the old functionaries flocked to its banner, and many members of other parties entered the Government service. The financially ambitious, however, were checked by the decree on Salaries of Government Employees, fixing the salaries of the People's Commissars—the highest—at five hundred rubles (about fifty dollars) a month. . . . The strike of Government Employees, led by the Union of Unions, collapsed, deserted by the financial and commercial interests which had been backing it. The bank clerks returned to their jobs. . . .

With the decree on the Nationalisation of Banks, the formation of the Supreme Council of People's Economy, the putting into practical operation of the Land decree in the villages, the democratic reorganisation of the Army, and the sweeping changes in all branches of the Government and of life,—with all these, effective only by the will of the masses of workers, soldiers and peasants, slowly began, with many mistakes and hitches, the moulding of proletarian Russia.

Not by compromise with the propertied classes, or with the other political leaders; not by conciliating the old Government mechanism, did the Bolsheviki conquer the power. Nor by the organized violence of a small clique. If the

5. A transliteration of TsIK, the Russian abbreviation for Central Executive Committee, the former Petrograd Soviet, which was extending its authority over the rest of Russia.

masses all over Russia had not been ready for insurrection it must have failed. The only reason for Bolshevik success lay in their accomplishing the vast and simple desires of the most profound strata of the people, calling them to the work of tearing down and destroying the old, and afterward, in the smoke of falling ruins, cooperating with them to erect the frame-work of the new.

The Bolshevik Victory in the Civil War

Moshe Lewin

In the following selection, Moshe Lewin, a Red Army veteran and professor of Russian history at the University of Pennsylvania, examines the political developments in Russia during the civil war of 1917–1922. He contends that while the war was inevitable, its outcome was far from certain and was shaped by the strengths and weaknesses of the factions involved: Lenin's Bolsheviks, the czarist Whites, and the panoply of leftist parties that were battling for dominance in the Russia of the 1920s. Even within the Communist Party, various camps were vying for control.

Lewin concludes that the key to the Bolshevik victory in the civil war was not ideology, or even popularity, but the seizure of the Russian heartland around Moscow and the ability of the Bolsheviks to win over the urban proletariat and millions of peasants with their slogan "Land, Bread, and Peace." With their enemies finally defeated by 1922, the Bolsheviks took advantage of a political vacuum to carry out a complete reworking of Russian society from the top down.

The civil war was, no doubt, a crucial period in the history of the new Soviet regime. The demarcation of this period is a matter for debate. It may be argued that it began in November 1917 and ended in the middle of 1922. These dates encompass all the most important trends and traits that produced the flavor and substance of the period, the particular ways of acting, and the specific culture of the emerging system and its leaders. By mid-1922, almost all the military operations of importance, including those directed against the widespread

Excerpted from *Russia/USSR/Russia: The Drive and Drift of a Superstate*, by Moshe Lewin. Copyright © 1995 by Moshe Lewin. Reprinted by permission of The New Press, (800) 233-4830.

bands of guerrillas and bandits, had ceased; the first reasonably abundant harvest had begun to supply enough food to start healing the country's terrible wounds, particularly the consequences of the atrocious famine of 1921; and the war economy was returning to more normal, peacetime functioning.

We are dealing therefore with a time-span of about four years, marked by upheavals, battles, slaughter—a protracted national agony during which the new system was created and took shape. For historians and for other students of social and political systems, it was not simply an important period but also a very exciting one. It seems easier to grasp the essential features of a regime at its inception rather than to try to extract them from the numerous accretions that accumulated at later stages of development.

Creating a Utopia

The system we are studying was not built methodically according to some preestablished blueprint. It was, rather, improvised under the pressure of constant emergencies, although ideologies and programs of the previous era did play their role. This is visible, notably, in some policy preferences such as distaste for markets and a special relation with the working class, to take just a few examples. But these ideological preferences produced more than just facts. They also engendered illusions that are best illustrated by the policies subsumed under the term *War Communism*. An "illusion in action" or, to use a better term, "utopia" is a powerful mobilizer, and yet its results can be—and were—quite different from what was hoped for. In any case, utopias of different kinds are often an important part of historical events and present an intricate subject for study.

We can state further that, although improvised, the key institution of the new system, the party—its only preexisting feature—was created or recreated in the course of the events under consideration, in a new garb, quite different from what it had been at the start. Party cadres, during their short history before October, had trained themselves to be leaders in a revolution that was not even supposed to be socialist. During this period they produced an ideology and a small number of dedicated cadres who, after October, engaged in activities and events, notably a bloody civil war, during which they organized and ran armies, built a state apparatus, and presided over a new state. As they became rulers of the improvised regime, they recreated themselves and acquired a new identity, even if initially this process was not self-apparent. Nevertheless, the transformation went on speedily in all facets of party life and in many of its principles, such as ties with the masses, organizational structure, modus operandi, social composition, ways of ruling, and style of life.

All this was not the main concern of the participants in the events, proponents or foes of the new regime. They, and observers abroad, were still absorbed by the novelties introduced by this newcomer into the family of world systems. Whether a separate peace with Germany, land to the peasants, workers' control, nationalization of banks and key industries, or less formalized but sharper and more frightening notions such as "rob from the robbers" (*grab' nagrablennoe*)—all of these developments were an outrage to domestic opponents and an insult to the Western world. Forced labor for the bourgeoisie did not improve matters. Under these conditions a civil war was inevitable. What was puzzling was the considerable calm that prevailed during the regime's first months in power. Some would explain it as a power vacuum that the Bolsheviks skillfully filled. But with the crumbling of the Provisional Government the power vacuum was filled, at least partly, by the networks of soviets that had helped the Bolsheviks into power and given them strong initial backing. As for the forces of the old regime and many who were undecided, they needed some time to regroup, to recover from the initial shock, and to reap the benefits of the new regime's predictable difficulties and errors—errors that did not fail to appear.

That civil war was likely can be hypothesized on grounds other than the sole challenge of the Bolshevik program. We know how deeply the Whites hated the forces that stood behind the Kerenskii government.[1] Social Revolutionaries

---

1. The Provisional Government, led by Alexander Kerenskii, which came to power after the fall of the czar in March 1917.

[SRs], Mensheviks, and later also the Liberals were considered by monarchists and nationalists, especially by the officers, to have been the main culprits of the Bolshevik takeover. It is therefore not an idle speculation to contend that a Constituent Assembly dominated by the SRs would have been dispersed; indeed, the SRs gave ample proof that they were incapable of mounting an effective defense. They did little when told to disperse by the Bolshevik sailors, and later, in their Samara stronghold, they failed again to produce a military force capable of sustaining them. They depended fully on the Czechoslovak units.[2] Their own forces were commanded by White officers who were just waiting for the chance to eliminate them, which is what happened somewhat later in Siberia, where White officers eliminated SR leaders, making clear how unwelcome they were in the White camp.

The basic reality of those years was that the battle was being waged not between democracy and authoritarianism but between two different authoritarian political camps that could field big armies and fight it out. Supporters of the Constituent Assembly could not do the same—and they were eliminated from the historical arena.

We are next faced with another riddle: Why did the Bolsheviks, whom we just described as unprepared for the job of ruling a huge country, nevertheless become victors in the Civil War? An easy answer comes to mind—which has a grain of truth in it: Their success owed mainly to the ineptitude of their opponents. Victor Shklovskii, in his riveting *Sentimental Journey*, said that it was not a matter of who was the stronger but, rather, who was less weak.[3]

But such an explanation will not do. The Bolsheviks worked feverishly to create a central government as well as important civilian services and local authorities; at the same time they organized a war machine, complete with an armament industry. To sum it all up, they created a state. This achievement testi-

2. Czech partisans operating in Russia after Russia's withdrawal from the war in the summer of 1918.   3. Victor Shklovskii, *Sentimental Journey* (Ithaca, N.Y., 1970), p. 187.

fied to a dynamism that the other side clearly lacked. Neither of the main White territories—the Siberian or the southern—managed to produce a credible state administration, despite their claim to superior experience in "statehood" (*gosudarst-vennost'*). Numerous documents, notably memoirs of White officers written during and after the events, attested to the sad state of affairs in the different central and local administrations of the White areas. One officer described the administration of the Stavropol region under the Whites as the rule of *pompadury*, corrupt and arbitrary little despots. The evidence from Kolchak country was not more cheerful. In the battle between the *pompadury* and the *komissary* [Bolshevik leaders], the latter certainly deserved to win. They turned out to have had a knack for state building that representatives of previously privileged classes lacked or lost. The deeper cause of this deficiency lay in their inability to convince their previously faithful subjects, especially the peasants, that they still had something to offer them. Their demise in October was not really an accident.

It is worth noting that the Bolsheviks were entrenched in the very heart of historical Muscovy, where they drew most of their support. Russia's heartland, and the resources of the nation and the state accumulated by history in this area, served them well in winning the war and, later, in reuniting the country. The huge border areas (*okrainy*) where the Whites operated, although well provided with raw materials, grain, and an excellent military resource—the Cossacks—did not give them the hoped-for chance to surround and take Moscow. The *okrainy* proved, on the contrary, too diversified, too distant from each other. Instead of being a base for victory, they turned into a morass that engulfed them.

The War of Classes

The sociohistorical study of this period, focusing on classes, nationalities, bureaucracies, and parties, as well as on the social composition of the armies, is an indispensable tool, although this kind of study is still in its infancy. Yet it is particularly noteworthy to the historian to learn that not just the Bolsheviks but also the key figures of the opposite camp, notably Paul Miliukov and General Denikin, looked to the social factors, including the class composition of the contend-ing camps and of the country as a whole, in order to explain the victories and defeats. The nefarious role of backward-looking *pomeshchiki* [landowners], the actions of the bour-geoisie, their policies in relation to the peasantry, the behav-ior and attitudes of workers—such were the factors Miliukov cited in his postmortem analysis of the Whites. And Denikin, although he denied that his side had a class charac-ter, admitted and regretted that it never managed to shed its class image in the eyes of the population, a derogatory image at that. Denikin also resented the duplicity and stinginess of the bourgeoisie who did not want to come up with the nec-essary means to save what they themselves declared to be their cause.

Such explanations are, in fact, indispensable, provided they are used flexibly and are based on good research. Both camps were coalitions, not neat, clearcut classes. Each side had an obvious, although not entirely monolithic, core, around which coalesced broader layers of the population that often hesitated, changed sides, returned to the fold again, or created a camp of their own. It was this flux that made the Civil War so unpredictable for its participants at the time and so complicated for the analyst today. Such a fluid state of affairs applied equally to both sides. We can cite many examples of military or partisan units, armed with red banners and commissars, turning against the Communists, even killing them, and going over to the other side, contin-uing on their own—or even staying . . . with the Reds.[4]

We know that there was a nucleus of workers, poor peas-ants, and *raznochintsy* [intellectuals] on the side of the Reds and a core of members of the formerly privileged classes, richer peasants, and, especially, military officers on the side of the Whites. The problem was who would emerge as the better social and political strategist, who could mobilize the support of large circles of the urban population and, more

4. For an example of a partisan unit from Antonov-Ovseenko's Red Army in the Ukraine that called themselves "Soviet" but that persecuted Communists, or, at best, prevented them from organizing cells in the unit, see V.I. Nevskii, ed., *Za sem' let* (Leningrad, 1921). There were many partisan, even regular, military units of this kind.

importantly, the small-scale peasant farmers. In this crucial task of social strategy the Bolsheviks proved superior. The Whites, on the other hand, who much of the time were stronger militarily, found themselves in trouble the moment they turned to the forceful drafting of peasants. According to Lenin, that was their undoing.[5] Their basic force became hopelessly diluted.

But social analysis makes us aware of yet another complexity and strain in the social environment of each side. The heat generated by the Civil War was such that the nucleus of both sides showed cracks at different moments, especially in the later stages of war. Dissension and decomposition settled into the White camp first, but neither were the Bolsheviks spared. Confusion, exhaustion, and signs of fragmentation finally hit the party—the tool that the Whites could not match—but luckily for the Reds, this occurred after the Whites' defeat.

What it all means is that the Reds were tested in the crucible as cruelly as anybody. The Civil War marked them as deeply as it marked the whole nation.

Building a New State

This was a time of incredible suffering, cruelty, and destruction. Terms like *time on the cross* and *via dolorosa*[6] were evocative of the age for many deeply religious people. Writers used such terms in their works about the period. The symbolists even posed the question of whose side Christ was on. The church, though, was quite firmly on the side of the Whites.

The human suffering resulted not only from the direct cruelties of the Civil War but also from its broader aspect: the widespread dislocation; destruction; decomposition of groups, classes, and parties—briefly a deeply morbid state of the whole social fabric. Shklovskii, again, in his strangely titled work written soon after the events, was particularly impressed, even fascinated, by the phenomena of morbidity—

5. V.I. Lenin, in *Deviataia konferentsiia VKP(b), sentiabr' 1920, protokoly* (Moscow, 1972), p. 12. He stated: "We defeated Kolchak and Denikin only . . . after their main, solid cadres were diluted in the mobilized mass of peasants."   6. In Christian theology, the route followed by Jesus Christ just before his crucifixion.

cruelty, the dissolution of social and human bonds, the sickening sight of a society in a state of disaggregation.

These important—and fatal—characteristics of the period have to be studied attentively. Without them, the problem of the aftermath and the legacy of the Civil War will remain unintelligible. We have emphasized that social strategy was a key aspect in the outcome of the war. But we have also mentioned one other aspect of the big game in which the Bolsheviks bested the Whites, namely, the domain of state building. Once the tsarist state collapsed and the Provisional Government was unable to shore it up or build a new one, the stage was set for the social forces in attendance to try their hand at recreating a new political organization. There is no need to repeat the well-known story about who tried and failed. The country was going to be reunited and the sociopolitical system would be established by the camp that could produce a state. In abstract terms, one can imagine situations where a large movement of the masses could win and could subsequently create a state. Historically, such seems to have been the case during "the time of troubles" (*smutnoe vremia*) in Russia at the beginning of the seventeenth century. During the no less tragic *smuta* of the twentieth century the (Bolshevik-run) state was produced, at first, hand-in-hand with a social movement, and soon ever more independently of it, or at least independently of the shifting moods of the sympathetic, neutral, or even hostile masses. An important feature of this process was that the new state was being erected amidst a disintegrating economy and a decomposing social fabric, at a catastrophic time for the whole country. Indeed, the state was emerging on the basis of a social development in reverse. The Bolsheviks were little aware at that time of this aspect of their achievement, but at the very moment of their triumph, the shadow of Pyrrhus was certainly present. . . .

The Party

It is time to turn our attention to the ruling party—an agency without precedent in the history of political systems before 1917. The opponents of the regime during the Civil

War did not have at their disposal any equivalent to it.

The party certainly was a versatile agency. It helped produce a central and local government, raised and organized an army, sustained the fighting military by an influx of dedicated party members, responded to mobilizations for all kind of tasks, and, finally, effectively carried out clandestine activities behind enemy lines.

Not unexpectedly, a tendency appeared among party leaders, with the exception of Lenin, to glorify, later even to "mythologize," the party. This certainly did not attest to its continuing good health. A political party has to be submitted to all the stringencies of sociohistorical and political analysis—and the tendency to turn the Bolshevik Party into some sort of superhistorical tool hindered analysis from early in the party's development. We know that the party went through rough times and acted in ever more complicated and changing situations. The impression given by Soviet and many Western presentations of an immutable "essence" called "the Communist Party" has to be dispelled. First, as we know, the party consisted of a network of clandestine committees, not more than 24,000 strong, at the beginning of 1917. During its short history, the number of its adherents had fluctuated widely. It was led, from abroad mostly, by its founder, Lenin. There also was leadership inside Russia, but it was often decimated by arrests.

Was the party before 1917 really the disciplined and centralized squad of "professional revolutionaries" who did as told by the top leader? Would this "classical" Leninist model withstand the scrutiny of a good monograph? The party represented more than just professional revolutionaries. There were elections, conferences, congresses, debates. As is often the case, a closer look may change many preconceived ideas. It is clear, though, that the Bolshevik Party was an unusual organization. It was not bracing itself to take power directly, because its leaders did not expect the coming revolution to be immediately socialist; at least, they were not at all sure what its character would be.

Dramatic changes occurred in this party in 1917. It became at the very least a different genus of the same species, if not an entirely different species. It was now a legal organization operating in a multiparty system; it grew in size to perhaps more than 250,000 members, and it operated as a democratic political party, under a strong authoritative leadership. Lenin was at the helm, but he was flanked at the apex by a group of leaders, below whom were influential networks of lower cadres who participated actively in policy making. If his colleagues accepted Lenin's line, it was mostly after lively debates and having sounded out the moods and opinions of the rank and file. Factions existed and were fully acknowledged as the party's normal way of doing business. At this stage, under Lenin's proddings, the party was aiming at power, but, again, not without serious differences of opinion about the modalities of taking and exercising it.

The Need to Run Things

Once the party was in power, in conditions of a civil war, another, deep transformation took place: the party became militarized and highly centralized, in a state of almost permanent mobilization and disciplined action. Its cadres were moved around where necessary by a newly created department, the *uchraspred*. Elections to secretarial positions ended, not to reappear in any meaningful way until [Mikhail] Gorbachev's [secretary of the Communist Party, 1985-91] efforts to reintroduce them. The center became all powerful, even if this development was often regretted as an unavoidable event in the circumstances of war. The situation did, in fact, demand it. Still, factionalism and intraparty debates continued, and conferences and congresses were regularly convened.

During the Civil War there was no sign of any "religious" reverence toward Lenin in the party caucuses. His prestige was enormous, but criticisms of party policies and of Lenin personally were often sharp. This aspect of the party tradition was unextinguished. There was hardly a leader or activist of any standing who did not engage in a polemic or even a serious challenge to Lenin's policies at one time or another.

Another important factor for change in the party was the fluctuating membership and shifting social composition characteristic of those years. We learned from one good source that there were 350,000 members between October 1917 and mid-1918; this figure subsequently dropped to 150,000 and then began to climb again, reaching 600,000 in the spring of 1921. Whatever the accuracy of such figures, one interesting phenomenon becomes obvious: the party entered a period of hectic growth at a time when mass support for the regime was at its lowest—in 1920 and 1921. Was this an aberration? Probably not.

By the end of the Civil War many would-be members and cadres perceived that the regime was here to stay. The growth of the party reflected the fact that no alternative was visible or possible anymore, despite the incredible furies of the uprisings. It also indicated the party's growing concern with the need of ruling and running things. Nobody spoke seriously anymore about "every crook" being able to run the state. Hence the influx into the party, including numbers of careerists and crooks, who would soon be removed by a powerful purge of unsavory elements, if such a feat was at all possible.

Toward the spring of 1921, party statistics showed that 90 percent of the membership was now of Civil War vintage.[7] Prerevolutionary cadres, even those who joined in 1917, were drowned in a mass of new entrants, many of them active participants in military and security operations and, quite naturally, imbued with a military, if not militaristic, political culture. The new recruits carried this attitude into the party, where it persisted, in different forms, for decades.

After the 1921 purge that discarded, probably, one-third of the membership, a new, powerful influx occurred, and during the next five years the membership reached the one million mark. The majority would now be made up of entrants who joined during the NEP [New Economic Policy], bringing to the party their own political culture and culture *tout court* [simply]. In the wake of these massive changes in social composition, the "old guard" was still at the top and running the

---

7. *Istoriia KPSS*, vol. 4, no. 2, p. 70, states that 90 percent of the membership at the beginning of 1921 joined in 1918–20. Thus, it is plausible to hypothesize that the party was built anew in those years and from a different human material.

show, but their numbers, stamina, even their health, were slackening. Could they assimilate, reeducate in their own image, the enormous mass of "crude" newcomers? If not, what would stop this mass from having a pervasive impact on the party and from transforming it in *its* own image?

There is evidence that many of the "old guard" despaired, overwhelmed and besieged as they were by huge numbers of people whose culture and mentality differed from their own. The Civil War entrants had brought to the party a military culture, whereas the culture of the newer entrants reflected the values of the NEP society. At the same time, the top layer, continuing an earlier Bolshevik tradition, still fought among themselves using terms and arguments that the bulk of the rank and file did not understand. It can be said that the "old guard" came to constitute a separate party within the larger party being formed around them. Finally, the new membership created a new model of a party run differently, and politically and ideologically transformed.

Chapter 2

Building the New State

The Creation of the USSR

M.K. Dziewanowski

The fall of the czar also meant an end to the Russian Empire, a result long and fervently hoped for by Lenin and his followers in the lean years before the revolution. From their exile in western Europe, the Bolsheviks saw the Empire as a bastion of the corrupt and antiquated capitalist system, which they hoped to replace with an international order of communist nations existing cooperatively. Once power was seized and held, however, the problems of nationalism and ethnicity confronted the Bolsheviks. If the peoples of nearby republics, such as the Georgians or Kalmyks, were allowed to go their own way and declare their independence, Soviet leaders feared, the Soviet state would find itself surrounded by enemies open to alliance with the Bolsheviks' enemies in the capitalist West.

This possibility could not be tolerated, so the Union of Soviet Socialist Republics (USSR) was created by the Tenth All-Russian Congress of Soviets on December 27, 1922. The new constitution, ratified in 1924, held out the promise of autonomy to the member republics but also created a powerfully centralized state in which regional concerns would be subordinated to the plans and policies of the party and its leaders in the capital of Russia. Aside from Russia, the union originally included Byelorussia, Transcaucasia, and Ukraine. Over the next two decades, the union would swell to include sixteen republics.

Author M.K. Dziewanowski, a professor and lecturer on Soviet history at the University of Wisconsin, describes the creation of the Union of Soviet Socialist Republics in the following excerpt from his book *A History of Soviet Russia and its Aftermath*. Dziewanowski explains

Excerpted from M.K. Dziewanowski, *A History of Soviet Russia and Its Aftermath*, © 1997. Reprinted by permission of Pearson Education, Inc., Upper Saddle River, NJ 07458.

how the creation of the USSR aided the consolidation of power by the Bolshevik Party, which as a result gained an empire of its own.

While reorganizing their economy and groping for a new international bearing, Soviet leaders were also reshaping the authoritarian structure of their state. At the time, Lenin was ailing, and the prospect of his death triggered the first jockeying for position of advantage by potential successors. The constitutional issue and the problem of succession were closely interconnected.

The Civil War resulted in the eventual reconquest of the Dnieper Ukraine, Belorussia, and the three Caucasian republics—Georgia, Armenia, and Azerbaijan—by what was until 1922 called the Russian Socialist Federal Soviet Republic (RSFSR). Through an agreement with Tokyo, the Far Eastern Province, temporarily a Japanese protectorate, also rejoined the RSFSR in 1922. Meanwhile, at Stalin's insistence and despite the fierce opposition of many Georgian Communists, Georgia, Armenia, and Azerbaijan were merged into a single Transcaucasian Republic. Thus, although a large segment of the multinational western fringe was lost, the remaining core of about 140 million people was about 48 percent non-Russian (64 million people). They represented a bewildering variety of ethnic groups at various stages of cultural and socioeconomic development. While the Great Russian heartland, especially its major cities, was fairly westernized, most of the seminomadic inhabitants of Central Asia, the Muslim tribes of the Northern Caucasus, and the inhabitants of Siberia were mostly backward, illiterate, and lacked a conscious feeling of nationality.

Federalism Versus Centralism

How to weld these areas and peoples together again was the subject of lively and often embittered discussion in the Party and in government circles in the early 1920s. The 1918 Constitution had already provided for a federal structure, as favored by Lenin himself. Once again, as with the peasant question, he followed the SR [Social Revolutionary] program. On the other hand, people like Trotsky, Stalin, and [Cheka (secret police) chief Feliks] Dzerzhinsky opposed federalism as making undue concessions to local nationalism and thus being fraught with great danger. Instead, they favored centralism, combined with limited autonomy if local conditions warranted. Yet the emerging Soviet Republic was very similar to the former Imperial Russia, at least in one respect: it was decidedly a multinational state.

Both Lenin and Stalin had observed how shallow and ineffective had been the old imperial policy of Russification, and how difficult it had been to impose Russian-Communist rule on the borderlands during the Civil War. In view of this, federalism seemed a better device to bribe the nationalities of the former Tsarist Empire to adhere to the Soviet State structure. Federalism was in accordance with the Bolshevik slogan of national self-determination so loudly proclaimed during the Civil War; it tended, moreover, to soften the impact of the reconquest of non-Russian areas by permitting the continued coexistence of various peculiarities in an ethnically heterogeneous republic, while the existence of an ethnic mosaic of peoples, some of them without developed national sentiments, provided an opportunity for Communist social engineering. In addition to these not inconsiderable advantages, federalism, if shrewdly presented abroad, would make the Soviet State a structure open to others who might wish to join it in the future.

All these assets were eventually recognized even by the opponents of federalism. On December 27, 1922, the Tenth All-Russian Congress of Soviets accepted Stalin's motion to establish the Union of Soviet Socialist Republics, or USSR. It was originally composed of four member-republics: Russia, the Ukraine, Belorussia, and Transcaucasus. In October 1924, the Russian Republic split and gave birth to two Central Asian Republics: Uzbek and Turkmen. In 1929 these six republics were joined by the Tajik Soviet Republic. In 1936 the Transcaucasian Republic was broken into three segments— Georgia, Armenia, and Azerbaijan—thereby transforming the USSR at that time into a union of nine federated segments. Within most Soviet republics, especially within the RSFSR, settlements of smaller ethnic groups were consolidated into autonomous areas in accordance with the long-range Soviet strategy of playing one ethnic group against another. The RSFSR, for instance, contained 12 regions, including, for instance, a Volga German autonomous republic and the autonomous territory of the Kalmucks.

The New Constitution of 1924

By 1923, the USSR had framed a new constitution. Ratified in 1924, it remained in force until 1936. The new charter was merely the former constitution of 1918 adjusted to the new federal structure of the Soviet State. The 1924 basic law differentiated between the governmental bodies of the USSR, or the Union, and those of the four previously mentioned individual Union Republics then in existence. The All-Union Congress of Soviets was made bicameral and was to be composed of the Council of the Union and the Council of Nationalities. While the Council of the Union was to be selected on the basis of population, the Council of Nationalities was to be composed of five delegates from each Union Republic and each autonomous republic, and one delegate from each autonomous area (*oblast*).

The Constitution provided for three kinds of ministries, then still called commissariats. There was the All-Union Commissariat for the USSR as a whole, and one for each Union-Republic or autonomous republic. The federal, or All-Union, government was given authority in questions of armed forces, war and peace, foreign relations, foreign trade, and fiscal matters, as well as for economic planning for the USSR as a whole. The authority of the constituent republics was limited to such powers as were not reserved for the All-Union government, and this was precious little. The new charter also provided for the establishment of a Supreme Court for the whole USSR.

It is worthwhile noting that the Russian Republic, comprising nearly three-quarters of the Soviet Union's territory, and containing its predominantly Great Russian population, had no separate Communist Party organization. Yet, gradually, the term "Russia" became a shorthand for "USSR," and the Russian language became the *lingua franca* of the Union. Nominally, all constituent republics had their individual Communist Parties; these were in fact subordinate to the All-Union, or Soviet Party.

The supreme power of the USSR theoretically was represented by the All-Union Congress of Soviets. The Congress, consisting of delegates from local soviets, was to be summoned every year by its Central Executive Committee. Only the delegates for the lowest tiers in the hierarchical pyramid, the village and city soviets, were to be elected by direct vote. All the higher soviets, the county, province, and republican ones, were composed of delegates selected by the soviets immediately below. All elections were strictly controlled by the Soviet Communist Party. The franchise was limited to people over eighteen involved in "productive work"; this included officials and soldiers but excluded former members of the bourgeoisie and priests. The Executive Committee was to be elected by the All-Union Congress from among its members and was to act as a governing body between congresses. The actual governmental functions of the Committee were to be performed by its Presidium, the chairman of which was to act as head of state. The first Chairman of the Presidium was Mikhail I. Kalinin, son of a poor peasant from the Tver province, a metal worker until 1917, and a man of flexible disposition. He was ideally suited to perform this purely symbolic function in full harmony with dictates of the ruling Party, as he was to do for well over twenty years.

Like the Constitution of 1918, the new charter bore only a vague relationship to political realities and power in the USSR and had a strong propagandistic ring. The preamble stated: "The family of brotherly peoples" of the USSR represents a "voluntary union of equal peoples, ready to embrace others who desire such association." The 1924 Constitution went so far as to provide for the right of each republic to secede freely from the USSR. Various semiofficial comments left no doubt, however, that a request for succession would be regarded as a hostile act opposed to the interests of the proletariat represented by the Soviet Communist Party. The Constitution also made specific provision for the admission of "all Socialist Soviet republics, both those now in existence, and those which will arise in the future."

Centripetal Factors

The outward decentralization allegedly resulting from the establishment of the federal system was a daring feat of political engineering. The operation was made possible by the preservation of the centralized and hierarchically organized All-Union, Soviet Communist Party, which reached from its Moscow headquarters into the remotest provinces, through its national branches. It was the All-Union Soviet Party that formed the firm infrastructure, the reliable nerve center of the USSR. The existence of this dictatorial Party allowed the construction of an alluring and impressive federal facade for the Soviet State, yet simultaneously rendered federalism illusory. Like the 1918 Constitution of the RSFSR, the new charter of the USSR made no direct reference to the real locus of power.

Another factor that permitted the Bolsheviks to put federalism into practice and implement an outwardly liberal ethnic policy was the overwhelming strength of its Great Russian hard core, the RSFSR. In 1923–1924 it comprised about three quarters of the territory of the USSR at that time, slightly over 76 million were Great Russians, who in turn constituted nearly 80 percent of the membership of the Communist Party. Moreover, within the territory of the Russian republic were situated most natural resources including most oil, natural gas, gold and diamond mines, as well as three of the four major industrial centers of the USSR: Petrograd, Moscow, and the Southern Ural region. Only the fourth industrial area, the Ukraine, was outside the Russian Republic.

From the Soviet point of view, the establishment of a federal state served several purposes. First, it helped to attract and maintain within the Union those ethnic elements for whom Communism would otherwise have had little appeal, such as the radical yet nationalistic segments of various minority groups. Second, the theoretically generous ethnic policy was a potentially effective instrument of foreign expansion, especially among the states to the west of the Soviet

Union like Poland, Romania, Czechoslovakia, and Turkey, where Ukrainian, Belorussian, or Armenian minorities lived without the benefit of a formally generous federal structure. In organizing their outwardly multinational federal state, the Bolsheviks were helped by their Civil War allies among the national minorities. The belief that national emancipation could be achieved through tactical, temporary cooperation with Communism was strong among leftist socialists, and even the radical democrats in various ethnic groups, especially the Ukrainians, the Belorussians, and some Moslems. Typical of them was the Ukrainian nationalist revolutionary leader Volodymyr K. Vinnychenko. He was convinced that by passing through the inevitable stage of "National Bolshevism" the Ukrainians might, perhaps, eventually achieve national independence. Among many Ukrainians this belief was strengthened by the development of their national culture, previously suppressed by the Tsarist administration and now flourishing under Soviet rule.

Lenin's Ethnic Policy

In the beginning, many of the pro-Bolshevik nationalists had reason to be optimistic because the Communist Revolution, with its principle of expropriation of all the means of production, was initially advantageous to the ethnic minorities, especially the Ukrainians and Belorussians. The upper classes in both regions were either Russian or Polish, and most of the capital, including the land, belonged to foreigners. During the period of the NEP [New Economic Policy], there was little forcible collectivization. Many petty traders and small industrialists were natives, and the Communist administration, short of qualified people, had to rely on whatever local talent was available, which often meant overlooking the political views of the people who were not anti-Communists. Economic planning could already boast some achievements. The figures, although often inflated, were outwardly impressive. From 1922 on, Soviet mass media constantly reported the building of new factories, highways, railroads, and canals, like those connecting the Dvina, the Niemen, and the Dnieper with the Volga. Electric light began to appear in the villages.

The NEP was paralleled by the policy of "taking native roots." Lenin in particular was determined to make the Communist system penetrate more deeply into the multinational fabric of the USSR. Consequently, national cultures were encouraged, education was fostered, native literatures were developed, often from scratch among some Central Asian tribes, and native tongues were revived. Lenin was in favor of teaching the national language and culture at State schools to every child of each nationality. On the other hand, he opposed separate political organizations (autonomous Communist parties) for each ethnic group.

Among the people who benefitted from the Leninist ethnic policy were not only Ukrainians and Belorussians, but also some three million Jews, formerly largely restricted to the Pale of Settlement[1] and cramped by its discriminatory legislation. As a result of the liberal revolution, the Jews had already obtained legal equality. The Bolsheviks officially condemned anti-Semitism and made it a punishable offense. Yiddish, the language of most Soviet Jews, was introduced into the Jewish schools. A Jewish press developed rapidly, and as early as the end of 1918, there were eighty-one Yiddish and ten Hebrew newspapers. A first-class Jewish theater was organized in Moscow. At the same time, however, religious Jews suffered from the official atheism of the new regime. Synagogues were being closed and rabbis often had to suffer indignities, not unlike the clergy of other denominations. At the same time, the Soviet regime, with the Jewish section of the Communist Party as its willing tool, was trying to assimilate the Jews into the surrounding population.

One method of assimilation was to diversify the hitherto rather one-sided socioeconomic structure of the Jewish population by encouraging Jews to leave the urban centers, settle in the countryside, and practice agriculture. And indeed, during the 1920s Jewish villages were set up in the Ukraine and in the Far Eastern segment of Birobijan. Jewish culture, like that in the Ukraine and Belorussia, enjoyed a brief period of expansion and flowering. The internationalist aspects

---

1. The region to which Jews were restricted under the czars.

of the Communist doctrine greatly appealed to many cosmopolitan Jews, who sincerely believed that they were undergoing a process of genuine amalgamation. They renounced their Jewishness not in order to become Russians or Ukrainians, but to be "New Soviet Men."

During the 1920s the Bolsheviks also paid a great deal of attention to the Muslim peoples, who numbered around 25 million. Kazakhs, Uzbeks, Turkmens, Tatars, and others were united by a common religion and the Arabic script. Mirza Sultan-Galiev, an able imaginative Muslim Volga Tatar and a member of the All-Russian Muslim movement, was largely instrumental in reconquering the Central Asian provinces for the Bolsheviks. Once in control of Central Asia, the Bolsheviks began to pursue a step-by-step policy of gradual secularization and integration of the native population. They gradually cut off the Muslims of the USSR from their brethren who lived south of its borders by discouraging travel and interpersonal contacts, and by replacing the original Arabic script first with the Latin and finally with the Russian. Secularization was fostered, initially without exaggerated zeal and excesses. "Don't paint nationalism red!" Lenin warned his comrades. Local cultures were to be "national in form but Marxist in content."

The Soviet ethnic policy was especially important in the Soviet Ukraine, the largest and most important of the federal republics. As long as Poland, Romania, and Czechoslovakia ruled over the western segments of the Ukrainian people, an outwardly liberal policy could serve as a means of pressure and diversion against these countries. The granting of cultural, if not political, autonomy to the ethnic minorities was also very useful to the Comintern [Communist International] in its propaganda; it could present the USSR as an attractive model for all peoples of the world to join eventually or at least emulate. One of the standard slogans of Soviet propaganda was: "We solved all ethnic problems."

The Formation of a New Ruling Bureaucracy

Leon Trotsky

In the history of revolutions, the term "Thermidor" sig-
nifies reaction. Thermidor was the month of the French
Revolution in which the nation's most radical leaders
went to their deaths on the guillotine and the revolutionary government was conquered by the moderate
Girondins—whom the Bolshevik theorists considered a
corrupt, self-seeking, and backward-looking clique of
opportunists. In a chapter entitled "The Soviet Thermidor," excerpted here, the Bolshevik leader Leon Trotsky
explains that he saw just such a reactionary period taking
place in the Soviet Union of the 1920s. According to
Trotsky, the Soviet masses were betrayed as the original
instigators of the revolution were replaced with a new
bureaucracy whose leaders were motivated more by self-
interest than by the ideals of the Bolsheviks.

A brilliant orator and tireless writer and propagandist,
Trotsky takes much of the credit for the victory of the Bolshevik (Red) Army in the Russian civil war. However, he
found himself overmatched in the intrigues among the
highest Bolshevik officials after the death of Vladimir
Lenin. After escaping the Soviet Union, Trotsky fled as far
as Mexico, where he continued to write articles and books
condemning Joseph Stalin and the direction the revolution had taken. The following passage is excerpted from
his book *The Revolution Betrayed: What Is the Soviet Union
and Where Is It Going?*

It is sufficiently well known that every revolution up to this
time has been followed by a reaction, or even a counterrev-

Excerpted from *The Revolution Betrayed: What Is the Soviet Union and Where Is It
Going?* by Leon Trotsky, translated by Max Eastman. Copyright © 1937, 1972 by
Pathfinder Press. Reprinted by permission.

olution. This, to be sure, has never thrown the nation all the way back to its starting point, but it has always taken from the people the lion's share of their conquests. The victims of the first reactionary wave have been, as a general rule, those pioneers, initiators, and instigators who stood at the head of the masses in the period of the revolutionary offensive. In their stead people of the second line, in league with the former enemies of the revolution, have been advanced to the front. Beneath this dramatic duel of "coryphées" on the open political scene, shifts have taken place in the relations between classes, and, no less important, profound changes in the psychology of the recently revolutionary masses.

Answering the bewildered questions of many comrades as to what has become of the activity of the Bolshevik party and the working class—where is its revolutionary initiative, its spirit of self-sacrifice and plebeian pride—why, in place of all this, has appeared so much vileness, cowardice, pusillanimity and careerism—[Bulgarian revolutionary Georgi] Rakovsky referred to the life story of the French revolution of the eighteenth century, and offered the example of [French revolutionary François Noël] Babeuf, who on emerging from the Abbaye prison likewise wondered what had become of the heroic people of the Parisian suburbs. A revolution is a mighty devourer of human energy, both individual and collective. The nerves give way. Consciousness is shaken and characters are worn out. Events unfold too swiftly for the flow of fresh forces to replace the loss. Hunger, unemployment, the death of the revolutionary cadres, the removal of the masses from administration, all this led to such a physical and moral impoverishment of the Parisian suburbs that they required three decades before they were ready for a new insurrection.

The axiomlike assertions of the Soviet literature, to the effect that the laws of bourgeois revolutions are "inapplicable" to a proletarian revolution, have no scientific content whatever. The proletarian character of the October revolution was determined by the world situation and by a special correlation of internal forces. But the classes themselves were formed in the barbarous circumstances of tzarism and backward capitalism, and were anything but made to order for the demands of a socialist revolution. The exact opposite is true. It is for the very reason that a proletariat still backward in many respects achieved in the space of a few months the unprecedented leap from a semifeudal monarchy to a socialist dictatorship, that the reaction in its ranks was inevitable. This reaction has developed in a series of consecutive waves. External conditions and events have vied with each other in nourishing it. Intervention followed intervention. The revolution got no direct help from the west. Instead of the expected prosperity of the country an ominous destitution reigned for long. Moreover, the outstanding representatives of the working class either died in the civil war, or rose a few steps higher and broke away from the masses. And thus after an unexampled tension of forces, hopes and illusions, there came a long period of weariness, decline and sheer disappointment in the results of the revolution. The ebb of the "plebeian pride" made room for a flood of pusillanimity and careerism. The new commanding caste rose to its place upon this wave.

The Rise of the Soviet Bureaucracy

The demobilization of the Red Army of five million played no small role in the formation of the bureaucracy. The victorious commanders assumed leading posts in the local Soviets, in economy, in education, and they persistently introduced everywhere that regime which had ensured success in the civil war. Thus on all sides the masses were pushed away gradually from actual participation in the leadership of the country.

The reaction within the proletariat caused an extraordinary flush of hope and confidence in the petty bourgeois strata of town and country, aroused as they were to new life by the NEP [New Economic Policy], and growing bolder and bolder. The young bureaucracy, which had arisen at first as an agent of the proletariat, began now to feel itself a court of arbitration between the classes. Its independence increased from month to month.

The international situation was pushing with mighty forces in the same direction. The Soviet bureaucracy became more self-confident, the heavier the blows dealt to the world working class. Between these two facts there was not only a chronological, but a causal connection, and one which worked in two directions. The leaders of the bureaucracy promoted the proletarian defeats; the defeats promoted the rise of the bureaucracy. The crushing of the Bulgarian insurrection and the inglorious retreat of the German workers' party in 1923, the collapse of the Esthonian attempt at insurrection in 1924, the treacherous liquidation of the General Strike in England and the unworthy conduct of the Polish workers' party at the installation of Pilsudski in 1926, the terrible massacre of the Chinese revolution in 1927, and, finally, the still more ominous recent defeats in Germany and Austria—these are the historic catastrophes which killed the faith of the Soviet masses in world revolution, and permitted the bureaucracy to rise higher and higher as the sole light of salvation. . . .

Stalin and the Ruling Caste

It would be naïve to imagine that Stalin, previously unknown to the masses, suddenly issued from the wings fully armed with a complete strategical plan. No indeed. Before he felt out his own course, the bureaucracy felt out Stalin himself. He brought it all the necessary guarantees: the prestige of an old Bolshevik, a strong character, narrow vision, and close bonds with the political machine as the sole source of his influence. The success which fell upon him was a surprise at first to Stalin himself. It was the friendly welcome of the new ruling group, trying to free itself from the old principles and from the control of the masses, and having need of a reliable arbiter in its inner affairs. A secondary figure before the masses and in the events of the revolution, Stalin revealed himself as the indubitable leader of the Thermidorian bureaucracy, as first in its midst.

The new ruling caste soon revealed its own ideas, feelings and, more important, its interests. The overwhelming majority of the older generation of the present bureaucracy had stood on the other side of the barricades during the October revolution. (Take, for example, the Soviet ambassadors only:

Troyanovsky, Maisky, Potemkin, Suritz, Khinchuk, etc.) Or at best they had stood aside from the struggle. Those of the present bureaucrats who were in the Bolshevik camp in the October days played in the majority of cases no considerable role. As for the young bureaucrats, they have been chosen and educated by the elders, frequently from among their own offspring. These people could not have achieved the October revolution, but they were perfectly suited to exploit it.

Personal incidents in the interval between these two historic chapters were not, of course, without influence. Thus the sickness and death of Lenin undoubtedly hastened the denouement. Had Lenin lived longer, the pressure of the bureaucratic power would have developed, at least during the first years, more slowly. But as early as 1926 [Lenin's widow Nadezhda] Krupskaya said, in a circle of Left Oppositionists: "If Ilych were alive, he would probably already be in prison." The fears and alarming prophecies of Lenin himself were then still fresh in her memory, and she cherished no illusions as to his personal omnipotence against opposing historic winds and currents.

The bureaucracy conquered something more than the Left Opposition. It conquered the Bolshevik party. It defeated the program of Lenin, who had seen the chief danger in the conversion of the organs of the state "from servants of society to lords over society." It defeated all these enemies, the Opposition, the party and Lenin, not with ideas and arguments, but with its own social weight. The leaden rump of the bureaucracy outweighed the head of the revolution. That is the secret of the Soviet's Thermidor.

Joseph Stalin Completes the Transition to Dictatorship

Theodore H. Von Laue

The Union of Soviet Socialist Republics was founded under the leadership of Lenin. But the modern Soviet Union, in large part, was the creation of Joseph Stalin, who guided the country through almost three decades of rapid industrialization, devastating war, and the rise to international superpower status. Stalin's reign was marked by brutal suppression of any opposition, a legacy that brought a reaction from his successor Nikita Khrushchev, who through his criticism of Stalin's "cult of personality" unwittingly brought about the modern era of dissidence, self-criticism, economic reform—and collapse.

In his book *Why Lenin? Why Stalin?*, author Theodore H. Von Laue traces the rise of Stalin to power in the 1920s. He reveals that Stalin's style as a politician was determined largely by Stalin's own personality—suspicious, devious, hardworking, and ambitious. Stalin had remained an obscure figure through the revolution and the civil war, but the confused period of time after Lenin's death provided him with opportunities best suited to his abilities. Von Laue explains how Stalin completed the transformation of Soviet government, begun under Lenin, from a one-party state to a dictatorship completely dominated by its charismatic leader.

Two traits stood out in the history of Russian communism as shaped by Lenin. The first was the boundless will to advance the country (not as an accidental base of world revolution but as Russia—Holy Russia) to a position of global pre-

Excerpted from pp. 202–210 of *Why Lenin? Why Stalin?* by Theodore H. Von Laue. Copyright © 1993 by Theodore H. Von Laue. Reprinted by permission of Pearson Education, Inc.

eminence, particularly in terms of industrial strength, the basis of modern civilization. Soviet socialism was the guarantee that this goal could be reached. The other trait was a fanatical reliance on organization, "our fighting method," as Lenin had called it in 1918. There were times, of course, when dire necessity, such as the ruin of Russia in 1921, set a limit to what organization could do. Yet the very retreat of NEP [New Economic Policy] led to a reaffirmation of this principle, as the tightening of party and state apparatus indicated. He, then, who could give vigor to these Leninist traits and advance them with the same monstrous impatience which Lenin had shown almost to the end of his career would be his true heir. In these essentials, Stalin was indeed the perfect Leninist by more than his own, all too brazenly proclaimed judgment. His rise to power did not mark, therefore, a Thermidorian [counter-revolutionary] reaction, but rather Fructidor, the high summer of fruition for the most dynamic and emotion-charged element of Bolshevism. If there entered with Stalin an element of retrogression, it came, inevitably, as the result of Russian backwardness.

Joseph Vissarionovich Djugashvili, known in the revolutionary underground as the Man of Steel or Stalin, did not possess the residual sensitivity of the Russian intelligentsia, the ear for the music of humaneness which Lenin had retained, however unwillingly. He came from the toughest ethnic stock in the [Russian] Empire, the Georgian mountaineers, who had feuded for centuries with each other and their neighbors. He was further hardened by his rise from a lowly station and by his subsequent career as a professional revolutionary. While Lenin had lived abroad in relative ease, Stalin had worked and suffered for the cause inside Russia. The [Bolshevik pre-revolutionary] exiles' mastery of Marxist theory and their cultural refinement were out of his reach. But he possessed an advantage over them by representing the agitators and organizers without whom they were impotent. To all appearances, he was a humble man who put the party before personality and honored Lenin with a steadfast loyalty; he was always calm and dependable. At the time of the Bolshevik Revolution, he did not match

Trotsky's brilliance but he was an indispensable member of the Bolshevik high command. As such, he received an important assignment in the new Soviet government as People's Commissar for Nationalities. Subsequently he also headed the Workers' and Peasants' Inspection, an agency which was to realize Lenin's dream of checking the abuses of bureaucracy by letting the toilers, even the housewives, take turns at public administration.

A Model Chairman

Yet his chief service always lay within the inner circles of the party. Here he proved without peers. He was appointed to the Politburo [Political Bureau or Supreme Council] and the Orgburo [Organizational Bureau, for making political appointments] when they were first constituted; he continued to serve on them even after he was named Secretary General. Thus he combined more vital functions in his own person than any other party official, including Lenin himself. He was a model chairman, tending to keep himself in the background and getting things done with a monumental capacity for work. Although Stalin quarreled bitterly with Trotsky during the civil war, his appointment to so many posts caused no controversy within the party; no one else seemed so well suited to perform the unwanted drudgery of party administration. It was he, then, who made the party into the model monolith by supervising the entire membership, appointing reliable men to key positions in the lower echelons, and keeping them alert and docile. And it was he who laid down the basic rules of power adjustment within this ever-growing leviathan which Kremlinologists have ever since watched as the key to Soviet policies.

What he lacked were the very qualities in which the former exiles excelled. He was not much of a writer or speaker. His style was stodgy, repetitious, interspersed with simple rhetorical questions to which, catechismlike, he gave simple answers, only occasionally lighted up by trivial jokes or a touch of folklore. Yet while devoid of flair, it was not ineffectual; like all the trappings of the Stalin regime as they evolved over the years, it catered to an audience of naïve,

slow-witted, overworked, and bewildered people who retained a fairy-tale wonder for the demigods who shaped
their destinies.

His style as an administrator was also several degrees too
rough, even for Lenin. But it was not Lenin who had to cope
with the stubborn realities of the new Soviet Empire. A
monolithic party composed of former revolutionaries who,
like most Russians, lacked the capacity of spontaneous mutual accommodation, was indeed no "girls' dormitory"; it required drastic methods of compulsion. And what was true of
the party was even more true of the country as a whole. All
the devils of disunity and division in the Empire that had
plagued the tsars also beset the Soviet regime. Stalin had no
respect for mass participation in public administration. What
counted in his eyes was masterminding the minute and un-
ending details of control, ob-
serving the drift of power at the
articulation points of organization, and being willing to go to
any lengths of ruthlessness for
the sake of success. Against the
Whites or the Georgian Mensheviks (as, later, against his opponents within the party and
potential enemies throughout
the body politic), Stalin showed
the extremes to which he might
go. His harshness in imposing

Joseph Stalin

Bolshevik rule on his native Georgia shocked even Lenin,
who during the last months of his life became rather critical
of the Secretary General's crudities. Yet were ruthlessness
and terror not part of the Leninist tradition, the price which
the Russian revolutionaries had always been willing to pay for
their ideals?

It was proof of Stalin's ability as an administrator that his
hold over the party was discovered only when it could no
longer be effectively challenged. In order to secure the succession, he merely needed to prove that he possessed the required support among the membership (which he largely

controlled) and then invoke party discipline against all dissenters. In this contest he drew on all the advantages of his cold-blooded endurance and superior craftiness in a game where everybody played for the highest stakes. Politics for Stalin was a round-the-clock, year-in, year-out watch on the quarter-deck. Those who could not stand the strain counted themselves out.

Necessary Qualities

There is no need here to relate the sordid tale of deceit, lies, defamation, threats, punishment, recantation, surrender, self-doubt, self-torture, and police torture which sum up the struggle for Lenin's succession. Suffice it to ask: Who among Stalin's rivals possessed the qualities necessary for carrying the Leninist heritage to its logical conclusion in a Soviet Russia? Trotsky, who possessed the strongest claim, was no statesman capable of sustaining the continuous burden of supreme responsibility. He did not even seem to comprehend the fact that effective leadership called for meticulous, large-scale, and unrelenting organization. Besides, he showed an amazing lack of nerve at the time of Lenin's death. Instead of brushing aside Stalin's objections and rushing at once to Moscow, he idled away his time at a southern spa where he had gone in order to cure an "indisposition." The other contenders counted even less. [Lev] Zinoviev was a coward, [Nikolai] Bukharin too soft. The rest did not really possess the proper format. And since there was no settled machinery of succession, every one of these men, had *he* risen to the top, would have had to eliminate his rivals by some form of wolfishness. A militant Communist party required a single head. No collegium could maintain in the long run the dynamic drive of the Communist myth. Thus Stalin emerged as the first complete heir of the Imperial autocrat. Under the prevailing conditions, Russian society did not manage to produce a more civilized dictator. The blame, if blame there must be, falls on the country and on circumstances rather than on the man.

Stalin completed the fatal progress toward dictatorship inherent in Lenin's concept of the Bolshevik party. Before the Revolution, the organization of the party had already taken the place of the party itself. Afterward the Central Committee—and later the Politburo—took the place of the organization, and finally, under Stalin, the dictator took the place of the Central Committee and even the Politburo. At the same time, Stalin became the charismatic "leader" and the all-wise "father" of the Soviet peoples, providing in these comforting symbols a better emotional resting place for his subjects' worries than the tsars had ever furnished.

No other man in the twentieth century has wielded such unlimited power over so many subjects during so long and critical a time. Needless to say, that incredible power corrupted him. It brought out the weaknesses in his character, his desire to revenge the condescension with which the intellectuals in the party had always treated him, his suspicion of rivals, and his penchant for brutal and primitive solutions. Yet for a mortal in that rare category of self-made Caesars, he bore his burden comparatively well, certainly better than Mussolini, Hitler, or even Napoleon. His deified public image always remained a propaganda façade. Having come to his high station relatively late in life (he turned fifty in 1929), he remained free of flamboyant megalomania or idle showmanship and retained the outward simplicity—and at least a shred of the inward humility—prescribed for a true Communist leader. Only in old age, after a life of superhuman perils, did the controls of common sense break down and his rule decay into crass tyranny.

Stalin's Resolution

At the time of Lenin's death, there had been need for a strong man. However completely the party now controlled the country, its future course was shrouded in doubts. Lenin had faded from leadership without indicating a successor or even leaving a clear-cut legacy. On the one hand, his followers remembered the Bolshevik militancy of his prime; on the other, they were bound by the hesitation and caution of his last years. His directives for NEP were unprecedently tame. They emphasized the need to appease the peasants and to make Soviet progress dependent on their willingness to change. He had also left open the basic question of whether Soviet Russia could, within the foreseeable future, move into full socialism. It had been generally assumed that a predominantly agrarian society like Russia's could be propelled into socialism only with the help of a socialist West (or at least a socialist Germany). Now that revolution in Europe was ruled out, was the Soviet regime merely to mark time?

Against these undercurrents of doubt and amidst the din of the struggle for the succession, Stalin sponsored, in an uncertain and fumbling way, a note of optimism which resumed the earlier buoyancy of Bolshevism. At the fourteenth party congress in December, 1925, a historic resolution was passed which again set the sights far ahead. The party pledged itself to carry on economic construction with the intention of "transforming the USSR from a country importing machines and equipment into one producing machines and equipment, so that the USSR under the conditions of capitalist encirclement cannot be made into an economic adjunct of world capitalism, but will represent an independent economic unit built in the socialist manner and capable . . . of serving as a powerful means of revolutionizing the workers of all countries and the suppressed peoples of the colonies and semi-colonies."

Subsequently the resolution stated the theoretical premise for the projected advance, saying that "Russia possesses all that is necessary for the construction of a socialist society." This was Stalin's famous doctrine of "Socialism in One Country," which taught that Soviet Russia could confidently go ahead by itself on the road to socialism.

In the following year (1926), another party gathering pointed even more emphatically toward industrialization as the fulfillment of Soviet ambition:

> The biggest historical task set before the dictatorship of the proletariat, the creation of socialist society, demands the concentration of all forces of the party, the government, and the working class on the problems of economic policy.

The goals of that policy were now set sky high. Nothing less would do than "overtaking and surpassing the level of industrial production in the leading capitalist countries in a relatively short span of time."

The Soviet Dilemma

Yet how were these ambitions to be put into practice? Party economists were sharply divided over the proper course of Soviet economic development. One group, led by N. Bukharin, proceeded from Lenin's directives for NEP. It wanted to give the peasants, particularly the [middle-class] kulaks, still more freedom. It resumed, as it were, [Tsarist-era Minister Peter] Stolypin's policy [of modernizing Russia's rural political system under an authoritarian monarchy]. Only when a strong and prosperous rural base had been established, so ran the argument, could—and should—industry grow. Yet this approach, echoing the criticism levied against the [Sergei] Witte system,[1] endangered the monolithic nature of the Soviet dictatorship. A house divided between a free peasantry and a regimented urban working class could not long survive; granting freedom to the peasants would push the regime back toward liberal democracy. And what, meanwhile, would become of Soviet Russia's security in a hostile, "capitalist" world?

The other group, led by Trotsky and E. Preobrazhensky, started like Witte from the need for rapid industrial growth. If agriculture was to produce more, it had to be supplied with more and better industrial goods. Yet this was bound to become more difficult as the existing industrial equipment, inherited from tsarist days, began to wear out. Under these conditions, even maintaining the current level of industrial production (which had steadily risen after 1921 without, however, regaining prewar levels) would be impossible, let alone advancing to socialist plenty. The escape from this difficulty, so this group argued, lay in deliberate industrial expansion. Unfortunately, this policy cost the country dearly. In the absence of foreign capital, the huge capital outlays could be obtained only by further lowering the standard of living,

---

1.Witte (1849-1915), minister of finance under Tsar Nicholas II, sought to modernize Russia on the western European model.

by "primitive socialist accumulation," as Preobrazhensky indiscreetly put it. That, from a political point of view, seemed suicidal. Had not the Soviet regime promised a higher income to the toilers of Russia? This school of thought thus ran into the same predicament that had forced Witte's dismissal from the Ministry of Finance. The Russian people would not tolerate any further sacrifices. In short, whichever direction economic analysis took, it ended in a cul-de-sac.

By 1928, when Stalin's power over the party was at last firmly entrenched, the problem of Soviet economic development could no longer be disregarded. While his own authority was limited and the experts had disagreed, he had straddled the fence, urging rapid industrialization yet also inclining toward Bukharin's side, not wishing to antagonize the peasantry. By 1928, however, Bukharin's policy had proved a fiasco. Under the freedom which the party allowed the peasants, they did not increase their production to the limit; on the contrary, they curtailed it. Were they thus to slow down the economic advance to which the party had repeatedly pledged itself ever since 1925, and was the entire regime to bog down in the peasant sloth? Furthermore, the loss of political momentum which accompanied the struggle over the succession was already spreading corruption in party circles.

At this point, as grave a crisis as faced Soviet Russia after the civil war, Stalin returned to the full fury of Leninism. Not possessing Lenin's ability to dramatize the new phase of Soviet policy with subtle theoretical premises, he changed course clumsily and crudely, relying more on will and brute force than on technical finesse. Yet the change contained all the ingredients of a major turning point. The first thing Stalin did was to paint the international scene, just then brightened by the "spirit of Locarno" and the Kellogg-Briand pact,[2] in dark and ominous colors. He wanted to conjure up again (on dubious evidence) the wartime phobia about "capitalist" invasion and the fighting mood of the

2. The Locarno pact of 1925 was signed by Germany, France, Belgium, Great Britain, and Italy. The Kellogg-Briand pact was signed in 1928. Both of these multilateral treaties were meant to guarantee peace in Europe.

early Comintern [Communist International] in order to prepare the peoples of Russia for the sacrifices to come.

Unjustified as this doctrinaire interpretation of "capitalist" policy appeared in 1928, its pessimism was more realistic than the optimism of the West. After the outbreak of the Great Depression in the next year, the international scene changed for the worse. In the wake of the depression, the flimsy precautions of collective security crumbled and most of the new democratic regimes established after the war perished, if they had not already done so. The trend toward dictatorship was running strong in the twenties, as events in Italy, Spain, Portugal, Poland, and Lithuania had shown; now it accelerated. The entire western tradition of promoting public welfare by private initiative seemed wrecked, as unemployment and poverty suddenly descended upon millions of unsuspecting peoples.

Out of these unprecedented calamities emerged the aggressive forces responsible for the second World War. In Germany, they brought to power a totalitarian movement not without parallels to Soviet communism, despite its diametrically opposed ideology. National socialism, too, was the product of the imperialist age. It thought in terms of global power—not of a class, to be sure, but of nationality and its supposed essence, race—and it throbbed with a national pride made fanatical by the recent defeat of Germany. It, too, was geared to the age of psycho-politics, with techniques of appeal and agitation often copied from Marxist experience. At the same time it aroused more spontaneous mass support than communism enjoyed even in Russia.

Stalin Launches the Great Terror

Ronald Hingley

One of the most remarkable events of Soviet history was the Great Terror of the 1930s, a wide-ranging purge of party officials and suspected opponents by the state security forces under the reign of Joseph Stalin. During the Great Terror, millions of Soviet citizens were arrested, tried, and sent to labor camps. Millions more were summarily executed or died in torture chambers or in prison cells. The entire Soviet population lived in fear of denunciation and arrest, an event they knew could occur anytime, anywhere, and for no reason at all.

Even Joseph Stalin, a dictator with absolute power in the Soviet Union, needed a justification for the fear and bloodshed that would be carried out. Writer Ronald Hingley reveals that Stalin found his cause in the murder of Sergey Kirov, a high Communist Party official who was gunned down outside his office on December 1, 1934. The murder gave Stalin's NKVD, or state police, the excuse it needed to unleash the purges. At the time, Kirov's murder appeared to be the act of a political opponent, an enemy of the state. However, Hingley reveals that the Kirov murder may have been a carefully planned act that had its approval at the highest levels of the Soviet government, potentially masterminded by Stalin himself. Hingley describes the possible intrigue surrounding the assassination and explains Stalin's intention to purge the Communist Party of any and all officials who might have rivaled him in popularity or importance.

Excerpted from *Joseph Stalin: Man and Legend,* by Ronald Hingley (New York: McGraw-Hill). Copyright © 1974 by Ronald Hingley. Reprinted by permission of Peters, Fraser & Dunlop Group Ltd., as agents for the author.

There are few dates more significant in Stalin's biography than 1 December 1934, when his friend and colleague Sergey Kirov, Politburo member and Leningrad Party boss, was shot dead by an assassin at 4.30 in the afternoon. The murder occurred in a corridor of the Smolny Institute, Kirov's Leningrad headquarters.

Not until twenty-one months later did the full purport of the assassination become apparent, when [Grigory] Zinovyev, [Lev] Kamenev and certain associates were executed after being sentenced to death at a Moscow show trial of Communist leaders—the first of three such major spectacles—on charges which included the murder of Kirov. As is now clear beyond doubt, the Zinovyev Trial was an act of murder performed by Stalin: an act advertised in advance and carried out by judicial means before the eyes of the world. The same may be said of the two succeeding trials at which [Georgy] Pyatakov and [Nikolay] Bukharin were the main defendants, and which also pivoted on the assassination of Kirov. Stalin's motive in staging these three great pageants was to set precedents calculated to extend his freedom of action yet further. Once he had demonstrated that he could openly exterminate Lenin's closest political allies, he would be free to repress all remaining rivals, however exalted. Kirov's murder accordingly helped to make possible the judicial extermination of Zinovyev and Kamenev, as later of Pyatakov and Bukharin—thus equipping Stalin with what he had so long sought: unlimited licence to kill. Though the slaughter of Kirov removed only one political rival, it therefore paved the way for removing all other rivals, actual or potential, numbering several million, in the Great Terror of 1937–8.

During these appalling years members of the Party Apparatus, from the highest to the lowest, were to qualify for liquidation. The Terror was also to destroy the Soviet administrative, managerial, governmental, military, trade union, *Komsomol* and cultural élites: a campaign so devastating that it may be considered yet another revolution, the second to be carried out by Stalin since Lenin's death. We have already observed the Secretary-General forcibly collectivizing and industrializing a backward country, from 1929 onwards, through the earlier of these upheavals. Now the second Stalinist revolution, inaugurated by Kirov's murder, will see the dictator turning his fury against those very seasoned Stalinists who have helped him to accomplish the previous transformation. That vast numbers of politically neutral citizens will also be caught up in the maelstrom need hardly be said.

Such, eventually, was to be the outcome of Kirov's murder. But what of the crime's origin? Was Stalin, who later openly paraded himself as the liquidator of Zinovyev and Kamenev, also the real, secret, assassin of Kirov?

Possible Methods of the Crime

It was not, of course, Stalin who discharged the murder weapon; there is no record of his ever performing so humble a chore. Leonid Nikolayev it was (a disgruntled, recently expelled minor member of the Leningrad Party) who fired a Nagan revolver at Kirov on the fateful December afternoon. But what was Nikolayev's motive? More important, who put him up to it? Who removed—who ordered the removal of—the bodyguards and security apparatus surrounding the victim? One account has the assassin as a jealous husband avenging himself on the notorious lecher Kirov, whom he once chanced to surprise in bed with the attractive Milda Nikolayeva. But could a mere cuckold, unaided by accomplices within Party and police, so easily have penetrated the heavily guarded Smolny building? How was it that the murderer had not been detained while making two previous attempts to approach Kirov on the same premises: the one some six weeks before the successful assault, the other a few days previously? That Nikolayev—a dismissed Party member, and one known to be nursing a grievance at that—had even been searched on one of these occasions, that he had been caught with a revolver and an incriminating notebook, yet was merely sent about his business without suffering detailed investigation . . . these and other details suggested that the assassin had not been acting on his own, but that members of the Leningrad NKVD had afforded him every facility short of actually pressing the trigger.

The officer immediately responsible for relaxing security measures in the Smolny was [Ivan] Zaporozhets, second-in-command of the Leningrad NKVD. He in turn had been briefed by [Genrikh] Yagoda (head of security police from 1934 until 1936), according to the official Stalinist version of the episode as developed at the Bukharin Trial. But who set in motion the chain leading from Yagoda through Zaporozhets to Nikolayev? Was this instigator indeed, as also stated at the Bukharin trial, the Leader's former crony [Abel] Yenukidze, who had since been conveniently liquidated? Or should we look further back? Even if Yenukidze *was* involved, may he not have been yet another go-between? Was the prime mover indeed Stalin himself?

The dictator's complicity has been accepted with varying degrees of conviction by leading Western authorities, also receiving confirmation by innuendo in certain statements made by [Nikita] Khrushchev. 'There are reasons for the suspicion [Khrushchev stated in 1956] that the killer of Kirov, Nikolayev, was assisted by *someone* from among the people whose duty it was to protect the person of Kirov.' Khrushchev returned to the theme again in 1961, pointing out that Kirov's main bodyguard (whose name was Borisov) had been murdered by NKVD agents in a fake traffic accident on the day following the assassination . . . murdered just as he was being taken to an interrogation which threatened to reveal too much about the real origins of the Kirov killing, as also about Borisov's mysterious absence from the scene and failure to protect his master. Then Borisov's killers had been exterminated in their turn; evidently '*someone* needed to have them killed in order to cover up all traces.' Since three such 'someones' (Zaporozhets, Yagoda, Yenukidze) had already been clearly identified at the Bukharin Trial, Khrushchev was now transparently hinting—in the language of one who longs to wound, yet fears to strike—at a fourth, previously unidentified, hand behind these murky proceedings: that of Stalin himself.

Another theory has also been put forward: that the assassination was indeed staged on Stalin's orders, but that it was all along intended as a fake attempt expressly designed to be 'narrowly averted' at the last moment, thus providing the dictator with the excuse to introduce severe emergency measures while yet leaving his old friend Kirov intact. Such a bogus assassination would have been a delicate affair indeed, and some last-minute failure in co-ordination might easily have led on to the real thing. In the absence of evidence for or against this version, one can only say that it is hard to square with Stalin's usual *modus operandi*. Rarely, if ever, do we find him seeking to be more subtle than the practical exigencies of his situation required.

The fact is that we simply do not know exactly how Kirov's murder came about, and we are still in no position to assess the degree of Stalin's complicity with any certainty. To state outright, as Robert Conquest does [in his book *The Great Terror*], that the dictator had decided in advance to murder Kirov is to go beyond the evidence which the Stalinist machine was so remorselessly engaged in destroying. Nor, in the light of Stalin's thoroughness as a suppressor of inconvenient information, are we ever likely to tap any new, mysteriously surviving source which might clear up this affair once and for all. We can merely speculate in the dark on the basis of the scanty evidence and of Stalin's known character, opportunities and motives.

That one who was to accomplish so many publicly flaunted judicial murders—those of Zinovyev, Kamenev and many another old comrade—that such a man would not have been deterred by mere scruple from ordering the earlier, secret extermination of his friend and colleague Kirov, need hardly be stated. There is no evidence that Stalin was ever influenced by considerations of morality or of loyalty to his associates, either in late 1934 or during any other phase of his march to supremacy. The dictator's opportunities for accomplishing such villainy undetected were considerable, too, owing to his total mastery of Soviet communications, not to mention the elaborately intermeshing security police organs which he maintained: all operating in secret, yet none being sufficiently close to the dictator to be certain that it was not itself under surveillance by some other body of custodians yet more clandestine.

The Murder Provides an Excuse

So much for Stalin's opportunities. With regard to his possible motives, we have already identified one of them, and the most significant in the long term, as the search for a general licence to kill. Kirov's popularity, his claims to be considered a potential alternative Number One, his grip on the Leningrad Party machine . . . these, too, have already been mentioned as features likely to have embarrassed the dictator. To them must be added Kirov's inconvenient posture as a focus for 'moderate' opinion—opposed to Stalin's extremism—within a Politburo consisting, before the assassination, of ten full members. Two other Politburo moderates were Kuybyshev and Ordzhonikidze, who had recently allied themselves with Kirov in urging a retreat from out-and-out pro-Stalinist positions. With regard to these so-called moderates, we should add that all three of them had long been prepared to sanction extreme mass violence so long as this had been applied to other people. They were 'liberals' in the highly restricted sense of seeking means to curb government by massacre only at the point where their own persons appeared to be threatened. Since other members of the Politburo have also been rumoured as vacillating in their support for Stalin, the importance of removing from the ten-man ruling caucus the three most disaffected among potential hostile voters can hardly be exaggerated. Every such individual removal increased Stalin's leverage within so small a body.

The murder of Kirov also provided the dictator with an excuse for decreeing an immediate state of emergency throughout the USSR. To combat political terrorism as exemplified by this assassination possibly or probably ordained by Stalin, it was arguably expedient to employ counterterrorist Terror most certainly ordained by Stalin. On receiving the news of Kirov's death, the dictator accordingly leapt into sudden action, hastening to extend his persecutions to fellow-Bolsheviks hitherto immune. Without waiting for the Politburo's approval he at once issued a decree accelerating the investigation of terrorism and ordering the immediate execution, without right of appeal, of those found guilty. This new directive helped to provide the rationale for the coming tidal wave of Stalinist atrocities.

After promulgating these measures, Stalin immediately left Moscow for Leningrad by train. He descended on the former capital at dawn on 2 December, taking over a floor of the Smolny Institute and personally assuming control of the 'investigation' into the murder. The main object of this inquiry was to exploit the case politically, while ensuring that the dictator's own involvement (great or small) should be buried deep with the bodies of any who might have inside knowledge of the background. The assassin Nikolayev was 'tried' *in camera* and then shot on 29 December, taking with him to the grave any information compromising higher authority which he may have possessed. The Leningrad NKVD chiefs were also arrested and sent to concentration camps, but under privileged conditions and with relatively short sentences; later, in 1937, when a few extra shootings could no longer attract attention, they were quietly liquidated.

These minor police officials were not particularly important to Stalin, and were presumably exterminated because they knew too much. Nor need we waste time puzzling over the hundred-odd alleged White supporters shot in Leningrad and Moscow soon after Kirov's murder, in accordance with an early official version of the outrage: that it was the work of anti-Soviet emissaries from abroad. Nor yet need we make more than passing reference to the forty-thousand-odd Leningraders deported to Siberia and the Arctic after Kirov's murder. The dictator's real targets were Zinovyev and Kamenev—as became evident barely a fortnight after Kirov's death, when these two senior victims-designate were arrested. In the following month they were secretly tried, for giving encouragement to the terrorist 'centre' supposedly responsible for Nikolayev's crime; they were persuaded to admit moral culpability, but received only prison sentences of ten and five years.

Convenient Deaths Among the Leaders

Though this was the 'first occasion (apart from the case of Sultan-Galiyev in 1923) . . . on which political opposition by Communists . . . was made the subject of an open criminal charge', and as such was a minor milestone in Stalin's career, measures so half-hearted were of little use to him at this stage. He had, one must suspect, already set his heart on exterminating Lenin's former comrades-in-arms, and nothing less would do. If, as seems likely, the dictator was already pressing hard for the physical annihilation of Zinovyev and Kamenev, he must have been thwarted by temporarily effective opposition within the Politburo. How convenient, therefore, when Kuybyshev died of a 'heart attack' within two months of Kirov's even more convenient demise. The police overlord Yagoda and various doctors were later to stand accused of murdering Kuybyshev—more strictly, of hastening his death by deliberately failing to give him correct medical treatment. But if Yagoda did indeed do away with Kuybyshev somehow or other, he may well have been acting on Stalin's orders . . . especially as the Leader is actually known to have been responsible, between 1934 and 1940, for the death of at least sixteen other persons who had been, at one time or another, members of the Politburo. We must also remember that, at the time of Kirov's and Kuybyshev's deaths, Stalin still had no means of removing Politburo members other than discreetly camouflaged murder. In any case the main point was that the disappearance, contrived or accidental, of every such 'moderate' brought the Leader one step nearer to the kind of Politburo which he needed: one with a dependable majority consisting of obedient flunkeys.

Stalin used more gradual methods to oust the genial Yenukidze, the old crony and fellow-Georgian who was eventually to be charged posthumously with ultimate responsibility for Kirov's murder. As a veteran Georgian Bolshevik, Yenukidze was guilty of one particularly heinous offence: that of knowing too much about Stalin's past as a member of the Caucasian Bolshevik underground. In particular, Yenukidze was all too well aware that the youthful Dzhugashvili's [Stalin's] role in early Party history had been obscure and inglorious. Though Yenukidze had since tried to atone for this by writing mendacious accounts of the Leader's heroic youth, he had never managed to catch up with the fast developing

Legend, and his own contributions to Stalin's fictitious biography were soon to be eclipsed by the yet more thorough-paced fabrications of [Laurenti] Beria. As first mooted, Yenukidze's public disgrace revolved about this very point: he admitted in *Pravda* of 16 January 1935 that he had been guilty of errors in describing early Bolshevik history in the Caucasus. Within a month or two he had been deprived of his various offices as a prelude to liquidation and posthumous vilification at the Bukharin Trial.

Signs also began to appear that the 'great' writer and humanist Maxim Gorky, who had done so much to bolster Stalin's reputation, was also in trouble. On 28 January *Pravda* published an attack on Gorky, who had hitherto been sacrosanct. Gorky was to die in June 1936, and since he too is known to have been a moderate, urging Stalin to be reconciled with Kamenev and other political enemies, the suspicion has arisen that he too may have been murdered. This was to be expressly asserted at the Bukharin Trial, at which Gorky figured as one victim in the series of medical homicides allegedly engineered by Yagoda. That Stalin had Gorky killed seems all too possible. . . .

The Party Smashed

Assaulting the governmental, technical, managerial, cultural and other élites, the Great Terror could not but take a high toll within the Party, since so high a proportion among the most prominent members of the various Soviet establishments consisted of card-holding Communists. Nor did the Party's inner core of full-time functionaries—the *apparatchiki*—escape Stalin's fury.

In Moscow, in Leningrad, at provincial centres within the RSFSR, as also in the Ukraine, Belorussia, the Caucasus and Central Asia . . . everywhere the Terror struck. While higher officials sought to cover up or buy time by zeal in liquidating lesser fry, these juniors themselves strove to forestall their fate by feverishly denouncing high-ups to still higher authority: all in vain. None, at any level, could count on immunity, though danger was fairly closely correlated with seniority. Thus the way was opened, as in the Army, for the rapid promotion of juniors. But such beneficiaries were, more often than not, soon dismissed and shot in their turn, to be succeeded by further doomed relays. Such was the general picture throughout Stalin's slave empire at this period, though many variations are recorded from one area to another: in timing: in the identity of the main purgers; in severity of impact; in the extent of our knowledge. . . .

How, in these chaotic circumstances, could any individual hope to preserve a whole skin? Certainly not by protesting to Stalin about the excesses of the Terror, for there was no quicker passport to liquidation. Nor might immunity even be guaranteed by excess of zeal in exterminating one's colleagues, since such arch-exterminators automatically qualified as convenient scapegoats against the inevitable day when Stalin should decide to pose as the advocate of restraint. Nor yet could the cultivation of passive unobtrusiveness—an attitude no less conspicuous, in this grotesque age, than any other—be relied upon to deflect the sword of injustice. Amid the raging Terror only one tiny group of persons retained immunity: Stalin's half dozen senior colleagues among full Politburo members: Andreyev, Kaganovich, Kalinin, Mikoyan, Molotov and Voroshilov. To them must be added three top-échelon touring purgers, slightly junior in Party rank, but soon to achieve Politburo candidate membership: Khrushchev, Malenkov and Beria. With these must be contrasted the ten Politburo members or candidate members, elected in 1934 or later, who fell by the wayside during the following years: the Kirov-Kuybyshev-Ordzhonikidze trio, early removed by murder or good luck; four Ukrainian Party chiefs (Postyshev, Kosior, Chubar and Petrovsky); the two Latvians Rudzutak and Eykhe; and—in the end—the chief author (under Stalin) of the Great Terror, Yezhov.

The two Politburo Latvians figure among those posthumously accorded martyr status by Khrushchev, who speaks of a secret trial of Rudzutak at which the latter denounced a conspiratorial centre 'as yet not liquidated . . . which is craftily manufacturing cases, and which forces innocent persons to confess'. Aware or not that he was denouncing Stalin himself with these words, Rudzutak was shot, his last accusation remaining buried for nearly twenty years in the archives. Eykhe, the other Politburo Latvian, was among the many physically tortured by NKVD officers; they exploited the knowledge that his 'broken ribs had not properly mended and were causing me great pain.' Physical torture was sanctioned by Stalin in the summer of 1937, and had been widely applied before that. Administered with extreme brutality, it was yet employed unsystematically on the whole, and in accordance with the individual NKVD interrogator's inspiration of the moment.

All in all, as many as a million Party members or former members may have perished in the Great Terror. Even so they probably contributed no more than 10 per cent of the grand total of fatalities, which may well have exceeded ten million. Forming so small a proportion among the totality of martyrs, card-holding Soviet Communists surely remain, among all Stalin's victims, those whose passing has least claim on the regrets of posterity. By whatever combination—of gullibility, misplaced idealism, careerism, corruption, conceit in trying to build a Utopia on their contemporaries' bones— each slaughtered Party man had in some degree contributed to his butcher's professional advancement. 'He that diggeth a pit shall fall into it.'

The Purge of 1937

Aleksandr I. Solzhenitsyn

Aleksandr I. Solzhenitsyn served his country well as an officer in the Soviet army during World War II. However, in 1945 he made a derogatory comment about Joseph Stalin in a letter to a friend. His mail was opened and read by a party official. He was promptly arrested, tried, and sent to a Soviet labor camp, where he served out a long term for his illegal opinions.

Solzhenitsyn's would have been one of many million such stories, unnoticed by anyone within or outside of the Soviet Union. Much to the chagrin of the Soviet government, however, he was also a skillful and ambitious writer. His powerful account of the Soviet prison system, *The Gulag Archipelago*, first appeared in an English translation in 1974. A best-seller in the West, while banned inside the Soviet Union, the book was the first of many such exposés of the Soviet system that embarrassed Soviet officials attempting to pursue détente with the West. It earned Solzhenitsyn a long exile to the United States, where he was treated as an anti-Communist hero and a wise oracle on Russian culture and history.

In the following excerpt, Solzhenitsyn describes the purges of 1937–38 engineered by Joseph Stalin. He vividly portrays the atmosphere of fear and suspicion that pervaded Soviet society while the government used the weapon of police terror to enforce party discipline and eradicate dissent.

Excerpted from *The Gulag Archipelago, 1918–1956: An Experiment in Literary Investigation I–II*, by Aleksandr I. Solzhenitsyn. Copyright © 1973 by Aleksandr I. Solzhenitsyn. English language translation copyright © 1973, 1974 by Harper & Row, Publishers, Inc. Reprinted by permission of HarperCollins Publishers, Inc.

The damascene steel of Article 58,* first tried out in 1927, right after it was forged, was wetted by all the waves of the following decade, and with whistle and slash was used to the full to deal telling blows in the law's attack upon the people in 1937–1938.

Here one has to make the point that the 1937 operation was not arbitrary or accidental, but well planned well ahead of time, and that in the first half of that year many Soviet prisons were re-equipped. Cots were taken out of the cells and continuous one- or two-storied board benches or bunks were built. Old prisoners claim to remember that the first blow allegedly took the form of mass arrests, striking virtually throughout the whole country on one single August night. (But, knowing our clumsiness, I don't really believe this.) In that autumn, when people were trustingly expecting a big, nationwide amnesty on the twentieth anniversary of the October Revolution, Stalin, the prankster, added unheard-of fifteen- and twenty-year prison terms to the Criminal Code.'

There is hardly any need to repeat here what has already been widely written, and will be written many times more, about 1937: that a crushing blow was dealt the upper ranks of the Party, the government, the military command, and the GPU-NKVD [state police] itself. There was hardly one province of the Soviet Union in which the first secretary of the Party Committee or the Chairman of the Provincial Executive Committee survived. Stalin picked more suitable people for his purposes.

Olga Chavchavadze tells how it was in Tbilisi. In 1938 the Chairman of the City Executive Committee, his first deputy, department chiefs, their assistants, all the chief accountants, all the chief economists were arrested. New ones were appointed in their places. Two months passed, and the arrests began again: the chairman, the deputy, all eleven department chiefs, all the chief accountants, all the chief economists. The only people left at liberty were ordinary accountants, stenographers, charwomen, and messengers. . . .

*Article 58 of the Criminal Code of the Russian Soviet Federated Socialist Republic defined counter-revolutionary crimes and set out punishments for such crimes as well as for treason, espionage, terrorism, and sabotage.

Here is one vignette from those years as it actually occurred. A district Party conference was under way in Moscow Province. It was presided over by a new secretary of the District Party Committee, replacing one recently *arrested*. At the conclusion of the conference, a tribute to Comrade Stalin was called for. Of course, everyone stood up (just as everyone had leaped to his feet during the conference at every mention of his name). The small hall echoed with "stormy applause, rising to an ovation." For three minutes, four minutes, five minutes, the "stormy applause, rising to an ovation," continued. But palms were getting sore and raised arms were already aching. And the older people were panting from exhaustion. It was becoming insufferably silly even to those who really adored Stalin. However, who would dare be the *first* to stop? The secretary of the District Party Committee could have done it. He was standing on the platform, and it was he who had just called for the ovation. But he was a newcomer. He had taken the place of a man who'd been arrested. He was afraid! After all, NKVD men were standing in the hall applauding and watching to see *who* quit first! And in that obscure, small hall, unknown to the Leader, the applause went on—six, seven, eight minutes! They were done for! Their goose was cooked! They couldn't stop now till they collapsed with heart attacks! At the rear of the hall, which was crowded, they could of course cheat a bit, clap less frequently, less vigorously, not so eagerly—but up there with the presidium where everyone could see them? The director of the local paper factory, an independent and strong-minded man, stood with the presidium. Aware of all the falsity and all the impossibility of the situation, he still kept on applauding! Nine minutes! Ten! In anguish he watched the secretary of the District Party Committee, but the latter dared not stop. Insanity! To the last man! With make-believe enthusiasm on their faces, looking at each other with faint hope, the district leaders were just going to go on and on applauding till they fell where they stood, till they were carried out of the hall on stretchers! And even then those who were left would not falter. . . . Then, after eleven minutes, the director of the paper factory assumed a businesslike expression and sat down in his seat. And, oh, a miracle took place! Where had the universal, uninhibited, indescribable enthusiasm gone? To a man, everyone else stopped dead and sat down. They had been saved! The squirrel had been smart enough to jump off his revolving wheel.

That, however, was how they discovered who the independent people were. And that was how they went about eliminating them. That same night the factory director was arrested. They easily pasted ten years on him on the pretext of something quite different. But after he had signed Form 206, the final document of the interrogation, his interrogator reminded him:

"Don't ever be the first to stop applauding!"

(And just what are we supposed to do? How are we supposed to stop?)

Now that's what [Charles] Darwin's natural selection is. And that's also how to grind people down with stupidity.

The Arrest Quotas

But today a new myth is being created. Every story of 1937 that is printed, every reminiscence that is published, relates without exception the tragedy of the Communist leaders. They have kept on assuring us, and we have unwittingly fallen for it, that the history of 1937 and 1938 consisted chiefly of the arrests of the big Communists—and virtually no one else. But out of the *millions* arrested at that time, important Party and state officials could not possibly have represented more than 10 percent. Most of the relatives standing in line with food parcels outside the Leningrad prisons were lower-class women, the sort who sold milk.

The composition of the hordes who were arrested in that powerful wave and lugged off, half-dead, to the Archipelago [prison camp system] was of such fantastic diversity that anyone who wants to deduce the rationale for it scientifically will rack his brain a long time for the answer. (To the contemporaries of the purge it was still more incomprehensible.)

The real law underlying the arrests of those years was *the assignment of quotas*, the norms set, the planned allocations. Every city, every district, every military unit was assigned a specific quota of arrests to be carried out by a stipulated time. From then on everything else depended on the ingenuity of the Security operations personnel.

The former Chekist [state police member] Aleksandr Kalganov recalls that a telegram arrived in Tashkent: "Send 200!" They had just finished one clean-out, and it seemed as if there was "no one else" to take. Well, true, they had just brought in about fifty more from the districts. And then they had an idea! They would reclassify as 58's all the nonpolitical offenders being held by the police. No sooner said than done. But despite that, they had still not filled the quota. At that precise moment the police reported that a gypsy band had impudently encamped on one of the city squares and asked what to do with them. Someone had another bright idea! They surrounded the encampment and raked in all the gypsy men from seventeen to sixty as 58's! They had fulfilled the plan!

This could happen another way as well: according to Chief of Police Zabolovsky, the Chekists of Ossetia were given a quota of five hundred to be shot in the Republic. They asked to have it increased, and they were permitted another 250.

Telegrams transmitting instructions of this kind were sent via ordinary channels in a very rudimentary code. In Temryuk the woman telegrapher, in holy innocence, transmitted to the NKVD switchboard the message that 240 boxes of soap were to be shipped to Krasnodar the following day. In the morning she learned about a big wave of arrests and guessed the meaning of the message! She told her girl friend what kind of telegram it was—and was promptly arrested herself.

(Was it indeed totally by chance that the code words for human beings were *a box of soap?* Or were they familiar with soap-making?)

Targets of the Purges

Of course, certain patterns could be discerned.

Among those arrested were:

Our own real spies abroad. (These were often the most dedicated Comintern [Communist International] workers and

Chekists, and among them were many attractive women. They were called back to the Motherland and arrested at the border. They were then confronted with their former Comintern chief, for example, Mirov-Korona, who confirmed that he himself had been working for one of the foreign intelligence services—which meant that his subordinates were automatically guilty too. And the more dedicated they were, the worse it was for them.)

Soviet employees of the Chinese Eastern Railroad, the KVZhD, were one and all arrested as Japanese spies, including their wives, children, and grandmothers. But we have to admit these arrests had already begun several years earlier.

Koreans from the Far East were sent into exile in Kazakhstan—the first experiment in mass arrests *on the basis of race.*

Leningrad Estonians were all arrested on the strength of having Estonian family names and charged with being anti-Communist Estonian spies.

All Latvian Riflemen and all Latvian Chekists were arrested. Yes, indeed, those very Latvians who had been the midwives of the Revolution, who just a short while before had constituted the nucleus and the pride of the Cheka! And with them were taken even those Communists of bourgeois Latvia who had been exchanged in 1921—and been freed thereby from their dreadful Latvian prison terms of two and three years. (In Leningrad, the Latvian Department of the Herzen Institute, the House of Latvian Culture, the Estonian Club, the Latvian Technicum, and the Latvian and Estonian newspapers were all closed down.)

In the midst of the general to-do, the Big Solitaire game was finally wound up. All those not yet taken were raked in. There was no longer any reason to keep it secret. The time had come to write "finis" to the whole game. So now the socialists were taken off to prison in whole "exiles" (for example, the Ufa "exile" and the Saratov "exile"), and they were all sentenced together and driven off in herds to the slaughterhouses of the Archipelago.

Chapter 3

Building Socialism

Turning|Points
IN WORLD HISTORY

Early Attempts to Manage the Economy

Peter Kenez

During the civil war that lasted roughly from 1918 to 1922, Lenin imposed an economic policy of "war communism," which included forced labor, grain confiscation, restrictions on trade unions, and state control of industry. Following the war, in an effort to revive the devastated economy, Lenin eased his control of the economy by instituting the New Economic Policy (NEP), which allowed small-scale private businesses to operate free of government control. In addition, the Russian peasants, who made up 80 percent of the population, were allowed to keep their land and freely market their products. In the following selection, Peter Kenez describes the challenges confronted by the Bolsheviks as they attempted to bring about the recovery of the agricultural and industrial sectors of the economy in the 1920s. Kenez is the author of *A History of the Soviet Union from the Beginning to the End*, from which this essay was excerpted.

In their effort to rebuild the economy the Bolsheviks returned to the principles of capitalism. After they made their first crucial and ideologically difficult concession, accepting private ownership, they showed considerable flexibility and were willing to use heterodox methods to bring about national recovery. Lenin, who had high hopes of attracting foreign capital by offering concessions, went further in promising foreigners the possibility of unhindered exploitation of the country's natural resources than some of the White leaders, such as for example General [Anton Ivanovich] Denikin.

Excerpted from *A History of the Soviet Union from the Beginning to the End*, by Peter Kenez. Copyright © Peter Kenez 1999. Reprinted with the permission of Cambridge University Press.

The young Soviet state, however, had little success in attracting foreign capital. Given the prevailing economic conditions and the understandable suspicions of capitalists, it is not surprising that only an insignificant amount of foreign capital entered the economy. Even at the end of the decade [the 1920s], when the Soviet economy was stable and the regime had shown its ability to survive, only a 0.6 percent of the total output of the economy was produced by foreign concessions. It is therefore fair to say that foreign help had played little or no part in the revival of the economy.

Recovery was blocked by bottlenecks: industry could not operate without a functioning transportation system, and the trains, in turn, could not run without fuel. Under the circumstances, the government had to concentrate scarce resources in the critical areas. The first priority was the production of coal—the miners in the Donets basin and elsewhere received extra food to enable them to perform their heavy work. Soviet Russia used its small supply of convertible currency to buy railway engines and rolling stock abroad. There was a high price to pay, however, for these necessary steps: providing one group with better nourishment could come only at the expense of others. Economizing with scarce resources and capital led to the closing of numerous inefficient factories. During war communism the workers had frequently received their wages in food; losing jobs often meant starvation. The immediate consequence of the introduction of the new economic policies meant increased hardship for many, and the standard of living of the working class fell even further. For some time the market did not function normally: the relationship between agricultural and industrial prices wildly fluctuated. (At a time of high inflation, all prices rose; the issue was the relationship of prices.) In the middle of 1922, as compared to the pre-war situation, the exchange was excessively favorable to agriculture. This imbalance was partially the result of the desperate need for food: at a time of famine, those who had surplus food could demand very high prices.

The relative decline of industrial prices, paradoxically, was also partially the consequence of the extreme disorganization of industry. The factories, suddenly denied resources from the government, desperately needed capital. Since the factories did not have a functioning network for selling their products, in some instances they were forced to trade in the streets of the cities in order to raise money. On occasion factories were even compelled to sell some of their machinery. At a time when Soviet industry produced only a fraction of what Russian industry had produced before the war, goods were unsalable.

In the following year, prices changed in such a way as to become grossly unfavorable to the village. This was because it was more difficult to reconstruct industry than agriculture: famine had been alleviated, but industry remained extremely inefficient, with low productivity and a high cost of production. In addition, the distribution system continued to perform poorly. The consequence of high industrial prices in a market economy was predictable. The peasants once again had little incentive to part with their products. This was the so-called scissors crisis—a name given by Trotsky, who had a knack for the vivid phrase. The two widening blades respectively stood for agricultural and industrial prices. Since in the Soviet economy all major economic issues had political overtones, the government, fearing another crisis in its ability to feed the cities, took energetic measures to force down industrial prices in October 1923.

A major step toward normalization was the stabilization of the currency. The Soviet government was not entirely responsible for the hyperinflation, which was as deep as the better-known German one. The depreciation of the currency began when the imperial government decided to cover war expenditures by printing more money; the revolution and the civil war greatly exacerbated the problem. At its nadir, the country was reverting to barter economy; paper money had become worthless. In order to save the situation, the government had to draw up balanced budgets and revive the banking system. Between 1922 and 1924 the government managed in several steps to create a stable currency based on gold.

After the first two or three years of the new economic system, the government had reason to be pleased with the results. Life was gradually returning to normal. Private enterprise dominated the economy, producing more than 50 percent of the national income. Agriculture was almost entirely in private hands: even at the end of the period, state farms and collective farms occupied less than 2 percent of the land under cultivation. Small-scale industry was private, while large-scale heavy industry was state-owned. The government retained control over the mines, the banking system, and foreign trade, and thus had a decisive influence in running the economy.

The rate of recovery was uneven in different sectors of the economy. Agriculture was first to catch up with pre-war production standards. Light industry (factories that produced consumer goods) was next to improve, and heavy industry was slowest to recover. Foreign trade revived, though it remained far below what it had been before the war. The mixed economy and the one-party state created a society profoundly different both from what had existed before the revolution and what was to come as a result of Stalinist industrialization.

The Arrival of the NEPmen

The revolution and its immediate aftermath brought about a great social leveling. In the new economic system, however, differentiation once again emerged. NEP spawned a new social phenomenon, the NEPman. This new social stratum came into being in order to take advantage of the economic opportunities offered by the regime. Enterprising people traveled to the villages, selling clothes, shoes, razor blades and so forth. The prices were high and the quality invariably low; nonetheless, at a time when the normal distribution network did not function, the NEPman provided a useful service. Peasants could not be expected to take their products to the consumer. The NEPman took this task on himself, frequently making exorbitant profit in the process. But food once again became available and plentiful in the cities, at least for those who could afford to pay the high prices.

The new class was a heterogeneous one. Its members

came from different social backgrounds: enterprising peasants, descendants of the pre-war petty-bourgeoisie, and even some former members of the aristocracy now tried to make a living in unaccustomed circumstances. Some of the NEPmen were well off. People who traded in the cities or operated factories could make a great deal of money, but others remained petty traders barely eking out a living. This social class was emblematic of the world of the 1920s. The newly rich were visible: conspicuous consumption in the midst of poverty was especially disturbing following a great revolution fought in the name of equality. For most Bolsheviks the NEPman represented everything they disliked: petty bourgeois desire for property and profit, lack of ideological interests, and a middle-class life style. In the second half of the decade, many of the NEPmen found that they could not continue their business activities. From the beginning such people had operated on the margins of legality, and as regulations became stricter and more numerous, as the government trade network was able to perform some of the tasks itself, the activities of the NEPmen seemed more and more like black market operations.

From the point of view of the working class, the results of the great revolution were ambiguous. In theory, Soviet Russia was a state of workers and peasants, and the Bolshevik party, in particular, claimed to represent the workers. It is impossible to say to what extent the workers accepted this claim at face value, but Bolshevik appeals were obviously not without effect. It may be that many workers derived psychological benefits from living in a political system that was described as the "dictatorship of the proletariat."

The NEP and the Workers

The workers did also have some tangible gains. The state was building a bureaucracy. There was constant need for functionaries, and the party, on the basis of its ideology, trusted the workers more than others and whenever possible attempted to promote them. Paradoxically, the greatest gain the workers enjoyed was the opportunity to cease being workers. The possibility of making a career in the new system was open to all intelligent and ambitious workers. One would guess that even those workers who had no ambition to leave the factory bench came to identify with the new state because they saw their friends promoted.

The labor legislation of the NEP modified the policy of war communism: forcible labor conscription was abolished. Workers could freely sell their labor in either the private or the state sector of the economy. The regime abandoned its early egalitarian policies. Skilled workers now received much better wages than the unskilled. The trade unions, at least in the private sector, regained a limited ability to protect the economic interests of the workers. Although strikes were legal, the party leadership above all was interested in reconstruction and therefore prevented the spread of strikes through its control over the trade unions. Labor legislation in other aspects was in advance of that existing at the time in capitalist countries: it limited the length of the working day, forbade child labor, and provided paid vacations and health insurance.

As far as concrete economic gains were concerned, the situation was not so favorable. The standard of living could not rise until the economy recovered, and that was a slow and painful process. In the first half of the 1920s the cities recovered their populations, with the exception of Petrograd. The new urban influx meant the housing situation deteriorated. Since labor productivity remained below pre-war standards, rising labor costs came at the expense of accumulating capital for industrialization. The government therefore resisted wage increases.

The most severe problem was unemployment. Even after the economy recovered, in the second half of the 1920s, unemployment did not diminish but worsened. Since the countryside was tremendously overpopulated, once conditions in the cities became bearable the peasants flocked into industry, just as before the war. Both private industry and state enterprises were cost conscious and conservative in hiring workers. Unemployment hit various sectors of the working classes unevenly. Older, skilled and experienced workers were less likely to suffer than young workers and women.

The Komsomol (the youth organization), however, was not allowed to champion the interests of the younger workers, for the regime feared setting one section of the working classes against another. Unemployment benefits depended on how long a worker had been employed. Consequently, seasonal workers and the young who had never held jobs remained ineligible. The chronic problems of industry, such as unemployment and inability to accumulate capital for industrialization, created an atmosphere of crisis. This atmosphere colored the debate concerning the economic future of the country.

Resistance Among the Peasants

In 1917 the Bolsheviks had allowed the peasants to take the land and cultivate it as if it were their own only because they had no choice. Like the provisional government before, the Bolsheviks lacked the strength to prevent forcible land seizures. In the course of the 1920s, however, they looked apprehensively at the countryside, where private property consciousness was taking ever firmer roots. In theory the Bolshevik solution was to persuade the peasants to give up their lands and join collective farms. In the utopian era of the civil war, agitators had made serious attempts to convince the peasants that collective agriculture was superior to individual. The agitation, however, had backfired. The peasants hated even the idea of collectives, and anti-Bolshevik propagandists took advantage of this hatred. They told their audiences that in case of Red victory everything would be collectivized. The Bolsheviks had to abandon even agitation for the time being.

During the great economic debates of the 1920s Bolshevik theorists returned to the topic of collective agriculture. They argued that once the state became rich enough to support collective farms with machinery and fertilizers, and the peasants could see the advantages of cooperation, they would voluntarily join. Since in fact the state was not in a position to support collective farms, the discussion remained theoretical. In reality there was no evidence whatever that the peasants would easily give up their land.

As the rural self government of the tsarist regime, the *zemstva*, was dismantled, and as the village soviets could not take their place, the traditional peasant village commune came to play a greater role than ever before. It was this institution rather than the village soviet that made the important decisions in the village, and the village communes continued to elude the influence of Soviet power. Although the Bolshevik government distrusted them, it took no immediate steps against them. As pre-war economists and politicians recognized, the commune was a hindrance to economic growth. A strange blend of communalism and individualism, the peasant commune periodically redistributed land; therefore the peasants had little incentive to improve their holdings. The very foundation of the commune was the egalitarian sensibility of the peasantry, which required that the better and worse agricultural lands be fairly distributed. The consequence of such distributions was that families often received small strips of land in different parts of the village, making efficient cultivation, especially mechanized cultivation, difficult if not impossible. It is likely, however, that the main reason for Bolshevik hostility to the communes was not their economic inefficiency, but the inability of the regime to control them.

Under the conditions of NEP, class differentiation in the villages—which had greatly diminished as a result of the revolution—started to increase again. Differentiation, however, remained very slight, the gap between the poor and the rich very narrow. The Bolsheviks, for reasons of their own, in their writings and discussions always exaggerated the extent of stratification. They feared and mistrusted the peasant class, but it was impossible for them to say this aloud, or perhaps even to admit it to themselves. Instead, they aimed their animosity at the richest layer of the peasant class, the kulaks, who made up approximately 5 percent of the peasantry. The kulak category remained ill-defined. Possessing some sort of agricultural machinery, or occasionally lending grain to poorer neighbors was sufficient to be considered a kulak. Since only 1 percent of the peasantry hired labor, it was impossible to define kulaks as peasants who exploited others.

The leaders of the regime faced exactly the same dilemma in connection with the kulaks as they did with the NEPmen. It was a dilemma at the heart of the contradictions of the NEP, one that led to the ultimate demise of the system. On the one hand, the Bolsheviks needed the services of the kulaks. Only the better-off peasants could produce for the market, and without them the regime could not properly feed the cities and would have no grain for export. On the other hand, as communists, they feared that the increased economic power of the kulaks would inevitably lead to political power. They explicitly considered the richest peasants hostile; implicitly they feared the entire peasantry, still 80 percent of the population. As a result governmental policies vacillated: at times the government issued regulations favorable to enterprising peasants, at other times unnecessary restrictions hindered the improvement of agriculture. Measures taken against the kulaks hurt the entire economy: the bulk of the peasantry understood that it was not worthwhile to strive to improve their lot, because there was a high price to be paid for economic success.

After a disappointing harvest in 1924, caused again by a drought, a series of good harvests followed. By the second half of the 1920s agriculture recovered, and overall production figures approached the pre-war level. These few years were the best years for the Russian peasantry. The weakness of Soviet power in the villages, and the political system of the NEP based on the theory of worker–peasant alliance, did not allow the government to tax the peasants as heavily as they had been taxed in imperial Russia. The consequence of agricultural improvement, lessened taxation, and lessened differentiation was that the bulk of the peasants were better off than before the war. But because they used their products primarily to feed themselves better, rather than selling them on the open market, the amount of grain that entered the market remained well below pre-war levels.

The peasants benefited from the revolution because they came into possession of all agricultural lands. Furthermore, the government, which they had always regarded as alien and hostile, was now too weak to interfere in their lives.

Never in modern Russian history was the peasantry as autonomous as in the 1920s. However, the revolution did not help to overcome the traditional problems of Russian agriculture: a backward peasantry, primitive methods of cultivation, and great agricultural overpopulation. In fact, the changes made by the revolution were a step backward. It was the most modern sector of agriculture that suffered the most. The destruction of industry meant that factories could not siphon away the great village overpopulation. The peasantry, satisfied with being left alone, showed little interest in innovation or improvement.

Lenin Institutes the New Economic Policy

Warren Bartlett Walsh

Lenin and the Bolsheviks instituted the policy of War Communism to cope with the drastic needs of the civil war. But the expropriations of food and the seizures of private businesses and factories had their effects: Russian industry was all but destroyed, a terrible famine raged in the countryside, and the country had to rely on foreign aid to fend off mass starvation. In Bolshevik-controlled areas, peasants and workers staged anti-Bolshevik demonstrations. The discontent reached its climax in the uprising of Russian sailors—considered loyal supporters of the Bolshevik revolution—at the Kronstadt naval station in 1921.

Instituted in 1921, the New Economic Policy (NEP) was designed as a temporary measure to reverse the economic disaster facing the early Bolshevik regime. In his book, *Russia and the Soviet Union*, historian Warren Bartlett Walsh describes the policy and gives the background of the central planning system that was put in place after NEP ended in 1928. Although NEP may have helped Soviet Russia recover, it also placed a large portion of the Russian economy out of the Bolsheviks' control—a result that the new government, founded on the basis of total centralization and regimentation, would not tolerate for long.

It certainly was never the intention of Lenin and his men to produce the situation [of increasing inefficiency, declining production, and shortages] which he described . . . to the [Tenth Party Congress of March 1921], nor was it altogether of their making. But they were the rulers of Russia and were

Excerpted from *Russia and the Soviet Union*, by Warren Bartlett Walsh. Copyright © by the University of Michigan, 1958. Reprinted by permission of the University of Michigan Press.

therefore held responsible. Discontent, often manifesting itself in violent outbreaks, had occurred throughout these first years. Now the outbreaks increased in violence and in frequency, and, moreover, became clearly anti-Communist. Government food reserves and other stock piles were looted. Food and supplies in transit were highjacked, and there was a mounting wave of crime. The peasants were among the most rebellious, although active discontent was not confined to them. Professor [N.S.] Timasheff has noted that during 1920–21 there were peasant revolts in 21 out of the 50 provinces of European Russia. One was so successful that the whole province was out of Moscow's control for over a year. The climax came a week before the meeting of the Tenth Party Congress, when the sailors at the Kronstadt naval base rose under the slogan "Soviets without Communists." Bolshevik histories blame this uprising upon "White Guards, in complicity with Socialist-Revolutionaries, Mensheviks, and representatives of foreign states." All these may have been involved, but the causes were neither as simple nor as malicious as that account would imply. Discontent was bona fide and justifiable. The revolt was serious enough in itself, and it also carried symbolic overtones. Kronstadt had been one of Bolshevism's strongholds in 1917, and men from there had taken an extremely important part in the Petrograd coup. Now men from the same base were in open revolt against the regime which sailors from Kronstadt had helped to create. Their revolt was suppressed and the revolutionaries were annihilated, but the widespread discontent did not diminish. Suppression of force by force was not enough. As the official *History* disingenuously puts it, "The Party was confronted with the necessity of working out a new line of policy on all questions affecting the economic life of the country, a line that would meet the new situation. And the Party proceeded to work out such a line of policy on questions of economic development."

The New Economic Policy

The decision was not as easy as this account makes it sound. Some of the Party leaders ascribed the faults and failures to too little War Communism. These leaders proposed to stand uncompromisingly in the way they had begun and to increase, rather than to relax, their controls. The other group held that the failures had been caused by too much control and not too little. They therefore demanded a "tactical retreat," that is, a compromise of immediacies but not of the ultimate goal. Since Lenin led this second group, and since he ruthlessly cracked the whip on his followers, its way prevailed. The Tenth Party Congress ordered the adoption of a New Economic Policy. The NEP, as this was customarily known, was in force from 1921 to 1928.

The resumption of private trade and small private industries and certain other capitalistic forms in the domestic economy of Russia misled many observers into supposing that Lenin had put Russia on the road back to capitalism. The NEP was hailed as proof (which it was) that the system introduced in 1917–18 had failed, and also as proof (which it was not) that Russia was about to "return to normalcy." The Communist leaders, in contrast, spoke of the NEP as the road to communism. Unless it is supposed that they meant their own brand of communism this must also be considered an erroneous interpretation. The official explanation of the change used to be that undue enthusiasm had led to a major error. It had been forgotten that, according to the Party's gospels, socialism was a necessary intermediate stage. It was not possible, said the doctrine, to jump directly from capitalism to communism. That, however, is precisely what had been attempted and, ran the official explanation, it was necessary to make a fresh beginning by frankly going back to the intermediate stage. Later Communist explanations have said that the NEP was not really a return to anything because what Russia had had between 1917 and 1921 was not real communism anyway. It was merely a situation created, as the Party history now puts it, by the war and the blockade [of Bolshevik Russia by the opposing White armies and their allies in the West]. This new explanation relieves the leaders of the onus of having made a bad blunder which they had to correct. Lenin was more honest.

Probably all these interpretations contain some part of

the truth, but none of them is wholly correct. The NEP was not one thing, but many things. There was certainly a restriction in the scope of the controls. The Committees of the Poor and the Food Requisitioning Squads [used to discover and requisition food from uncooperative peasants] were disbanded. The class war in the villages was stopped, and the confiscation of foods was ended. The peasants were now required to give only a part of their produce to the state, and were allowed to keep or sell the rest. They were, however, required to pay a tax which was somewhat higher than it had been in the tsarist period. The middle peasants (*seredniaks*) were now favored instead of the poor peasants (*bedniaks*). Gifts or loans of seed and implements and new laws on landownership and use were employed to encourage the middle peasants. Private trading in the domestic market was permitted under a licensing system, and private traders (who were called NEPmen) were encouraged to do business. They did so with great enthusiasm. About three-quarters of the retail trade in 1922–23 was carried on by private merchants. Small industrial concerns—those employing less than 20 workers—were released to co-operatives or to individual private ownership. But here one of the other aspects of the NEP becomes apparent.

Between 91 and 92 per cent of all the industrial concerns in Russia were given over to co-operative or private or combined state and private control. But the 8.5 per cent of the industries which continued to belong to the government employed almost 85 per cent of all industrial workers. The government, in other words, kept the larger share. It also tightened rather than loosened its controls. All banking and credit facilities, all transportation, all foreign trade, most large-scale domestic trade, and all large-scale industry remained in the hands of Lenin's organization. So did the machinery of government. These things were held more tightly than ever before. The Supreme Economic Council [SEC] was made responsible for large industry, and was given authority commensurate with the responsibility. Each segment of industry was placed under the direct management of a trust which was run by a committee somewhat like a board of directors. The number of such trusts finally reached 486. Each trust was required to submit plans and reports to the SEC for approval, and 50 per cent of the profits of every trust were assigned to the state. Legally, however, each trust was an independent enterprise which was to be operated for profit, and which was free to buy or sell to state organizations (including other trusts) or to private businessmen. The trusts soon engaged in vigorous competition for funds, supplies, labor, and sometimes for markets. Super-trusts, or syndicates, were then created to regulate prices, competition, the distribution of goods, and the allocation of raw materials. It was a complex and complicated system, which was not very efficient, but which worked, after a fashion. . . .

Economic Planning

Long-range economic planning on a national scale did not go into effect in the Soviet Union until 1928, but its beginnings predate the NEP. Some authorities trace the origins of large-scale planning to a Russian engineer named [B.G.] Grinevetsky. Grinevetsky, who incidentally was anti-Bolshevik, published in 1919 a suggestion for the planned development of heavy industry. Other writers trace the origins to Lenin's dream of rural electrification. This was one of his pet projects. "Communism," Lenin told the Eighth Party Congress, "is the Soviet government plus the electrification of the whole country." Later he wrote the then chairman of the State Planning Commission, "We must make propaganda for electricity. How? . . . [by] popularizing it. For this purpose a plan must be worked out at once for the installation of electric light in every house in the R.S.F.S.R. That will be a long business. . . . Nevertheless, we need a plan at once. . . ." Lenin then went on to suggest a plan which was crude in the extreme because of his ignorance of the technical difficulties involved. But the plan prodded the experts into action, which was what he wanted. A special body, called the State Commission for Electrification (GOELRO), was created and given the task of producing the plan Lenin demanded. This plan was later used by the State Planning Commission. That commission in 1925–26 published its first set of "control figures," which established approximate goals for the main branches of the economy. Control figures were also prepared for 1926–27 and for 1927–28. The Supreme Economic Council presented its own draft plan in January, 1927.

Meanwhile, Lenin and his successors were using private enterprise under the NEP. Gradually the national economy recovered. By 1926 the national income was slightly above the 1913 level, which meant that it had increased tremendously over both the 1921 and the 1917 figures. (The increase between 1921 and 1926 was 13 billion rubles.) The gross output of all industry had reached the prewar level by 1926, and agricultural production had increased beyond the prewar records. It has been generally assumed that this recovery was due to Lenin's New Economic Policy. Perhaps it was. It may have been the cumulative result of the efforts of millions and millions of people who worked very hard for many years. At any rate, there was a recovery, the regime was saved, and it became possible to resume the attack upon private enterprise.

The Centrally Planned Economy Was Inefficient

Peter Rutland

At its heart, Soviet Communism was a set of directions for running an efficient economy, which Marx and his followers believed could best be done from a single place. The centrally planned economy would eliminate waste by using the talents of experts and planners, who would allocate resources and production wherever they were most needed. The result would be a society provided with all of its necessities and lacking the economic injustice of "haves" and "have-nots."

In his description of the centrally planned economy, historian Peter Rutland, a professor of government at Wesleyan University, begins with the end: the Soviet collapse and the rise of Russian president Boris Yeltsin and his economics minister, Yegor Gaidar. Rutland contends that the foundation of the modern Soviet economy lay in the crash industrialization that took place under Stalin. According to Rutland, the many decades of iron-fisted central planning had left Gorbachev and Yeltsin with a "house built on sand," a terminal economic illness rooted in inefficiency, corruption, and the sheer illogic of running a modern industrial economy through the diagrams of central planning.

Six years after [Mikhail] Gorbachev took office, his programme of economic reform was overtaken by political and economic disintegration. The attempted coup of August 1991 [in which hard-line communists tried to take control of the country] was a reaction to this political and economic

Excerpted from "The Economy: The Rocky Road from Plan to Market," by Peter Rutland, in *Developments in Russian and Post-Soviet Politics*, edited by Stephen White et al. Copyright 1994, Peter Rutland. All rights reserved. Reprinted by permission of Duke University Press.

collapse, and to the failure of Gorbachev's policies. The new leadership which took over in the wake of the coup decided that there was no alternative but to break with the old model and move the Russian economy in the direction of market economics. In October 1991 President [Boris] Yeltsin appointed Yegor Gaidar as First Deputy Prime Minister in charge of economic reform. The political vacuum created by the collapse of the USSR and the dismantling of the Central Committee apparatus, which had previously steered the planned economy, gave Yeltsin and Gaidar a window of opportunity to introduce radical economic reform.

Gaidar was a 35-year-old former academic who had been an editor at several Communist Party publications, but who had not been directly involved with the reform programmes proposed under Gorbachev. He decided to take as his model the shock therapy launched in Poland in January 1990, and moved swiftly to introduce similar measures in Russia. The price liberalisation introduced in January 1992, in the event, failed to stabilise the Russian economy. Instead, the economy slid into hyperinflation while simultaneously experiencing a sharp fall in output and a slump in living standards. Ensuing anger with the impact of the economic reform deepened the political confrontation between Yeltsin and the Russian parliament. Thus the events of 1991-2 set in train a downward spiral of political and economic interactions from which Russia has still not recovered.

It is important to view the economic policies of the Gaidar government in the context of the disastrous economic situation that they inherited. The system of central planning which Stalin imposed in the 1930s at tremendous human cost ground on for five decades and transformed the economy of the USSR in all its aspects: geography, institutions, social structure and psychology. After 1985, the old system started to break down. The power of central planners steadily eroded, with enterprises and republics behaving in an increasingly independent manner. From 1988 on, the previous macroeconomic and foreign trade balance of the Soviet economy also collapsed. These processes have left the post-Soviet economy in something of an institutional vacuum: it is neither a market nor a planned economy, but a curious hybrid whose laws of motion are as yet unclear. . . .

The Origins of the Soviet Economic System

How was it possible that the world's second superpower, capable of conquering space and building a formidable arsenal of nuclear weapons, was unable to feed its own people and provide them with the basic necessities of modern urban life? In order to grasp the paradoxes of the Soviet economy, it is necessary to view it in its historical context.

Since the 1930s the USSR operated under a centrally planned economy, or CPE. This was a highly distinctive form of economic organisation, in which the conventional laws of supply and demand, taken for granted in the West, did not apply. After all, the CPE was the result of a political struggle in which property rights were taken away from social classes and vested in the state. Stalin tried to establish a state monopoly over all forms of economic activity. Private ownership of productive assets (stores, workshops, farms, tools, factories) was abolished, to the maximum feasible extent. All such assets became the property of the state, managed by directors who were answerable to the industrial ministries based in Moscow, and to the network of political monitoring agencies (the party and the secret police) which spread down into every factory.

The CPE had its roots in Marx's vision of a unified economy which would run itself like a giant factory, free from the anarchy of the capitalist market. The New Economic Policy (NEP) which Lenin persuaded the Communist Party to accept in 1921 was a retreat from the utopian Marxist vision. NEP replaced state food requisitioning with a market in grain, and thus recognised the need for the state and private sectors to coexist (at least in the short run). In 1928 Stalin abandoned NEP, and set out to construct an economic system which would guarantee the CPSU's [Communist Party of the Soviet Union] monopoly of political power, and enable him to impose his development goals on the economy. Independent peasants were forced to join collective farms (*kolkhozy*), whose produce was requisitioned by the state.

The farmers scratched out a living from the small private plots that they were allowed to retain.

During the first 5 year plan (1928–32) Stalin launched the USSR on the path of 'extensive' growth, pumping capital and labour out of agriculture and consumption and pouring it into heavy industry. The coal mines, steel mills and power stations were seen as the key to economic growth and military preparedness. 'Intensive' growth (the expansion of production thanks to the more efficient use of resources) made only a marginal contribution at this stage.

Thanks to the vast natural and human resources of the USSR, Stalin's industrialisation strategy turned the USSR into the world's second largest economy. But Soviet citizens saw precious few of the benefits. Real living standards halved during the 1930s, and only regained the 1928 level by the late 1950s. By 1960 it was clear to the Soviet leadership that the scope for further extensive growth was exhausted. Capital accumulation was at maximum levels, and the labour reserves of the country were fully mobilised. The running down of the rural economy meant that the USSR became a net importer of food in 1963, while popular pressure for improved living conditions was mounting. Attention turned to reforms designed to shift the Soviet economy onto a path of intensive growth.

The Soviet Economy Under Brezhnev

Through the 1960s and 1970s, however, things continued pretty much as before. During the Brezhnev era (1964–82) the annual growth rate slowly declined, from 6.5 per cent to 2 per cent a year—but was still positive. Thus consumers saw their living standards roughly double. Most families acquired a television and refrigerator, although only 1 in 20 owned a car. An informal 'social contract' meant that everyone was guaranteed a job, a minimal subsistence income and rudimentary housing. The deficit of consumer durables meant that by 1990 consumers had accumulated 280 billion rubles (R280 bn) in savings accounts, a sum equivalent to 7 months' retail spending. This monetary overhang exacerbated the persistent goods 'famine'. Purchasing power comparisons show the average Soviet citizen's living standard was roughly 25 per cent of that prevailing in the developed capitalist economies. One has to go to a country such as Turkey or Mexico to find a comparison favourable to the USSR in these terms.

The economic stability of the USSR during the Brezhnev years was misleading: Soviet economic achievements were a house built on sand. Resources were poured into maintaining high output levels in heavy industry and defence plants, while investment in the social and economic infrastructure was neglected. The crunch came in the late 1970s, with crises in agriculture, transport and energy. The exhaustion of easily accessible natural resources led Brezhnev to launch hugely expensive projects in oil, gas and atomic power. At the same time, the big-spending ministries and regional party organisations forged ahead with costly prestige projects such as the Baikal-Amur railway and the 1982 'Food Programme'. Squeezed by these massive and unproductive investments, the economy stalled. There was probably zero overall growth between 1980 and 1985. After 1978 rationing of key food items was introduced in many outlying regions.

By 1985, when Gorbachev came to power, it was clear that the sorry condition of the economy threatened the status of the USSR as a superpower. By 1980 the USSR had lost its claims to be the world's second largest economy, having been overtaken by Japan (with half the population and none of the USSR's vast natural resources). By 1986 the USSR occupied first place in the world league table only in the production of oil, steel, iron ore, potatoes and sugar— hardly the sinews of a 21st century superpower. They occupied sixth place in the production of radios (just behind Singapore), and of passenger cars (behind Italy and France). Given what is known about poor product quality and false statistics, the real situation was even worse.

Gorbachev's poor economic management added a new problem to the list of economic woes: a growing fiscal crisis. In 1988 the government ran a R36 bn deficit on a R500 bn budget, a sum equal to 7.3 per cent of Soviet GNP [gross national product]. Previously, one of the few advantages of the

CPE had been tight control over the government budget. Budget discipline eroded after 1985, due to increasingly erratic behaviour by the political leadership, who subjected the bureaucracies to a series of bewildering reorganisations. Also, production costs were steadily rising, while prices were held constant. The gap was filled with government subsidies (food subsidies, for instance, rose from R2 bn in 1965 to R73 bn in 1990). These structural imbalances were compounded by a series of exogenous shocks. Falling world oil prices meant a loss of $40 bn export revenues, while cleaning up after Chernobyl and the Armenian earthquake cost another R20 bn.

It was clear, however, that the Soviet economy was not merely suffering from poor political leadership. Nor was it facing a cyclical crisis that would clear up on its own accord after a few years. The economy experienced a steady, long-run decline in productive efficiency, which was in turn the product of deep-seated contradictions within the central planning system itself. The problem was that despite these chronic economic problems, all the key political and economic elites had a strong vested interest in the preservation of the status quo. This meant that the political leadership found it impossible to build a coalition in favour of market reform.

The Centrally Planned Economy

How, then, did central planning work? At the centre stood the State Planning Committee, Gosplan, which drew up a grid chart matching the flow of available inputs (labour, capital, and raw materials) with the set of desired outputs. Beneath Gosplan were some 60 economic ministries, supervising 120,000 factories, farms and other units in industry, construction, commerce and agriculture.

The ministries allocated output targets to enterprises in the form of an annual plan. Plans were altered so frequently that the 5 year plan was little more than a forecasting exercise: the annual plan was the operational document. The inputs which factories needed to fulfil their output targets were provided by the State Committee on Supplies (Gossnab). In addition to the economic ministries, there were 20 State

Committees supervising functional aspects of the economy (prices, labour, etc.). Beneath the ministries, regional soviets had control of a limited amount of local industry.

This system of central planning was incredibly complicated and difficult to manage. The national leadership steered the economy through a network of political agencies which paralleled the economic bureaucracies. There was the Communist Party, which ran a network of branches in every farm and factory. Powerful regional party officials used their political muscle to play a trouble-shooting role in the local economy: forcing through a local construction project, helping a factory acquire scarce supplies, persuading factory directors to help with the harvest and so forth. The personal networks between local political and economic managers were very important to the smooth functioning of the system. The party tried to use its monopoly of political authority to lay down priorities—such as saving energy, or building a pipeline. Unfortunately, there were so many 'priorities' in force that the centre lost the ability to make much of an impact.

The huge quantity of information flowing up and down the pyramid of planning institutions had to be simplified and made manageable. The planners relied on crude, physical measures of output (thousands of cars or tons of coal). Managers knew that output targets had to be met, even if it came at the expense of other goals set by their ministry (such as introducing new products or conserving energy). The central plan targets paid little attention to product quality—only 15 per cent of their manufactured goods met current world standards for quality and reliability. Soviet consumers had little choice but to accept whatever products were made available to them. Crude physical targets may have suited the Soviet economy of the 1930s, when it revolved around a few simple products (coal, oil, steel), but they are grossly inappropriate for a modern economy.

The biggest headache facing Soviet managers on a daily basis was the unreliability of supplies. The Soviet economy seemed to operate under conditions of permanent shortage. Plans were so 'taut' that even the smallest interruption in deliveries could threaten plan fulfilment, and in response managers hoarded stocks or traded on informal networks to procure the supplies they needed.

A striking feature of the CPE was the passive role played by money and prices. Planning took place in physical terms, and money flows were only calculated after the basic plan was constructed. Prices bore scant relation to production costs—retail prices covered only about one-third of the cost of producing food, for example. Managers worried about meeting output targets, and did not care whether or not they made a profit. They knew that at the end of the year their ministry would always cover their losses. Firms faced what Hungarian economist Janos Kornai termed a 'soft budget constraint'. Capital investment was treated as a gift from above, and there were no incentives to using it efficiently.

The planners tried to make their job easier by concentrating production in a handful of very large enterprises, such as the Kama truck plant, which had 120,000 employees in a single location. In most product categories two or three monopolists dominated the Soviet market. Supplies and equipment would be hauled over hundreds or even thousands of miles—at subsidised transport rates. These oversized firms created massive company towns, building their housing and even running their own farms to provide for their own workers.

An important behavioural feature of the Soviet planning system was the 'ratchet effect'. Productivity gains would earn firms handsome bonuses for the initial year, but would mean higher targets in subsequent years. Thus there were few incentives for managers and workers to show initiative and innovate, which meant that the CPE strongly inhibited technological progress. While the USSR enjoyed some spectacular successes such as Sputnik, it lagged 6–10 years behind the United States in leading-edge electronic and computer technology despite the vast amount of resources poured into scientific institutions.

The CPE suited some economic sectors better than others. The system had been designed to maximise the growth of the military-industrial sector, which accounted for at least

25 per cent of Soviet industry. Mining and heavy industry also did fairly well, but agriculture, construction, and consumer goods and services were all severely deformed. Agriculture was the Achilles heel of the Soviet economy. While labour productivity in Soviet industry was about 30–50 per cent of the U.S. level, in agriculture it was 5–10 per cent. Despite having 20 per cent of the labour force in agriculture, the USSR still had to import about 10 per cent of its food needs.

The Soviet Government's Control of Culture

Richard Pipes

The Bolsheviks saw their movement as an all-encompassing remaking of Russian society, in which no aspect of the country would emerge unchanged. By this philosophy, art, writing, and music, as well as agriculture and industry, were reshaped at the direction of Communist officials in order to fulfill revolutionary ideals and create the "workers' state." Central planning, control, and censorship entered the lives of creative artists, who found themselves working in praise of the Bolshevik revolution or working not at all.

Historian Richard Pipes, a widely recognized author and expert on the Russian Revolution, explores Bolshevik culture in the following excerpt from his book *A Concise History of the Russian Revolution*. He describes the strict control of all information and expression by the new state, the new concept of proletarian (working-class) art, and the Bolshevik campaign against all forms of bourgeois expression—held to be any work of art or music that celebrated the individual rather than the collective. On this basis, the Bolshevik revolution destroyed many of Russia's artistic icons of the past and replaced them with the perpetrators of socialist realism, a style of work that explored revolutionary slogans rather than style and propagandic function rather than form.

The Bolshevik leaders viewed culture in purely instrumental terms: it was a branch of government concerned with molding minds and promoting attitudes favorable to the construction of a socialist society. Essentially, its function was propaganda in the broadest sense of the word. This was the objective of literature, of the visual and performing arts, and, above all, of education.

The Bolsheviks, of course, did not invent propaganda. It had been practiced at least since the beginning of the seventeenth century, when the papacy established the Congregatio de Propaganda Fide to spread Catholicism. During World War I, all the belligerent powers engaged in it. The Bolshevik innovation consisted in assigning propaganda a central place in national life: previously employed to touch up or distort reality, in Communist Russia propaganda became a surrogate reality. Communist propaganda strove, and to a surprising extent succeeded, in creating a fictitious world side by side with that of everyday experience and in stark contradiction to it, in which Soviet citizens were required to believe or at least pretend to believe. To this end, the Communist Party asserted a monopoly over every source of information and opinion and, in time, severed all contacts of its subjects with the outside world. The effort was undertaken on such a vast scale, with such ingenuity and determination, that the imaginary universe it projected eclipsed for many Soviet citizens the living reality, inflicting on them something akin to intellectual schizophrenia.

Early Soviet cultural history reveals a striking duality: on one level, bold experimentation and unrestrained creative freedom; on another, relentless harnessing of culture to serve the political interests of the new ruling elite. While foreigners and historians focused on the whimsical creations of Bolshevik and fellow-traveler artists, the more significant phenomenon was the silent rise of a "cultural" bureaucracy for whom culture was only a form of propaganda, and propaganda the highest form of culture. In the 1930s, with Stalin firmly in control, the experimentation abruptly ceased and the bureaucracy took over.

The issue dividing the Bolsheviks over cultural policy in the early years of the new regime concerned the legacy of the past. One group, associated with the Proletarian Culture (Proletkult) movement, which had arisen before the Revolution, declared the creations of the "feudal" and "bourgeois" periods irrelevant to Communist society. They were best destroyed, or at least ignored, in order to unshackle the full creative powers of the working class. The leaders of the Proletkult, who enjoyed the powerful patronage of the Commissar of Enlightenment, Anatolii Lunacharskii, proceeded to translate their theories into action with great energy. They opened studios at which workers learned to draw and paint as well as "workshops" where they composed poetry.

On the content of the new culture, the theorists of Proletkult were vague, leaving its definition to the spontaneous creativity of the masses. On one thing, however, they agreed: they had no use for individual "inspiration," which they viewed as a "bourgeois" illusion. Culture grew out of economic relations among human beings and their never-ending struggle with nature. In a socialist society, based on the principle of collectivism, culture would necessarily assume a collective character. A prominent member of Proletkult, Aleksei Gastev, a metalworker turned poet and theorist, had visions of a future in which people would be reduced to automatons identified by ciphers instead of names, and divested of personal ideas and feelings:

> The psychology of the proletariat is strikingly standardized by the mechanization not only of motions, but also of everyday thinking. . . . This quality lends the proletarian psychology its striking anonymity, which makes it possible to designate the separate proletarian entity as A, B, C, or as 325, 075, and 0, et cetera. . . . This signifies that in the proletarian psychology, from one end of the world to the other, there flow powerful psychological currents, for which, as it were, there exists no longer a million heads but a single global head. In the future, this tendency will, imperceptibly, render impossible individual thinking.

Some Proletkult theorists saw the daily newspaper as a model of collective creativity. They tried in "poetry workshops" to produce composite poems by having each participant contribute one line. At its best, Proletkult provided adult education for people who had never had any contact with art or literature; at its worst, it wasted time in dilettant-ish experiments that produced nothing of lasting value.

Its undoing was politics. Lenin viewed skeptically the whole notion of "proletarian culture." He had a very low opinion of the cultural level of the Russian masses and little faith in their creative potential. The task facing his govern-ment, as he perceived it, was to inculcate in the masses mod-ern scientific and technical habits. He thought it absurd to discard the artistic and literary heritage of the past for the immature creations of amateur writers and artists recruited among workers. But he tolerated the activities of the Pro-letkult until he became aware of its political ambitions. Alexander Bogdanov, the founder and chief theorist of the movement, believed that cultural organizations should be independent of political institutions and coexist, on terms of equality, with party organizations. Owing to Lunacharskii's friendship, the network of Proletkult cells, which at their height enrolled 80,000 active members and 400,000 sympa-thizers, enjoyed exemption from supervision by the Com-missariat of Enlightenment, which financed them. As soon as this fact was brought to his attention (this happened in the fall of 1920), Lenin ordered the Proletkult organizations to subordinate themselves to the Commissariat. Gradually the movement faded out of the picture.

The Control of Information

The Communist regime under Lenin controlled cultural ac-tivities through two devices: censorship and strict monopoly on cultural organizations and activities.

Censorship was an old tradition in Russia. Until 1864, it had been practiced in its most onerous "preventive" form, long abandoned in the rest of Europe, which required every manuscript to be approved by a government censor prior to publication. In 1864, it was replaced by "punitive" censor-ship, under which authors and editors faced trial for the publication of material judged seditious. In 1906, censor-ship was abolished.

It is indicative of the importance which the Bolsheviks at-tached to controlling information and influencing opinion that the very first decree they issued on coming to power called for the suppression of all newspapers that did not recognize the legitimacy of their government. The decree met with such resistance from all quarters, however, that it had to be suspended. In the meantime, the printed word was controlled by other means. The new government declared a state monopoly on newsprint and advertising. A special Revolutionary Tribunal of the Press tried editors who published information that was judged hostile to the authorities. Despite these impediments, a free press managed to survive; in the first half of 1918, several hundred independent newspapers appeared in Russia, 150 of them in Moscow alone. But they lived on borrowed time, since Lenin made no secret of the fact that he intended to shut down the entire free press as soon as conditions permitted.

The occasion presented itself in July 1918, following the Left SR [Social Revolutionaries] uprising in the capital. Immediately after crushing the rebellion, the government closed all non-Bolshevik newspapers and periodicals, some of which had been founded in the eighteenth century. The unprecedented action eliminated, in one fell swoop, Russia's sources of independent information and opinion, throwing the country back to conditions that antedated Peter the Great, when news and opinion had been a monopoly of the state.

Like the tsarist regime, Lenin's government showed greater leniency toward books since they reached a relatively small audience. But in this field, too, it severely restricted freedom of expression by nationalizing printing presses and publishing houses. All books had to have the endorsement of the State Publishing House (Gosizdat).

Such piecemeal control of information and ideas by the state culminated in June 1922 with the establishment, under the Commissariat of Enlightenment, of a central censorship office innocuously called Main Administration for Literary Affairs and Publishing and popularly referred to by the abbreviation Glavlit. Except for materials emanating from the Communist Party and its affiliates, and the Academy of Sciences, all publications were henceforth subject to preventive censorship by Glavlit. Glavlit had a section that censored the performing arts. Russians quickly learned the art of self-censorship, submitting only material that experience had taught them might have a chance of obtaining a license. In the 1920s, Glavlit did not strictly enforce book censorship, but the apparatus was in place. In the 1930s, it would be used to eradicate every semblance of independent thought.

The new regime eagerly courted Russia's writers, but it encountered in this milieu almost unanimous antagonism. Apart from a few poets and novelists willing to collaborate, Russian authors reacted to the restrictions imposed on their craft in one of two ways: they either emigrated abroad or withdrew into their private world. Those who chose the latter path faced extreme material hardships, freezing in the winter and starving year-round. Submission to the new authorities alone guaranteed minimal living standards but, to their credit, few writers sold out. . . .

Revolutionary Drama

In a country in which much of the population could neither read nor write, the printed word reached few. Given their interest in influencing the masses, the Bolsheviks preferred other means of spreading their ideas. Of these, the most effective proved to be the theater and the cinema, art forms in which they encouraged experimentation. Alongside the traditional theater, the Communists relied on unconventional spectacles ranging from political cabarets and street presentations to outdoor reenactments of historical events.

Revolutionary drama was intended to generate support for the regime and, at the same time, instill contempt and hatred for its opponents. To this end, Soviet directors borrowed from Germany's and other Western countries' innovative techniques. They strove, above all, to abolish the barrier between actors and spectators by eliminating the formal stage and taking their plays to city streets, factories, and the front. Audiences were encouraged to interact with the performers. The line separating reality from fantasy was all but obliterated, which had the effect of obliterating also the distinction between reality and propaganda.

Agitational-propaganda, or "agit-prop," theater vulgarized

the protagonists by reducing them to cardboard specimens of perfect virtue and unalloyed evil. The mental and psychic conflicts occurring within and among individuals which form the essence of genuine drama were ignored for the sake of primitive clashes between "good" and "bad" characters acting as their class status dictated.

Plays of this genre were often staged outdoors by professional actors disguised as casual bystanders to ridicule the old regime along with foreign "capitalists." They appealed to xenophobia and envy, fanning these feelings into open resentment and then idealizing them as expressions of class consciousness. . . .

A kind of spectacle much favored in 1920 presented, under the open sky and with the participation of thousands of extras, reenactments of historic events in a manner favorable to the Communists. The most celebrated of these was performed on the third anniversary of the October coup in the center of Petrograd, with 6,000 extras, under the title *The Capture of the Winter Palace*. Later made into a film by [Sergei] Eisenstein, it culminated in an assault of Red Guards on the Winter Palace, stills from which to this day appear as alleged depictions of an event that actually never took place.

Because such spectacles were prohibitively expensive, the government increasingly resorted to the cinema. The greatest influence on early Soviet cinema was that of the American D.W. Griffith. Russian filmmakers found especially attractive his techniques of close-ups and montage because they found them useful in stirring powerful emotions in audiences.

Soviet Art, Architecture, and Music

Artists, architects, and composers working for the new regime did not lag in adapting their skills to the country's revolutionary changes.

The most influential art movement of the 1920s, known as Constructivism, sought, like the early Communist theater, to break down the barriers between art and life. Inspired by the German Bauhaus, Russian Constructivists rejected formal art and attempted to inject aesthetics into the everyday.

They worked in painting and architecture, industrial and ty-pographic design, couture, and advertising. They aggres-sively rejected traditional "high art" in all its forms. Alexan-der Rodchenko turned out three "canvases" covered with nothing but the three primary colors, and declared painting to be dead.

Museums fell into disfavor as attention shifted to street art. Posters received much attention. During the Civil War they proclaimed the inevitable triumph of the Red Army over the enemy, who was depicted as repulsive vermin. Later, they served such didactic purposes as combating reli-gion. In 1918 and 1919, artists in Soviet employ covered en-tire public buildings and residences as well as trains and streetcars with graffiti bearing propagandistic slogans.

Avant-garde architects believed that Communist struc-tures had to be built of materials appropriate to the new era: declaring wood and stone "bourgeois," they opted for iron, glass, and concrete. The best-known example of early archi-tectural design was Vladimir Tatlin's projected monument to the Third International. A leading Constructivist, Tatlin wanted "proletarian" architecture to be as mobile as the modern metropolis. Accordingly, he designed his monument as a structure in permanent motion. The building was to have three levels. The lowest rotated once a year, the middle once a month, and the highest once a day; 400 meters (1,200 feet) tall, it was designed to exceed the highest building in the world. It was never built. Tatlin also designed a man-powered flying machine that never got off the ground.

Musical activity declined as Russia's best composers and performers emigrated abroad. Those who remained concen-trated on innovation. They staged "musical orgies" in which the instruments were not the discarded "bourgeois" winds and strings, but motors, turbines, and sirens. An officially designated "Noisemaster" replaced the conductor. "Sym-phonies of Factory Whistles," performed in Moscow, pro-duced such bizarre sounds that the audiences could not rec-ognize even familiar tunes. The new genre had its greatest triumph in the presentation in Baku in 1922, on the fifth an-niversary of the October coup, of a "concert" performed by units of the Caspian Fleet—foghorns, factory sirens, two batteries of artillery, machine guns, and airplanes.

The creations of writers and artists subsidized by Lenin's government had next to nothing in common with the taste of the masses, their intended audience. The latter's culture remained rooted in religion. Studies of Russian reading habits indicate that both before and immediately after the Revolution, peasants and workers read mainly religious tracts; their tastes in secular reading ran to escapist literature. The experiments in novel and poetry, painting, architecture, and music reflected the European avant-garde, and as such catered not to popular tastes but to those of the cultural elite. Stalin understood this very well. On attaining absolute power, he cut short experimentation and imposed literary and aesthetic standards which—when they did not merely reproduce creations of the past, whether the literary classics or "Swan Lake"—in crude realism and didacticism surpassed the worst excesses of the Victorian era.

Improving the Status of Women

Walter Duranty

One of Lenin's long-stated goals for the Bolshevik revolution was to end centuries of repression of Russian women.
The Communist revolution did bring down legal barriers
to employment, and women were suddenly free to enter
professions that had always been reserved for men. Certainly the Soviet medical profession benefited from this
revolution, as females would eventually make up the majority of physicians in modern Soviet Russia. Education
and medical care also were reformed to the benefit of Russian women, who enjoyed newfound rights to vote, to
study at a university, to apply for a divorce, to hold bank
accounts in their own name, and to hold positions of authority in workplaces and local governments.

In the following excerpt from *U.S.S.R.*, his journalistic
account of Soviet Russia in the 1940s, Walter Duranty argues that because the status of women was much lower
than that of men in czarist Russia, women benefited more
from the egalitarian reforms of the revolution. Although
very few women obtained high-ranking positions in the
Soviet government or in the Communist Party, Duranty
concedes, many women achieved great success in the middle ranks of Soviet life.

It is a singular fact that although the Bolsheviks from the beginning had decreed full legal, political, economic and social
equality between men and women in Russia, there were no
female defendants in any of the treason trials [of the 1930s].
By that time, nearly twenty years after the Revolution,
women were playing an increasingly prominent rôle in Soviet affairs, both inside and outside the Communist Party,

Excerpted from chapter 21 "Woman's Place," of *U.S.S.R.: The Story of Soviet Russia*, by Walter Duranty. Copyright © 1944 by Walter Duranty. Reprinted by permission of HarperCollins Publishers, Inc.

and it was only natural to expect that there would be some women members of the disloyal Opposition. Why there were not can perhaps be explained by the generalization that women as a sex benefited more than men from the Bolshevik Revolution. If it is true that in the final instance Lenin and Stalin won the support of the Russian masses because the masses believed that the two Bolshevik leaders were honestly trying to improve their lot, the same must be still more true about the women of Russia, whose lot—amongst the masses—was worse than that of the men.

Students of national psychology have not failed to remark a peculiar frustration and inner negativeness in the Russian character during the later decades of Tsarism, as depicted by such realistic writers as [Fyodor] Dostoyevsky and [Ivan] Turgenev. They ascribed this frustration to the fact that the absolutist, rigid and historically obsolete nature of the Tsarist State prevented men of intelligence and goodwill from taking any practical part in the direction of their country's destinies, and drove them into futile opposition or the wilderness of philosophic negation. In the simplest terms, man's function in the modern world can be defined as follows: to protect and provide for his wife and family, to defend and fight for his country, and, last but not least, to have a voice in his country's government. That voice was denied to Russian men by the Tsarist system. Politically they were impotent.

Until the most recent times, the function of women has not been considered political. Even Athens, the cradle of Democracy, did not permit votes for women, although one of Aristophanes' keenest comedies showed the strength of the feminist movement. In Tsarist Russia the function of women was to care for husband and children, and in the ranks of peasants and workers, which formed eighty percent of the population, to share man's physical toil. Among the peasants especially, women worked harder than men, because in addition to their responsibilities for "kids and cooking," as the Germans say, they had to work, and did work, in the fields. In short, from a psychological viewpoint they were performing their natural function, without any major frustration, that is, they were closer to life, and lived a more real life, than their husbands, fathers and brothers.

The American Relief Administration employed in one way or another more than a hundred thousand Russians, men and women, in its two years' fight against the Famine of 1921. The Americans were unanimous in saying that their women employees, whether members of committees to apportion the distribution of food or engaged in physical labor, were vastly superior to the men, from a standpoint of trustworthiness, regularity and general efficiency. This unbiased testimony cannot be disregarded, although there was much disagreement among the Americans about the reasons for it. Some said, "Well, of course, there's a famine, which affects first and most directly women and children and the home. So naturally Russian women feel more strongly about it than their menfolk." Other Americans declared simply that Russian women were more serious and patriotic than Russian men, and much more sober. "Lots of the men," they said, "will drink anything on sight, and if they can't get vodka will try to loot our stores of medicinal alcohol. The women never do that." To this I can add a point from my twenty years' experience of Russia, that I have seen hundreds of intoxicated Russians, including one who lay "dead drunk" in the gutter on a cold and wintry night, and when I came back that way three or four hours later, he was dead and cold forever. In all those years I never saw a Russian woman make of herself a public spectacle through inebriety.

It is impossible and absurd to set an arbitrary distinction between the sexes. Everyone knows that male children are apt to take after their mothers and female children after their fathers, and that thus a balance is preserved by Nature. Nevertheless, the fact remains that if the vast majority of the Russian population was downtrodden and unhappy under the Tsars, the burden fell heaviest upon the women. In consequence, they had intrinsically more to gain from a revolution than men and were, as I said before, more realist and less frustrated than men, when the Revolution confronted them with new problems and opportunities.

Opponents of the Soviet State, or conservative souls who

were shocked by equal suffrage of both sexes introduced by the Bolsheviks, complained that women have no political sense, that they are liable to be influenced by the male members of the family, that they are flighty and irresponsible, that more than men they are subject to the superstitions and pressures of the Church, and shouldn't, in fact, be allowed to think for themselves or speak for themselves, much less vote for themselves, without grave danger to the State. This biased view hardly needs refutation, although it is true that the level of feminine education in Russia, especially among the masses, was far below that of the men. Which accounts for the fact that although the Bolsheviks demolished all sex barriers, there were, and are still today, few women in the upper hierarchy of the Communist Party or Soviet Government. There have been such exceptions as the late Madame Krupskaya, wife-secretary and widow of Lenin, who played a prominent rôle in Bolshevik affairs before and after her husband's death, although she never formally held high rank in either Party or Government. And Madame [Alexandra] Kollontai, at one time member of the Central Committee of the Communist Party and for many years Ambassador of the U.S.S.R. in Sweden, where she overcame the deep-rooted prejudice, anti-Russian as well as anti-Bolshevik, of a proud and stiff-necked people. Madame Kollontai is a well-educated and intelligent woman, an early leader in the world feminist movement, who has written notable books. Like her diplomatic colleague [Maxim] Litvinov, she eschewed political controversy, although she was one of the "Old Bolsheviks" who opposed Stalin as a group, and thus escaped the fate which overcame so many Soviet ambassadors and foreign envoys. [Foreign minister Viacheslav] Molotov's wife, Madame Zhemchukina, was for some years head of the Cosmetic Trust of the U.S.S.R., which did a thumping business in Russia and the Middle East and brought in large amounts of much-needed foreign currency. She was a competent woman, well able to rank with her colleague-competitors, Elizabeth Arden and Helena Rubinstein, whom she met on a trip to the United States in 1936 or thereabouts. After establishing the Cosmetic Trust on a sound and successful basis, she was unexpectedly transferred to chairmanship of the Fish Trust, which doubtless smelt less sweet, and then in the Purge years faded somehow from the Soviet picture, for reasons which remain unknown. . . .

Women's Resistance to the New System

Lenin, the philosophic atheist and destroyer of old things, was neither mad nor evil when he attacked the wealth and corruption of the Orthodox Church of Russia, its servile support of Tsarism and its superstitious hold upon peasant ignorance. Lenin's motives were altruistic when he decreed that children would fare better if taken from squalid peasant hut or city tenement, where their hard-worked mother could give them no proper care, and placed in orphan asylums. He was altruistic when he decreed that marriage and divorce had been too expensive and remote for the downtrodden masses of Russia, and must now be free to all, without any cost in money. He wished to liberate his people from the chains of money and superstition, to make, if you please, every Soviet citizen a cog in a great machine, but—such was the paradox—a free cog, with self-respect. Even the bearing of children was, he said, a matter of individual choice, for woman alone to decide, and he legalized abortion.

Lenin's motives, I repeat, were undoubtedly altruistic, but his well-meant reforms did not suit the women of Russia. The old cliché, "Be it ever so humble there's no place like home," was stronger than Lenin's theories; they wanted their kids at home, no matter how squalid it was. The women of Russia were women; they didn't like abortion, nor the free-love system of marriage and divorce, which was only the scratch of a pen, costing a dime or less, to regulate the most profound, important and permanent of human relationships. And so the laws were changed. Abortion was abolished, and the system of marriage and divorce was set back upon a basis far more liberal than of old, but far more solid than the first Bolshevik program of free-love short-term contract and unlimited promiscuity.

Women's influence in Russia must also have had its part in the wartime "Recognition" and "Pact of Friendship" between the Soviet Government and the Church. It need not be said that women are more superstitious than men, but no one can deny that most of them sit at home when their sons and husbands and brothers go forth to fight a war. They sit at home and wait, in anxious dread. The words "In the time of our trouble we called upon the Lord" are never so true as in wartime. When her man may be killed tomorrow, what can a woman do for hope and consolation? I know there are good political reasons for rapprochement between State and Church in Russia. The Church is a force of unity, and the Orthodox Church of Russia can have vast influence over its allied communities in Bulgaria, Serbia, Greece and Rumania; but, as with marriage-divorce laws and the status of home and family, so too with the Church in Russia: the swing back from Bolshevik theory to ancient habit and practice has been made for the women of Russia.

If it be true, as of course it was, that the victory of Bolshevism depended upon and was decided by the winning of the peasants to a Socialist regime, the support of the women in the villages was unquestionably one of the prime factors in Stalin's successful effort to socialize agriculture. The woman farm-worker today presents her book of work-hours on full equality with men, she shares with them the advantages of opportunity through education, and perhaps surpasses them in patriotism. Nevertheless, women do not stand fully equal with men in the U.S.S.R. In office, professional and industrial work their wages are still somewhat lower than those of men in equivalent positions, and efforts made to correct this inequality have not yet been wholly successful. . . .

New Opportunities Under the New Regime

It cannot be wholly denied that there has been in the U.S.S.R. an atavistic prejudice against feminine equality in capacity, politics and wage rates. On the other hand, equality and freedom of Opportunity through education have produced a great number of successful and competent women in the middle ranks of Soviet life, in every phase of endeavor. It is still too soon, considering the handicap under which they had started, for women to have reached the highest points; but the very fact of that handicap has made them most devoted to the Soviet regime which removed it. To take a simple instance, but one which applies to nearly three-fourths of the women, that is the peasant women, in Soviet Russia today, the collective farm system has made a vast difference in their lives and pursuit of happiness. In the old days Russian peasant women worked like men in the fields and had in addition to look after their husbands and children, prepare food, wash clothes, and clean house. Even the youngest babies were set out alone in the grain fields in order that their cries of hunger and distress might scare off marauding crows. Hundreds of Russian women have told me that the period from spring to autumn in their villages was one long grind of overwhelming work, gave them no time to rest, and left them too exhausted almost for sleep. "Today," they said, "that's all gone. Now the farm work is done by brigades; each group in the whole Collective has its allotted task. Some do the cooking, some look after the children, some take care of the poultry and the pigs, and others work in the fields. But for all of us there's a seven-hour shift, with time for meals, and overpay during the harvest if we work longer than that. We have the same rights as the men, the same book of 'labor-days' by which our share in the harvest is apportioned. Can't you see why we stand firm for Lenin and for Stalin, who have brought about this change, who have made us human beings instead of hopeless drudges?"

I make bold to say that the support and adherence, the courage and self-devotion of the women of Russia has been the greatest factor in the progress of the nation from its depths of degradation and defeat in 1917 to its victorious resistance in 1943, for the best and most excellent of reasons. First, that Russian women as a sex benefited proportionately more than men from the Bolshevik Revolution; second, that being less frustrated than men and therefore more closely attuned to the realities of life, they were able to see more clearly what Bolshevism had done for them and their children, to give them something to fight for, dearer than life itself.

As I said earlier, women in Russia have not yet, for the most part, reached high office or positions of dominant importance, although the middle ranks of scholarship, science, business, and even industrial management, show a large and growing number of feminine executives. For obvious reasons they have not, either, played a prominent role in warfare. The "Women's Death Battalion" of the grotesque Kerensky period has no place in Soviet realism. Theoretically, women are admitted to the armed services on the same level as men, and I personally have known women members—in one case a commander—of bombing and fighting airplane squadrons. I have met a woman cavalry captain, no less competent and respected than her masculine fellow-officers. There have been women sharpshooters in the Regular Army, and women leaders of guerrilla bands. But speaking generally, women in the Red Army have the same auxiliary function as the WACs and other feminine branches of the American armed services.

During the war Russian women have undertaken men's functions in agriculture and industry to a far greater extent than has been the case in the United States, for the obvious reason that the war has been fought on Russian soil, with a terrific drain on manpower. This cannot fail to have a corresponding effect upon the position of women in Russia. It will jump them from actual and economic inferiority to the full legal equality established by Soviet law. Most significantly, this change will accord with the movement of the U.S.S.R. towards conservatism. It will not lead to matriarchy as such, but it cannot fail to contribute to a more genuine companionship and equality between the sexes, and offer an example which may be of no small value to the Western world.

It is, however, interesting to remark that the stress of war—with its attendant problem of homeless refugee children—has produced a surprising change in the Soviet system of education. This educational system had already one important change when it was decided, in the middle thirties, that the study of history, Russian and foreign, of law and of the "humanities," should replace the original Bolshevik concept that history began with the Revolution of 1917, and that everything must depend upon the rigid doctrine of Marxian economic determinism. This second, war-time, change involves a difference of education between girls and boys of what would be called in America high-school age. Instead of following, as heretofore, an identical curriculum, the education of high-school boys is now directed along specifically masculine lines, that is pre-military training and technical or professional courses in agriculture, industry and so forth. Girls, however, are now directed towards such feminine vocations as housekeeping, cooking, sewing, and the care of children. Ostensibly, this is a war measure, but it may well represent a definite and interesting recognition of the fundamental difference between the natural and basic functions of men and women.

Chapter 4

The Soviet Union and the World

Turning | Points

IN WORLD HISTORY

Soviet and U.S. Misperceptions Led to the Cold War

Ronald Grigor Suny

After World War II, the two strongest military powers on earth adhered to their incompatible political and economic systems—capitalism and communism—making conflict virtually inevitable. In the following excerpt from his book *The Soviet Experiment*, historian Ronald Grigor Suny describes how this ideological division led to the start of the cold war in Eastern Europe. In reviewing the events of the late 1940s—and the words and actions of leaders on both sides—Suny explains that the cold war was the result of suspicions and distorted perceptions on both sides. While the United States looked on the Soviets as a threat to their democratic allies, the Soviets saw the United States and its European allies as a menace to their own spheres of influence around the world.

With the old ruling classes either having been killed off or dispersed and Soviet officers and officials the most powerful actors in the region, the real question was not *whether* the Soviet Union would dominate East-Central Europe—that was a foregone conclusion given military realities and Soviet notions of security—but rather *how* Stalin would dominate his borderlands. Would it be through "friendly governments," as in Finland, or through allied but autonomous Communist-led states, as in Czechoslovakia and Bulgaria, or through fully Stalinized, Soviet-controlled police regimes as were finally established in the years 1949 to 1953?

In the initial postwar period, from 1945–47, the Soviet government agreed to the formation of coalition govern-

From *The Soviet Experiment: Russia, the U.S.S.R., and the Successor States*, by Ronald Grigor Suny. Copyright © 1997 by Ronald Grigor Suny. Used by permission of Oxford University Press, Inc.

ments of democratic, socialist, and Communist parties. As early as September 1944 a pro-Soviet Communist-dominated coalition, called the Fatherland Front, came to power in Bulgaria. In March 1945 coalition governments, with Communists and socialists as members, were formed in Czechoslovakia and Rumania. On June 28, 1945, the Polish government based on the Lublin Committee[1] was reconstituted. Now led by a socialist, it included the peasant party leader [Stanislaw] Mikolajczyk as deputy prime minister. In Hungary national elections resulted in a Peasant Party majority, but the Communists and Social Democrats, each receiving 17 percent of the vote, were included in a coalition government.

East-Central Europe was ripe for social change. Though the region was basically agricultural, it experienced near famine in 1944–45. As the most backward part of Europe, it still maintained semifeudal structures in some places. One of the first tasks of the new Soviet-backed governments was land reform. In Hungary, for example, where less than 1 percent of the population owned 48 percent of the land, the Soviet Army ordered the "abolition of feudalism," and, against the resistance of the Catholic church, which alone held 17 percent of the land, it confiscated and distributed over 3 million hectares[2] to 663,000 peasants, many of whom had been landless. In September 1944, 1 million hectares of large Polish estates were redistributed to peasants. Later 5.5 million Poles were resettled on former German lands in the west from which Germans were expelled. Rumania distributed over 1 million hectares to individual landholders. Through the land reform the left-leaning governments and the Soviet occupiers gained some sympathy and support from a generally hostile population.

Rather than spontaneous change arising from below, Communists preferred governmental initiative. In many places workers and students favored radical reforms, but the Communists in government worked with other parties to

1. The Polish Committee of National Liberation, or Lublin Committee, was formed by 15 Communist and leftist Polish leaders on July 21, 1944, as a provisional Polish government.   2. A hectare equals about 2.5 acres.

quash the revolutionary workers' councils and liberation committees that had arisen at the end of the war. They agreed to outlawing strikes and promoting social order rather than revolution. They pushed for nationalization of industry, particularly foreign and German-owned companies. In late 1945 and early 1946 Czechoslovakia and Poland nationalized most of their industry, to the protests of the United States.

A Sphere of Influence in Eastern Europe

Eastern Europe quickly became the major bone of contention between the United States and the Soviet Union. [U.S. president Harry] Truman opposed the Soviets building a sphere of influence there and was concerned about the economic isolation of the region as well as the violations of democratic norms. The Americans had very little direct economic interest in Eastern Europe; their holdings amounted to just over a half a billion dollars, only 4 percent of U.S. investments abroad. Nevertheless, the American minister to Hungary feared that that country would soon "become an economic colony of [the] USSR from which western trade will be excluded and in which western investments will be totally lost." For most American officials, however, the damage to these investments and to trade was less worrisome than the threat to its goal of unrestricted world trade and the elimination of economic and political spheres of influence. The Soviets, on the other hand, were primarily concerned with state security. Stalin was comfortable with a sphere-of-influence policy in which the Soviets would have the dominant political say, but he was willing to have the West trade and invest in Eastern Europe. For the first few postwar years no economic Iron Curtain cut Eastern Europe off from the West. The Soviet Union, too poor, underdeveloped, and devastated by the war to supply East-Central Europe's economic needs, wanted trade, loans, and investment from the West to develop the area but stopped short of allowing its neighbors to be integrated into a Western economic bloc.

From 1943 on, the Soviet government made it clear that it hoped to be granted a large American loan, perhaps $1 billion, at low interest to aid the USSR in its postwar reconstruction. As the war wound down, [Vyacheslav] Molotov made a formal request for a postwar loan. [U.S. president Franklin D.] Roosevelt delayed deciding on the loan, and no mention was made of such a credit at the Yalta Conference. When Soviet-American relations cooled after Roosevelt's death, the probability of a loan like the one granted to Great Britain in early 1946 faded fast. In March 1946 the State Department announced that the Russian loan request had been "lost" since August of the previous year. The United States told the Soviets that it would be willing to discuss a loan of a billion dollars but that such a discussion would require examination of Soviet relations with Eastern Europe and the promise of the USSR to join the International Monetary Fund and the World Bank and adopt their rules in international commerce. The Soviets found such terms impossible. They argued that complete free trade as advocated by the United States would result in a reproduction of the prewar economic division of Europe into an advanced, industrialized Western Europe and a backward, agrarian Eastern Europe. Protectionism, they contended, was necessary to develop industry in Eastern Europe, which Stalin wanted to develop in cooperation with the Soviet Union. The USSR concluded bilateral trade treaties with its neighbors and began setting up joint-stock companies that combined the interests of East European and Soviet firms. These agreements heavily favored the Soviet economy. The Soviet sphere of influence in East-Central Europe was to be both political and economic.

Western Leaders' Views of the Soviet Union

Three important statements in early 1946 shaped the coming Cold War decisively: Stalin's so-called pre-election speech, George F. Kennan's "Long Telegram," and Winston Churchill's "Iron Curtain speech" in Fulton, Missouri. On February 9, 1946, Stalin spoke to a packed house at the Bolshoi Theater in central Moscow. Stalin characterized the recent war as originating in the conflicts between monopoly-capitalist states over raw materials and markets, which had led to the formation of two hostile capitalist camps. Both world wars had been imperialist wars bred by a great crisis in capitalism, but the Second World War differed from the First in that the fascist powers were antidemocratic, terroristic, and expansionist. World War II, therefore, had the character of an antifascist war of liberation with the task of reestablishing democratic freedoms. Freedom-loving countries, like the USSR, the United Kingdom, and the United States formed an antifascist coalition to destroy the armed might of the Axis Powers. Though the speech was a fairly conventional statement of the Soviet interpretation of the causes of war, it was read by many in the West as an aggressive statement of Soviet hostility to the West. Supreme Court Justice William O. Douglas called the speech the "declaration of World War III."

A few weeks later George F. Kennan, the U.S. chargé d'affaires in the Moscow embassy, sent his famous "Long Telegram" to the State Department. This memo, with its clear and forceful presentation of Soviet ideological premises, was extraordinarily influential on the subsequent American thinking on policy toward the USSR. Kennan began by noting that the Soviets were concerned about "capitalist encirclement," which he saw as "not based on any objective analysis of [the] situation beyond Russia's borders" but arising "mainly from basic inner-Russian necessities which existed before [the] recent war and exist today."

> At bottom of [the] Kremlin's neurotic view of world affairs is [the] traditional and instinctive Russian sense of insecurity. . . . Basically this is only the steady advance of uneasy Russian nationalism, a centuries old movement in which conceptions of offense and defense are inextricably confused.

For Kennan Soviet thinking could be explained as a kind of "self-hypnosis," with no belief in objective truth. The Soviets were "impervious to the logic of reason" and "highly sensitive to the logic of force." Soviet policy was aimed at increasing its own power and weakening that of the capitalist powers.

> We have here a political force committed fanatically to the belief that with [the] US there can be no permanent modus

vivendi, that it is desirable and necessary that the internal harmony of our society be disrupted, our traditional way of life be destroyed, the international authority of our state be broken, if Soviet power is to be secure.

In contrast to the United States and its values, Kennan concluded, "world communism is like [a] malignant parasite which feeds only on diseased tissue."

On March 5, 1946, former British prime minister Winston Churchill addressed students and faculty at the small Westminster College in Fulton, Missouri. He had been invited by President Truman, who sat on the stage. Though at the time no country then occupied by Soviet troops had a purely Communist government and in many there would be years of relatively free elections ahead, Churchill intoned dramatically that Eastern Europe had been lost to the West:

> From Stettin in the Baltic to Trieste in the Adriatic, an iron curtain has descended across the continent. Behind that line lie all the capitals of the ancient states of central and eastern Europe. Warsaw, Berlin, Prague, Vienna, Budapest, Belgrade, Bucharest, and Sofia, all these famous cities and the populations around them lie in the Soviet sphere and all are subject in one form or another, not only to Soviet influence but to a very high and increasing measure of control from Moscow. Athens alone, with its immortal glories, is free to decide its future at an election under British, American, and French observation.

Besides the disagreements over Eastern Europe in 1946, the West was also nervous about Soviet intentions in the northern Middle East. Soviet troops were occupying northern Iran in line with a Soviet-Iranian treaty, but at the same time Azerbaijani radicals were being encouraged to create their own autonomous state in the region. The USSR also made territorial claims on Turkey, first on the behalf of Armenia and later of Georgia, and demanded a base in the Dardanelles. Stalin's muscle-flexing in Iran and Turkey only drove the governments of those countries into the Western camp and confirmed the West's demonic vision of the Soviet Union as a state with an insatiable appetite for expansion. In

March 1946 the Soviet Union agreed, under Western pressure, to withdraw troops from Iran and ceased pushing the claims to Kars and Ardahan in eastern Anatolia. But the image of the Soviets as expansionist was by this time indelibly etched into the minds of Western policymakers. In a long memorandum to the president in September, a key advisor wrote, "The language of military power is the only language which disciples of power politics understand." More ominously, he went on, "In order to maintain our strength at a level which will be effective in restraining the Soviet Union, the United States must be prepared to wage atomic and biological warfare." When Truman read the memo, he told his advisor that it was too hot to be circulated and locked it away in his office safe.

Soviet views on the United States were in many ways ideological mirror images that reflected back the same distorted images of Soviet aggression and expansionism that were becoming fixed in American minds. The Soviet ambassador to the United States sent his own "long telegram" to Moscow, in which he accused American "monopolistic capital" of "striving for world supremacy." Truman was seen as "a politically unstable person but with certain conservative tendencies." The ambassador's greatest fear was that hundreds of U.S. bases were to be built around the globe, demonstrating the "offensive nature of [American military's] strategic concepts" and the "plans for world dominance by the United States."

The Division of Europe

On March 12, 1947, President Truman spoke before Congress for a brief eighteen minutes about international affairs and dramatically changed the direction of American foreign policy for decades to come. He talked of "the gravity of the situation which confronts the world today" and of the need for the United States to aid Greece as a "democratic" and "free" state. Turkey, which was not spoken of as democratic, nevertheless needed to have its "integrity" defended.

> We shall not realize our objectives . . . unless we are willing
> to help free peoples to maintain their free institutions and

their national integrity against aggressive movements that seek to impose upon them totalitarian regimes. . . .

I believe that it must be the policy of the United States to support free peoples who are resisting attempted subjugation by armed minorities or by outside pressure.

Truman's speech marked the end of American retreat and isolation and the acceptance of what it considered its global responsibility. The president accentuated the anti-Communist tone in his speech in order to assure passage of his aid program to Greece and Turkey through Congress, which it did by lopsided majorities. A Gallup poll showed that three-quarters of Americans favored Truman's new policy. The Soviet response to Truman's speech was cautious. Molotov told his ambassador in Washington that "the President is trying to intimidate us, to turn us at a stroke into obedient little boys. But we don't give a damn." Yet within a few months Soviet policy toward the West, and East-Central Europe, began to harden, in part in response to a bold new initiative on the economic front by the United States.

On June 5, 1947, Secretary of State [George C.] Marshall announced at Harvard University that the United States was willing to offer grants to European states if they worked out plans for economic integration. American policymakers were concerned that European poverty made Western Europe both a poor trading partner for the United States and a potential target for the Left. Desperate to trade its postwar surpluses, the United States through the Marshall Plan could establish stable, viable trading partners in democratic states. The offer seemed to be open to the USSR as well as other East European states, though there was divided opinion among American leaders about the wisdom of including the Soviets. A very influential group around George Kennan was convinced that the West must form its own bloc, which would include Western-occupied zones in Germany. Three weeks later the foreign ministers of the Great Powers met in Paris to discuss a joint proposal for American aid. Molotov wanted the aid to be given without preconditions, but the Western ministers agreed with the American advisors that a coordinated plan for the entire European economy should be drawn up. The Soviet Union was unwilling to integrate their state economy into an international capitalist system, and Molotov claimed that the American conditions would allow foreign interference into the internal affairs of states.

Molotov left the conference without an agreement, convinced that the Marshall Plan would subordinate the Soviet Union and Eastern Europe to Western capitalism, but Foreign Trade Minister [Anastas] Mikoyan tried to convince Stalin of the advantages of joining the Plan. As he remembered in his memoirs,

> His only reaction was: "We shall be dependent on the West." In vain I argued that we were independent enough politically, and that with the aid from the USA we would be able to restore the economy of the European part of the country, which was in ruins, much faster and on a new technological level. Which would have made us more independent! But Stalin, a clever man able to understand economic issues when one explained them to him, could be also stubborn as a donkey, to the extent of being a fool.

Once Stalin had made up his mind, the Soviets forced their East European allies, including the Czechoslovaks, who were particularly anxious to receive Marshall Plan aid, to reject the American offer. Stalin warned [Czech foreign minister] Jan Masaryk, "If you take part in the conference you will prove by that act that you allow yourselves to be used as a tool against the Soviet Union." By August the East European states were coordinating their own mutual trade ties as a separate trade bloc. The "Molotov Plan" was adopted, and Europe split into two antagonistic economic blocs. From that point on, an even closer political and economic integration of Eastern Europe with the USSR became inevitable.

In late September 1947 leading Communists met at Szklarska-Poreba in Poland to work out a common strategy in the Cold War world. Stalin's principal representative was Andrei Zhdanov, who mapped out the division of the world into two major camps: the anti-imperialist and democratic camp versus the antidemocratic and imperialist. He stressed, as Stalin had, that war between the two was not inevitable. But his major aim was to stiffen the back of European Communists for a more militant struggle ahead. He attacked the French and Italian Communist parties for their mild and conciliatory policies and praised the Yugoslavs as the most militant and revolutionary party. The meeting ended with the formation of a Communist Information Bureau, or Cominform, which included the parties of the East-Central European states (with the exception of Greece) plus the French and Italian parties. The Cominform conference marked as clearly as any event the turn of the Communist movement toward a more militant strategy.

Despite Stalin's overwhelming authority, the Soviet Union did not have a single, consistent foreign policy in the Cold War years. Stalin had no blueprint for Eastern Europe and up to 1947 played with various possible arrangements for the countries in the region. But in the last years of the decade he tightened his grip on the neighboring regimes, and the options narrowed rapidly. Calculating that Truman was a weak leader and that anti-American sentiments were growing in Europe, the Soviets overreacted in 1947, underestimated the power of the American economy, and adopted a new defensive policy that consolidated the division of Europe.

The Cuban Missile Crisis Was a Victory for Socialism

Nikita Khrushchev

The cold war confrontation between the West and the Soviet Union reached a dangerous climax during the Cuban Missile Crisis of October 1962. To reinforce the defenses of Cuba, a crucial ally in the Western Hemisphere, the Soviet Union ordered the installation of nuclear weapons on the island. When the United States discovered the missile silos and transports through aerial reconnaissance, a showdown developed, in which one misstep could have brought the two superpowers to war. After a tense standoff, the Soviet Union agreed to remove its missiles from Cuba.

As he explains in the following excerpt from his memoir *Khrushchev Remembers*, Soviet premier Nikita Khrushchev had the original idea to place missiles in Cuba, only ninety miles from the U.S. coast and within range of major American cities, including New York and Washington, D.C. As first secretary of the Communist Party, Khrushchev had been in control of the Soviet Union since the mid-1950s. By the early 1960s, he was confident and brash, and was convinced that the Soviet Union would eventually overtake the United States and that communism would spread around the world. As for Cuba, he calculated that the missiles would deter American aggression and solidify his country's alliance with Cuban leader Fidel Castro. But he did not fully anticipate the U.S. reaction. Although he acknowledges making concessions in removing the missiles from Cuba, Khrushchev insists that the episode was a victory for socialism because it protected Cuba from future U.S. aggression.

Excerpted from *Khrushchev Remembers*, by Nikita Khrushchev, translated by Strobe Talbott. Copyright © 1970 by Little, Brown and Company, Inc. Reprinted with permission from Andrew Nurnberg Associates Ltd.

The fate of Cuba and the maintenance of Soviet prestige in that part of the world preoccupied me even when I was busy conducting the affairs of state in Moscow and traveling to the other fraternal countries. While I was on an official visit to Bulgaria, for instance, one thought kept hammering away at my brain: what will happen if we lose Cuba? I knew it would have been a terrible blow to Marxism-Leninism. It would gravely diminish our stature throughout the world, but especially in Latin America. If Cuba fell, other Latin American countries would reject us, claiming that for all our might the Soviet Union hadn't been able to do anything for Cuba except to make empty protests to the United Nations. We had to think up some way of confronting America with more than words. We had to establish a tangible and effective deterrent to American interference in the Caribbean. But what exactly? The logical answer was missiles. The United States had already surrounded the Soviet Union with its own bomber bases and missiles. We knew that American missiles were aimed against us in Turkey and Italy, to say nothing of West Germany. Our vital industrial centers were directly threatened by planes armed with atomic bombs and guided missiles tipped with nuclear warheads. As Chairman of the Council of Ministers, I found myself in the difficult position of having to decide on a course of action which would answer the American threat but which would also avoid war. Any fool can start a war, and once he's done so, even the wisest of men are helpless to stop it—especially if it's a nuclear war.

It was during my visit to Bulgaria that I had the idea of installing missiles with nuclear warheads in Cuba without letting the United States find out they were there until it was too late to do anything about them. I knew that first we'd have to talk to [Cuban leader Fidel] Castro and explain our strategy to him in order to get the agreement of the Cuban government. My thinking went like this: if we installed the missiles secretly and then if the United States discovered the missiles were there after they were already poised and ready to strike, the Americans would think twice before trying to liquidate our installations by military means. I knew that the

United States could knock out some of our installations, but not all of them. If a quarter or even a tenth of our missiles survived—even if only one or two big ones were left—we could still hit New York, and there wouldn't be much of New York left. I don't mean to say that everyone in New York would be killed—not everyone, of course, but an awful lot of people would be wiped out. I don't know how many: that's a matter for our scientists and military personnel to work out. They specialize in nuclear warfare and know how to calculate the consequences of a missile strike against a city the size of New York. But that's all beside the point. The main thing was that the installation of our missiles in Cuba would, I thought, restrain the United States from precipitous military action against Castro's government. In addition to protecting Cuba, our missiles would have equalized what the West likes to call "the balance of power." The Americans had surrounded our country with military bases and threatened us with nuclear weapons, and now they would learn just what it feels like to have enemy missiles pointing at you; we'd be doing nothing more than giving them a little of their own medicine. And it was high time America learned what it feels like to have her own land and her own people threatened. We Russians have suffered three wars over the last half century: World War I, the [Russian] Civil War, and World War II. America has never had to fight a war on her own soil, at least not in the past fifty years. She's sent troops abroad to fight in the two World Wars—and made a fortune as a result. America has shed a few drops of her own blood while making billions by bleeding the rest of the world dry.

All these thoughts kept churning in my head the whole time I was in Bulgaria. I paced back and forth, brooding over what to do. I didn't tell anyone what I was thinking. I kept my mental agony to myself. But all the while the idea of putting missiles in Cuba was ripening inside my mind. After I returned to Moscow from Bulgaria I continued to think about the possibility. Finally we convened a meeting and I said I had some thoughts to air on the subject of Cuba. I laid out all the considerations which I've just outlined. I presented my idea in the context of the counterrevolutionary invasion which Castro had just resisted [Bay of Pigs invasion, April 1961]. I said that it would be foolish to expect the inevitable second invasion to be as badly planned and as badly executed as the first. I warned that Fidel would be crushed if another invasion were launched against Cuba and said that we were the only ones who could prevent such a disaster from occurring.

In the course of discussions inside the Government, we decided to install intermediate-range missiles, launching equipment, and Il-28 bombers in Cuba. Even though these bombers were obsolete, they would be useful against an enemy landing force. The Il-28 was too slow to fly over enemy territory because it could easily be shot down, but was well suited for coastal defense. The Il-28 was our first jet bomber. In its time it had been god of the air, but by the time we gave military assistance to Cuba, the Il-28 had already been taken out of production.

The Boiling Point

Soon after we began shipping our missiles to Cuba, the Americans became suspicious. Their intelligence told them that the number of our ships going to Cuba had suddenly and substantially increased and that our own people were unloading the ships once they reached Cuban ports. We didn't allow the Cubans to do any of the unloading or installation of the missiles themselves. While the Americans had no direct information about what we were delivering, they knew that whatever we were doing, we were doing with our own hands. It was not long before they concluded on the basis of reconnaissance photographs that we were installing missiles. They also knew about our Il-28 bombers which had been flown to Cuba.

The Americans became frightened, and we stepped up our shipments. We had delivered almost everything by the time the crisis reached the boiling point.

There are people who argue with the benefit of hindsight that antiaircraft missiles should have been installed before the ballistic missiles so as to close the airspace over Cuba. This doesn't make sense. How many surface-to-air missiles can you fit on a tiny sausage-shaped island? There's a limit to the number of missile installations you can put on an island as small as Cuba. Then, after you've launched all your missiles, you're completely unprotected. Moreover, antiaircraft missiles have a very short range. Antiaircraft batteries can easily be knocked out from the sea and air.

I want to make one thing absolutely clear: when we put our ballistic missiles in Cuba, we had no desire to start a war. On the contrary, our principal aim was only to deter America from starting a war. We were well aware that a war which started over Cuba would quickly expand into a world war. Any idiot could have started a war between America and Cuba. Cuba was eleven thousand kilometers away from us. Only a fool would think that we wanted to invade the American continent from Cuba. Our goal was precisely the opposite: we wanted to keep the Americans from invading Cuba, and, to that end, we wanted to make them think twice by confronting them with our missiles. This goal we achieved—but not without undergoing a period of perilous tension.

When the Americans figured out what we were up to in Cuba, they mounted a huge press campaign against us, claiming that we were threatening the security of the United States and so on and so forth. In short, hostility began to build up, and the American press fanned the flames. Then one day in October President [John F.] Kennedy came out with a statement warning that the United States would take whatever measures were necessary to remove what he called the "threat" of Russian missiles on Cuba. The Americans began to make a belligerent show of their strength. They concentrated their forces against Cuba, completely surrounding the island with their navy. Things started churning. In our estimation the Americans were trying to frighten us, but they were no less scared than we were of atomic war. We hadn't had time to deliver all our shipments to Cuba, but we had installed enough missiles already to destroy New York, Chicago, and the other huge industrial cities, not to mention a little village like Washington. I don't think America had ever faced such a real threat of destruction as at that moment.

Meanwhile we went about our own business. We didn't let

ourselves be intimidated. Our ships, with the remainder of our deliveries to Cuba, headed straight through an armada of the American navy, but the Americans didn't try to stop our ships or even check them. We kept in mind that as long as the United States limited itself to threatening gestures and didn't actually touch us, we could afford to pretend to ignore the harassment. After all, the United States had no moral or legal quarrel with us. We hadn't given the Cubans anything more than the Americans were giving to their allies. We had the same rights and opportunities as the Americans. Our conduct in the international arena was governed by the same rules and limits as the Americans'.

We had almost completed our shipments. As the crisis approached the boiling point, the Western press began to seeth with anger and alarm. We replied accordingly, although not so hysterically. Our people were fully informed of the dangerous situation that had developed, although we took care not to cause panic by the way we presented the facts.

I remember a period of six or seven days when the danger was particularly acute. Seeking to take the heat off the situation somehow, I suggested to the other members of the government: "Comrades, let's go to the Bolshoi Theater this evening. Our own people as well as foreign eyes will notice, and perhaps it will calm them down. They'll say to themselves, 'If Khrushchev and our other leaders are able to go to the opera at a time like this, then at least tonight we can sleep peacefully.'" We were trying to disguise our own anxiety, which was intense.

An Exchange of Notes

Then the exchange of notes began. I dictated the messages and conducted the exchange from our side. I spent one of the most dangerous nights at the Council of Ministers office in the Kremlin. I slept on a couch in my office—and I kept my clothes on. I didn't want to be like that Western minister who was caught literally with his pants down by the Suez events of 1956 and who had to run around in his shorts until the emergency was over. I was ready for alarming news to come any moment, and I wanted to be ready to react immediately.

President Kennedy issued an ultimatum, demanding that we remove our missiles and bombers from Cuba. I remember those days vividly. I remember the exchange with President Kennedy especially well because I initiated it and was at the center of the action on our end of the correspondence. I take complete responsibility for the fact that the President and I entered into direct contact at the most crucial and dangerous stage of the crisis.

The climax came after five or six days, when our ambassador to Washington, Anatoly Dobrynin, reported that the President's brother, Robert Kennedy, had come to see him on an unofficial visit. Dobrynin's report went something like this:

"Robert Kennedy looked exhausted. One could see from his eyes that he had not slept for days. He himself said that he had not been home for six days and nights. 'The President is in a grave situation,' Robert Kennedy said, 'and he does not know how to get out of it. We are under very severe stress. In fact we are under pressure from our military to use force against Cuba. Probably at this very moment the President is sitting down to write a message to Chairman Khrushchev. We want to ask you, Mr. Dobrynin, to pass President Kennedy's message to Chairman Khrushchev through unofficial channels. President Kennedy implores Chairman Khrushchev to accept his offer and to take into consideration the peculiarities of the American system. Even though the President himself is very much against starting a war over Cuba, an irreversible chain of events could occur against his will. That is why the President is appealing directly to Chairman Khrushchev for his help in liquidating this conflict. If the situation continues much longer, the President is not sure that the military will not overthrow him and seize power. The American army could get out of control.'"

I hadn't overlooked this possibility. We knew that Kennedy was a young President and that the security of the United States was indeed threatened. For some time we had felt there was a danger that the President would lose control of his military, and now he was admitting this to us himself. Kennedy's message urgently repeated the Americans' demand that we remove the missiles and bombers from Cuba. We could sense from the tone of the message that tension in the United States was indeed reaching a critical point.

We wrote a reply to Kennedy in which we said that we had installed the missiles with the goal of defending Cuba and that we were not pursuing any other aims except to deter an invasion of Cuba and to guarantee that Cuba could follow a course determined by its own people rather than one dictated by some third party.

While we conducted some of this exchange through official diplomatic channels, the more confidential letters were relayed to us through the President's brother. He gave Dobrynin his telephone number and asked him to call at any time. Once, when Robert Kennedy talked with Dobrynin, he was almost crying. "I haven't seen my children for days now," Robert Kennedy said, "and the President hasn't seen his either. We're spending all day and night at the White House; I don't know how much longer we can hold out against our generals."

We could see that we had to reorient our position swiftly. "Comrades," I said, "we have to look for a dignified way out of this conflict. At the same time, of course, we must make sure that we do not compromise Cuba." We sent the Americans a note saying that we agreed to remove our missiles and bombers on the condition that the President give us his assurance that there would be no invasion of Cuba by the forces of the United States or anybody else. Finally Kennedy gave in and agreed to make a statement giving us such an assurance.

I should mention that our side's policy was, from the outset, worked out in the collective leadership. It wasn't until after two or three lengthy discussions of the matter that we had decided it was worth the risk to install missiles on Cuba in the first place. It had been my feeling that the initial, as well as the subsequent, decisions should not be forced down anyone's throat. I had made sure to give the collective leadership time for the problem to crystallize in everyone's mind. I had wanted my comrades to accept and support the decision with a clear conscience and a full understanding of what the consequences of putting the missiles on Cuba might be—namely, war with the United States. Every step we had taken had been carefully considered by the collective.

Good Sense Prevails

As soon as we announced publicly that we were ready to remove our missiles from Cuba, the Americans became arrogant and insisted on sending an inspection team to the island. We answered that they'd have to get the Cuban government's permission to do that. Then the Chinese and American press started hooting and shouting about how Khrushchev had turned coward and backed down. I won't deny that we were obliged to make some big concessions in the interests of peace. We even consented to the inspection of our ships—but only from the air. We never let the Americans actually set foot on our decks, though we did let them satisfy themselves that we were really removing our missiles.

Once the evacuation was begun, there was some question in our minds whether the Americans would pull back their naval forces which surrounded the island. We were worried that as soon as we retreated the Americans might move in on the offensive. But no, good sense prevailed. Their ships started to leave Cuba's territorial waters, but their planes continued to circle the island. Castro gave an order to open fire, and the Cubans shot down an American U-2 reconnaissance plane. Thus another American spy, just like Gary Powers,[1] was downed by one of our missiles. The incident caused an uproar. At first we were concerned that President Kennedy wouldn't be able to stomach the humiliation. Fortunately, however, nothing happened except that the Americans became more brazen than ever in their propaganda. They did everything they could to wound our pride and to make Kennedy look good. But that didn't matter as long as they pulled back their troops and called off their air force.

The situation was stabilizing. Almost immediately after the President and I had exchanged notes at the peak of the crisis, our relations with the United States started to return

1. U.S. pilot Gary Powers had been shot down over the Soviet Union while flying a U-2 reconnaissance plane in May 1960.

to normal. Our relations with Cuba, on the other hand, took a sudden turn for the worse. Castro even stopped receiving our ambassador. It seemed that by removing our missiles we had suffered a moral defeat in the eyes of the Cubans. Our shares in Cuba instead of going up, went down.

We decided to send [Anastas] Mikoyan to Cuba. "We have no better diplomat than Mikoyan for a mission like this," I said. "He will discuss the situation with the Cubans calmly." Not everyone understands what Mikoyan is saying when he talks, but he's a reasonable man. He had, over the years, played an important role in the development of our foreign trade and had proved himself a skillful negotiator.

Then Castro came out with his four or five conditions for normalizing relations with the United States. We whole-heartedly supported him in his demand that the Americans should give up their naval base at Guantánamo Bay. To this very day we support him in this demand, but the Americans are still there and no one knows when they will leave.

Kennedy and Castro

In our negotiations with the Americans during the crisis, they had, on the whole, been open and candid with us, especially Robert Kennedy. The Americans knew that if Russian blood were shed in Cuba, American blood would surely be shed in Germany.[2] The American government was anxious to avoid such a development. It had been, to say the least, an interesting and challenging situation. The two most powerful nations of the world had been squared off against each other, each with its finger on the button. You'd have thought that war was inevitable. But both sides showed that if the desire to avoid war is strong enough, even the most pressing dispute can be solved by compromise. And a compromise over Cuba was indeed found. The episode ended in a triumph of common sense. I'll always remember the late President with deep respect because, in the final analysis, he showed himself to be sober-minded and determined to avoid war. He didn't let himself become frightened, nor did he be-

2. U.S. military forces were stationed opposite Soviet troops in East Germany.

come reckless. He didn't overestimate America's might, and he left himself a way out of the crisis. He showed real wisdom and statesmanship when he turned his back on right-wing forces in the United States who were trying to goad him into taking military action against Cuba. It was a great victory for us, though, that we had been able to extract from Kennedy a promise that neither America nor any of her allies would invade Cuba.

But Castro didn't see it that way. He was angry that we had removed the missiles. All the while, the Chinese were making a lot of noise publicly as well as buzzing in Castro's ear, "Just remember, you can't trust the imperialists to keep any promises they make!" In other words the Chinese exploited the episode to discredit us in the eyes of the Cubans.

After consulting with Mikoyan on his return from Havana, I decided to write a letter to Castro, candidly expressing my thoughts about what had happened. "The main point about the Caribbean crisis," I wrote, "is that it has guaranteed the existence of a Socialist Cuba. If Cuba had not undergone this ordeal, it's very likely the Americans would have organized an invasion to liquidate Cuba's Socialist way of life. Now that the climax of the tension has passed and we have exchanged commitments with the American government, it will be very difficult for the Americans to interfere. If the United States should invade now, the Soviet Union will have the right to attack. Thus we have secured the existence of a Socialist Cuba for at least another two years while Kennedy is in the White House. And we have reason to believe that Kennedy will be elected for a second term. Consequently, he may be in office for another six years altogether. To make it through six years in this day and age is no small thing. And six years from now the balance of power in the world will have probably shifted—and shifted in our favor, in favor of Socialism!"

My letter to Castro concluded an episode of world history in which, bringing the world to the brink of atomic war, we won a Socialist Cuba. It's very consoling for me personally to know that our side acted correctly and that we did a great revolutionary deed by not letting American imperialism intimidate us. The Caribbean crisis was a triumph of Soviet foreign policy and a personal triumph in my own career as a statesman and as a member of the collective leadership. We achieved, I would say, a spectacular success without having to fire a single shot!

A number of years have passed, and we can be gratified that the revolutionary government of Fidel Castro still lives and grows. So far, the United States has abided by its promise not to interfere in Cuba nor to let anyone else interfere.

I remember my very last conversation with Comrade Fidel Castro. We were at Pitsunda [a resort in the Caucasus, the site of a government dacha] and were discussing Cuba's sugar crop. Castro's eyes burned with the desire to get started as soon as possible with the task of revolutionizing Cuban agriculture. He knew that the only realistic way to elevate the Cuban economy was to increase the sugar output, and in order to do that he needed tractors, harvesting combines, and modern sugar refineries. During our conversation Castro said his goal was to dominate the international sugar market. I pointed out to him that world sugar prices, which were sharply inflated after the blockade against Cuban sugar,[3] would undoubtedly return to normal when other countries expanded their own sugar production to meet the world demand. It turned out that I was right: the inflated sugar prices, which would have been so lucrative for Cuba if the transitory market situation which caused them had lasted longer, quickly fell back to normal.

But the fact remains that Cuba has done extremely well. I've read in the newspapers that Cuba assigned itself the task of producing a sugar crop of ten million tons for 1970, a year which is significant for all progressive humanity because it is the one hundredth anniversary of the Great Lenin's birth. I'm very happy for the Cuban people that they have come this far.

Today Cuba exists as an independent Socialist country, right in front of the open jaws of predatory American imperialism. Cuba's very existence is good propaganda for other

3. The United States embargoed Cuban sugar imports starting in 1960.

Latin American countries, encouraging them to follow its example and to choose the course of Socialism. Other Latin American peoples are already beginning to realize what steps they can take to liberate themselves from American imperialists and monopolists. Hopefully Cuba's example will continue to shine.

As for Kennedy, his death was a great loss. He was gifted with the ability to resolve international conflicts by negotiation, as the whole world learned during the so-called Cuban crisis. Regardless of his youth he was a real statesman. I believe that if Kennedy had lived, relations between the Soviet Union and the United States would be much better than they are. Why do I say that? Because Kennedy would have never let his country get bogged down in Vietnam.

After President Kennedy's death, his successor, Lyndon Johnson, assured us that he would keep Kennedy's promise not to invade Cuba. So far the Americans have not broken their word. If they ever do, we still have the means necessary to make good on our own commitment to Castro and to defend Cuba.

Foreign Adventures and Domestic Turmoil Prompted Gorbachev's Reforms

Geoffrey Hosking

If Russia's entry into World War I signaled the beginning of the end of the old Russian monarchy, the invasion of Afghanistan in 1979 may have sounded an early death knell for the Soviet regime. The invasion was an attempt to support a new socialist government. However, Soviet forces were unprepared for the guerrilla warfare brought against them by well-armed Afghan opponents, and what was supposed to be a quick campaign turned out to be a drawn-out disaster.

In his book *The First Socialist Society*, author Geoffrey Hosking describes the bloody stalemate in Afghanistan and the far-ranging effects the war had on the Soviet government. By highlighting the regime's short-sightedness and incompetence, the Afghanistan campaign prompted the election of a new premier, Mikhail Gorbachev, a dedicated young party member who promised to bring some energy and vision to the creaking Soviet bureaucracy. Gorbachev quickly instituted liberal social, political, and economic reforms designed to restore the government's legitimacy while leaving its authoritarian structure intact. Instead, these reforms set the union on a course toward complete collapse. By 1990, Soviet troops had withdrawn from Afghanistan, the Soviet Union was reaching new agreements with the United States and western Europe, and Gorbachev had declared an end to the era of the cold war confrontation. By the end of 1991, the Soviet Union had disintegrated into fifteen autonomous nations and Gorbachev had resigned from office.

Excerpted from *The First Socialist Society*, by Geoffrey Hosking (Cambridge, MA: Harvard University Press). Copyright © 1985, 1990, 1992 by Geoffrey Hosking. Reprinted with permission from David Higham Associates on behalf of the author.

In December 1979 the Soviet army invaded Afghanistan, renewing, after a break of almost exactly a century, the advance into Central Asia which the tsars had pursued. It was the first time the Soviet Union had intervened in a country not assigned to their sphere of influence by the Yalta and Potsdam agreements at the end of Second World War. For that reason, it provoked a wave of indignation and hostility both among the Western powers and from the Islamic world, with both of which the Soviets had previously seemed anxious to cultivate good relations.

Background to the Invasion

What induced the Soviets to do it? Basically, the invasion of Afghanistan was another invocation of the Brezhnev doctrine, that a state which has once become socialist shall not be permitted—especially if it lies adjacent to the Soviet Union—to relapse into non-socialist political forms. In April 1978 a military coup brought to power in Kabul a pro-Soviet Marxist party bitterly divided internally by factions. The Khalq (or People) faction, which came out on top, tried to carry out major social transformations very rapidly, regardless of opposition. By implementing land reform without proper preparation they unleashed bitter village disputes and undermined traditional elites in the countryside. Their attempt to reform the marriage laws by abolishing the kalym [bride-price paid by the groom] upset the generally accepted basis of family contracts and hence the relationships between families. Campaigns for primary education and universal literacy on Soviet Marxist lines affronted Islamic believers. Symbolically most objectionable of all, the new rulers replaced the Islamic green flag with a red one.

All these brusquely executed reforms encountered tremendous popular hostility. The situation was similar to that in the Islamic areas of Soviet Russia in the early twenties, with headstrong reformers cramming ill-prepared changes down the throats of a population mostly determined to stick to its old way of life. And the response was the same. To avoid having to pay heavy taxes, forfeit family plots of land, or put their children in 'godless' schools, villagers took to the hills with their horses and with weapons acquired on the black market. Regular bands of guerrilla fighters formed—the *mujahidin*—like the Basmachi of the twenties, devoted to Islam and to national independence. And if the latter had received many of their supplies and weapons from over the border in Afghanistan, the whole conflict now moved one stage further south, with Pakistan acting as the source.

By this time the Soviet Union had numerous military and civilian advisers in Afghanistan, and was linked to it by a friendship treaty, signed in December 1978. Eventually, the Soviets decided that the socialist regime in Kabul was in danger from the vehement popular resistance. In December 1979, some 100,000 troops invaded, bringing with them Babrak Karmal, leader of the alternative Parcham (or Flag) faction, to form a new government. His policies were more moderate than those of the Khalq regime, whose political prisoners he at first released. He promised to 'respect the sacred principles of Islam', including 'family unity' and 'lawful private ownership', and even restored the green flag. But the Soviet troops behind him belied his words, and he was soon imprisoning political opponents no less indiscriminately than his predecessors, and moreover introducing a harsh conscription law to raise enough troops for an Afghan army to fight alongside the Soviets.

A Grim Stalemate

Thus by the 1980s the Soviets found themselves fighting a long anti-guerrilla campaign in Central Asia, as they did in the 1920s, only now under even less favourable circumstances, in a country not accustomed to Russian rule and with a formidable record of resistance to imperialist invaders (hitherto mostly British). In their initial optimism, the Soviet authorities sent in troops from their own Central Asian republics, many of them Uzbek, Tadzhik or Turkmen, and thus able to speak some of the languages of the Afghan population: the expectation evidently was that they would be able to rally the natives to the Soviet side. In the event, these Central Asian troops proved unreliable, and had to be withdrawn. Reportedly, all the personnel of at least one Soviet unit were executed for refusing to fight against fellow Muslims. Furthermore, the Afghan army itself turned out to be often unreliable, so that the Red Army found itself taking over the rural pacification campaigns which the Afghans themselves were supposed to perform.

The result, once again, was a grim stalemate. Limiting themselves to about 100,000 men—perhaps to sustain the pretence that they faced only a limited number of politically motivated rebels—the occupants never extended their control much beyond the cities and main roads, and sometimes it was shaky even there. In the attempt to do more, they sometimes drove the population out of their villages and made them uninhabitable. However, the Soviet army had not enough personnel to secure the areas thus cleared. Sometimes the peasants were able to return and rebuild their homes, sometimes they went to swell the numbers of the *mujahidin*. But very many—at least a fifth of the population—became refugees, mostly in Pakistan. Whatever their original aims, the Soviets were prepared to risk genocide in order to achieve them. . . .

Gorbachev Comes to Power

Faced with stagnation at home and stalemate abroad, in March 1985 the Politburo took its courage in its hands, and for the first time elected a member of the younger generation as General Secretary. Mikhail Gorbachev, 54 at the time of his election, came from the fertile southern region of Stavropol, an area of Cossack traditions and rich peasant farming. . . .

The election of Gorbachev testified to the Politburo's recognition that the country was in a very serious long-term crisis which would eventually jeopardize its standing as a great power alongside the United States. He was the candidate of those who wanted change, or who realized at any rate that it could no longer be postponed. Prominent among them was the KGB, perhaps the least corrupt of the major political institutions under [Leonid] Brezhnev, and the one in the best position to appreciate the depth of the crisis. Gorbachev's patron and mentor in the party hierarchy had been [Yuri] Andropov, and during his first year or so in office he continued his policies. He launched the slogan of 'acceleration' and tightened labour discipline, invoking the legendary feats of Alexei Stakhanov, and establishing an official quality control inspectorate, *Gospriemka*, which had power to reject badly made goods and cut the pay of those deemed responsible. He intensified the drive to investigate, dismiss and prosecute corrupt officials. He initiated a campaign against 'non-labour income', that is, against any earnings not acquired in officially recognized employment. He sharply restricted the sale of alcoholic drinks and banned their consumption on official occasions, even at celebrations. Mineral water was substituted, an affront to Russian traditions of hospitality and conviviality which earned Gorbachev the prim and disapproving nickname of 'Mineral Secretary'.

This was, if you like, Perestroika [restructuring] Mark 1, the fruit of Gorbachev's long years in the party apparatus and of his association with the KGB. It was launched to the catchy accompaniment of *glasnost*, or 'publicity', which at this stage meant little more than a new and livelier style of presentation, encouraging the media to probe the deficiencies of corrupt officials in what was becoming known as the period of 'stagnation' under Brezhnev. . . .

Symbolic of the new mood was the release of Academician Sakharov from exile in Gorky in December 1986. The letter which he had written to Brezhnev in 1970 may be said to contain the first sketch of what was now emerging as Gorbachev's Perestroika Mark 2, at the centre of which was the notion of an alliance between the party leadership and the country's scientific and cultural intelligentsia, including those who had hitherto been execrated as 'dissidents'. After his return to Moscow, Sakharov was not restricted in any way in his comments, but was permitted to make known his views on political issues, even where he was critical of Gorbachev and the party leaders. His boldness was gradually imitated by others, until journals like *Ogonek* and *Moskovskie novosti* became forums for authentic and wide-ranging public debate on all the issues facing Soviet society. . . .

In foreign and military policy, Perestroika Mark 2 meant

moving away from ideological rigidity and from security through armed strength. The cost of the arms race, the threat of nuclear war, and the prospect of ecological disasters acknowledging no boundaries all contributed to this radical reassessment. Gorbachev's 'new thinking' explicitly down-graded the class struggle and asserted 'the priority of all-human values, a world without violence and wars, diversity of social progress, dialogue and cooperation for the sake of development and the preservation of civilization, and move-ment towards a new world order.' In pursuit of these goals, the Soviet Union executed a carefully phased withdrawal during 1988–9 from its expensive and demoralizing war in Afghanistan. It reached agreement with the United States on the reduction of strategic and conventional arms and the scrapping of intermediate-range nuclear missiles. The War-saw Pact was disbanded, and in November 1990 the Soviet Union signed the Charter of Paris, under which it was agreed that 'the era of confrontation and division in Europe has ended': signatories promised to 'build, consolidate and strengthen democracy, to protect human rights and to create free-market economies.' In a real sense, by these agreements the Soviet Union joined the international community, of which it had previously been only a grudging and semi-detached member.

These changes meant that the party was quietly dropping its insistence on the primacy of the class struggle and the building of socialism in favour of 'all-human values', the rule of law and international peace. At times Gorbachev made a positive virtue of this abandonment of dogma. During a visit to Siberia in 1988, he was confronted by an earnest young man who asked him 'What stage of socialism have we reached now?' Gorbachev replied good-humouredly 'You've all got used to thinking like that: you're a young fellow, and all you're interested in is stages! (Laughter) I believe we are at the stage of restructuring that which we have so far cre-ated. That's the stage we're at.'

The Russian Revolution Had a Positive Impact on the World

Mikhail Gorbachev

A loyal party *apparatchik*, or official, Mikhail Gorbachev rose to party boss in his hometown of Stavropol, a national minister of agriculture, and finally general secretary of the Politburo—the last head of state in the history of the Soviet Union. Determined to keep a share of the world's spotlight, Gorbachev still writes and gives speeches around the world and has his own website dedicated to his thoughts and activities.

In the following excerpt from his book *On My Country and the World*, Gorbachev looks back on the October revolution of 1917 as a still-committed revolutionary. He remains convinced that the Bolsheviks and the nation they shaped helped to end the era of European colonialism, served as an example to those fighting for political freedom and justice, and in significant ways contributed to social and economic progress around the world—even in the United States. Gorbachev concludes that superpower rivalry between the Soviet Union and the United States was unnecessary and that the two nations could, theoretically, have coexisted peacefully and to their mutual benefit.

One of the basic features of the twentieth century has been the division of the world community into two opposing camps, East and West. By this I mean the dividing line drawn, first, between the Soviet Union and the West and, later, after other states began taking the road first traveled by the Soviet Union, between the countries of the so-called socialist camp and the developed Western countries.

Excerpted from *On My Country and the World*, by Mikhail Gorbachev, translated by George Shriver. Copyright © 2000 Columbia University Press. Reprinted with permission of Columbia University Press via the Copyright Clearance Center.

This division has fundamentally determined the whole course of world history since 1917. It did not, however, have an equal effect on both sides. The negative consequences are obvious and have been much studied. The positive consequences—and there were some—have so far remained in the realm of propaganda. I think that historical science still has a long way to go toward making a genuinely objective and dispassionate analysis of all the ups and downs of the century now drawing to a close.

It is not of course a question of speculating on what the world might have been like if the October revolution had not happened. There is no basis for scientific analysis in that. But to try to weigh the actual effect of the USSR on the course of international relations—that would be an important undertaking.

Was Peaceful Coexistence Possible?

Let us ask a question: While it was impossible to prevent the division of the world into two opposing systems after the victory of the revolution in Russia, might it not have been possible to avoid those extreme consequences that ultimately resulted in an endless series of confrontations culminating in the Cold War?

Reasoning theoretically, one might say: Yes, it would have been possible if both sides, immediately after the civil war in Russia and the failure of Western military intervention, had taken the road of recognizing each other's right to exist. In the real world, however, it proved impossible. Especially because, not only in Russia but to a considerable extent in what one might call the popular consciousness worldwide, the victory of October was seen as the beginning of a "new era." The division of the world into two opposing social systems was depicted by Communist ideologists as a good thing. Lenin spoke of it as final and irreversible. This is fully understandable in view of the "model" of social development the Bolsheviks were seeking to put into effect.

They took as their starting point the view that October was the beginning of a worldwide revolution. Following their example, similar revolutions would be victorious in

Western Europe, then in other countries, and finally the whole world would "go socialist." But the world revolution did not happen. "Soviet" revolutions (or insurrections) were defeated in several countries. At the end of his life Lenin admitted this fact and proposed that a new course be taken, oriented toward the prolonged existence of the Soviet state under "capitalist encirclement." A new policy was proclaimed—"peaceful coexistence" (Lenin's own term) with the capitalist world.

First, the West had no confidence in this "new course." Although the West recognized the USSR diplomatically and economically, it continued its attempts by various means to overthrow the Bolsheviks. Second, the Soviet leadership—both secretly and openly—continued to support revolutionary forces whose aim was to overthrow capitalism.

The Twentieth Congress of the CPSU [Communist Party of the Soviet Union] renounced the idea that a new world war was inevitable and spoke in favor of "peaceful coexistence." Yet five years later the party's new program, adopted at its Twenty-second Congress, declared peaceful coexistence to be "a form of the class struggle." This formula was not renounced until 1986, when a new version of the party program was adopted at the Twenty-seventh Congress.

Until that time the old orientation remained in force. In the name of an ideology that placed the peoples of the Soviet Union in hostile opposition to most of the world, our country increased its participation in the arms race, exhausting its resources and turning the military-industrial complex into the primary factor governing all politics and public consciousness in the USSR. We were feared, and we considered this to our credit, because the enemy should be afraid. And it was not just a question of our immense nuclear arsenal but also the provocative actions in which the Soviet Union engaged, such as the invasion of Czechoslovakia and intervention in Afghanistan.

All this is true, but the responsibility for the many decades of tension cannot be laid solely at Soviet feet. In the West, from the very beginning of the Russian revolution, a policy was adopted of trying to suppress that revolution.

Intersection by the West

In December 1917, for example, Leonido Bissolati, a minister of the Italian government, stated: "The influence of the Bolsheviks has reached proportions that are not without danger for us. If in the near future the Russian government does not fall, things will go badly for us. O Lord, punish the Bolsheviks!" In March 1918 [British statesman] Arthur Balfour, summing up the results of the London Conference of prime ministers and foreign ministers of France, Italy, and Britain, wrote the following in a dispatch to U.S. President Woodrow Wilson: "What is the remedy? To the Conference it seemed that none is possible except through Allied intervention. Since Russia cannot help herself [!], she must be helped by her friends." In early 1919 President Wilson also spoke in very definite terms: "We must be concerned that this [Bolshevik] form of 'rule by the people' is not imposed on us, or anyone else."

Wilson's "concern" was expressed in the deployment of armed expeditionary forces on the territory of Soviet Russia. And it must be acknowledged that this was not done merely to prevent "rule by the people" from spreading to other countries. The intentions of the Western powers went much further, as historical documents show.

On October 30, 1918, President Wilson approved a document (not for publication of course!) with commentary on the famous Fourteen Points, the American peace program. In this document the recommendation was made that Russia not be regarded as a unitary state. The document suggested that separate states, such as Ukraine, should arise on Russian territory. The Caucasus region was seen as "part of the problem of the Turkish empire." Another suggestion was that one of the Western powers be authorized to govern Central Asia as a protectorate. As for the remaining parts of Russia, the idea expressed in this document was to propose to Great Russia and Siberia that a government "sufficiently representative to speak in the name of these territories be created."

All this happened eighty years ago. But to judge from certain lightly tossed-off phrases and the highly "selective" diplomacy pursued by some Western countries, one gets the impression that even today "nothing has been forgotten."

I will not pursue this theme further. The documents and facts on this issue are numerous. The main point is to recognize that both sides, over the course of all the years since the revolution, have engaged in rough confrontation, sometimes openly, sometimes secretly. After World War II this was expressed in the arms race, above all, the nuclear arms race (although both sides feared it and neither side wanted a head-on military clash, especially not with weapons of mass destruction). This struggle was also expressed in rivalry on other continents (a race to see who could win more supporters or allies). Only after perestroika* began did the situation start to change. Both sides altered their approach and, to a certain extent, sought to meet each other halfway. This led to the end of the Cold War.

I should note that surviving elements of that era of confrontation have not been eliminated to this day. Most of the "holdovers" are found in the West, but in Russia, too, not all the prejudices and habits of that era have been overcome. That, however, is a separate topic.

It was apparently not possible to avoid the world's many decades of confrontation and division. But it is important to draw lessons from the past for future use. This mutually confrontational approach to international relations does no one any good; everyone has to pay the price. It should not be forgotten, moreover, that a hostile, confrontational attitude by each side toward the other only embitters both and intensifies all the dangers that may arise.

The Impact of the Revolution

More than seventy years of confrontation, as we have said, left their mark on the entire course of world history. Even under these conditions, and despite all the contradictory aspects of the Soviet past, in which tragedy and heroism were interwoven, giving rise to totally unexpected situations, the existence and development of the Soviet Union had an enormous impact on the rest of the world.

---

* A policy of economic reforms pursued during Gorbachev's rule of the Soviet Union.

At first, in the years right after October 1917, this impact took the outward form of mass movements that swept like waves across many countries. October inspired hope in a great many people, especially working people, that improvement in the conditions of their lives was possible. That was when the Communist movement was born, the best organized of all mass movements known to history.

We cannot close our eyes of course to the fact that Soviet Russia was a bulwark of decisive support and aid to these movements, but we also cannot keep quiet about the main consideration: What was involved was a spontaneous reaction by working people to the example set by October, on whose banners were inscribed the same kind of slogans for which they themselves had been fighting for decades in their own countries.

As Karl Kautsky wrote in 1920:

> If the low level of economic development in Russia today still rules out a form of socialism that would be superior to advanced capitalism, still the Russian revolution has performed a truly heroic feat, freeing the peasantry from all the consequences of feudal exploitation from which it had been suffocating. No less important is the fact that the Russian revolution instilled the workers of the capitalist world in a consciousness of their own power.

After World War II there emerged a large group of countries (the so-called socialist camp), representing nearly one-third of the human race. These countries not only took up the ideas of October; they also borrowed forms of government from the Soviet Union. The question of the nature of the revolutions that took place in Eastern Europe and East Asia deserves further study, particularly regarding their origins: What was the "balance" between the native popular movements in those countries and Soviet policy in bringing them into existence?

The creation of democratic, antifascist regimes was the natural result of the defeat of fascism in World War II and of the fact that the forces that had collaborated with the fascists were completely discredited. The subsequent stage, however, in which for all practical purposes one-party systems were established on the Soviet model (or something close to it), was not such a natural result. It was the result of open or secret pressure from Moscow. This also had to do with the Stalinist conception of proletarian internationalism and ideological unity among all Communist parties. Those parties, too, bear their share of responsibility for what happened. In addition, we cannot forget about the Cold War—that is, the responsibility the West also had for the policies Moscow pursued in relation to its allies.

When we began perestroika, one of the first steps we took was to declare an end to intervention in the internal affairs of our allies, to what was known as the Brezhnev doctrine. It could not have been otherwise. Having charted a course toward freedom, we could not deny it to others. Reproaches are often directed at me today, asking what I "gave up" or who I "gave it up" to. If such terminology is to be used, then we "gave up" those countries to their own people. We "gave up" that which did not belong to us. In general, I consider freedom of choice indispensable for every nation and one of the most meaningful principles in politics today.

In the opinion of George F. Kennan, the Russian revolution unquestionably accelerated the disintegration of the European colonial empires. Here, too, it was not a question of "exporting the Russian revolution." The anticolonial revolutions unfolded as a reaction to the emancipation of the nationalities of Russia, to the transformations that began to take place in the former borderlands of the tsarist empire. It was precisely the presence of the Soviet Union as part of the world balance of forces, and the attractive force of the Soviet example for the people in the colonies, that forced the colonial powers in a number of cases to make concessions to the liberation movements and grant independence to the colonies. From this point of view it is interesting to hear the opinion of a respected specialist Victor Gordon Kiernan, a professor at Edinburgh University. He wrote: "The fear that India would start to lean too far toward Moscow and socialism explains, in many respects, the granting of independence to India in 1947. Fear of the expansion of Soviet influence in the final analysis forced the West to take the road of decolonization in general."

Even from the point of view of sober-minded Westerners who are not socialists, this aspect of Soviet influence cannot be underestimated. What was involved here was a genuine quickening of the pace of social progress on a world scale.

Communism as a Catalyst for Progress

The existence of the Soviet Union had an impact on the capitalist world itself, on everyday life in the West. As many Westerners have admitted, social policy in the Soviet Union acted as a stimulus toward the introduction of similar social programs in the West, the granting of social benefits that had not existed before October or that had generally been considered unacceptable. It turned out to be simply impossible, even dangerous, to lag behind "Communism" in such matters.

I will cite testimony from sources connected with two quite different ideological tendencies. In a Belgian socialist magazine, *Le Socialisme*, we find the following: "There is no question that the Russian revolution of 1917 and the general rise of the revolutionary movement after World War I forced the capitalists to make numerous concessions to the workers, concessions that otherwise would have required much greater effort to extract." Here, on the other hand, is a statement by Walter Lippmann, the well-known columnist, who for several decades was one of the chief molders of opinion in American society: "But we delude ourselves if we do not realize that the main power of the Communist states lies not in their clandestine activity but in the force of their example, in the visible demonstration of what the Soviet Union has achieved."

Both statements come from the period before the dissolution of the Soviet Union. Have opinions changed since then? In 1997 I had an interview with Arrigo Levi, a prominent Italian writer and commentator. Our conversation dealt with the eightieth anniversary of October. The interview was later shown on television. I can recall verbatim much of what was said, especially Levi's comment: "Communism was unquestionably a powerful catalyst for progress in other countries."

Yes, that was so. Now, on the other hand, with Russia in

its present condition of crisis, when the power of its social example has faded, a new policy is gaining strength in many Western countries, a policy of cutting back on people's social rights and benefits, a desire to solve all problems connected with intensified global competition by making cutbacks in social programs at home. The French authors Jean Francois Kahn and Patrice Picard have written in this regard:

> The pathetic fiasco of the collectivist utopia had the inevitable result of spurring on the savage race for individual success, a race that of course proceeds on unequal terms. If the illusory successes of Communism contributed at first to a rejuvenation of capitalism, there is no question that the downfall of the Soviet system hastened the emergence of ultraliberal tendencies.

These are "tendencies" that in the final analysis can prove to be extremely dangerous. . . .

In recent years, especially after the dissolution of the Soviet Union and the changes in Eastern Europe, some people have triumphantly proclaimed that everything has returned to the way it should be. (This was done particularly by Francis Fukuyama in *The End of History?*) But to take this approach is a profound error. Today's world is an entire solar system in which the West is only one of the planets. The influence of October has been very great, as seen in the fact that the world has changed so strikingly and irreversibly. A process of change on a world scale began in October 1917. The world continues to change. And it is in no one's provenance to turn back the course of history.

The many years' experience since October allows us to consider matters more broadly and to draw lessons from the past for the sake of the future.

Appendix of Documents

Document 1: Meeting of the Petrograd Soviet of Workers' and Soldiers' Deputies

Prompted and inspired by Vladimir Lenin, the Bolsheviks struck at Russia's vacillating Provisional Government on October 25, 1917. On that day, Lenin gave the following report to the Petrograd Soviet on the coming tasks of the revolutionaries.

1. *Report on the Tasks of the Soviet Power* (Newspaper Report)

Comrades, the workers' and peasants' revolution, about the necessity of which the Bolsheviks have always spoken, has been accomplished.

What is the significance of this workers' and peasants' revolution? Its significance is, first of all, that we shall have a Soviet government, our own organ of power, in which the bourgeoisie will have no share whatsoever. The oppressed masses will themselves create a power. The old state apparatus will be shattered to its foundations and a new administrative apparatus set up in the form of the Soviet organizations.

From now on, a new phase in the history of Russia begins, and this, the third Russian revolution, should in the end lead to the victory of socialism.

One of our urgent tasks is to put an immediate end to the war. It is clear to everybody that in order to end this war, which is closely bound up with the present capitalist system, capital itself must be fought.

We shall be helped in this by the world working-class movement, which is already beginning to develop in Italy, Britain and Germany.

The proposal we make to international democracy for a just and immediate peace will everywhere awaken an ardent response among the international proletarian masses. All the secret treaties must be immediately published in order to strengthen the confidence of the proletariat.

Within Russia a huge section of the peasantry have said that they have played long enough with the capitalists, and will now march with the workers. A single decree putting an end to landed proprietorship will win us the confidence of the peasants. The peasants will understand that the salvation of the peasantry lies only in an alliance with the workers. We shall institute genuine workers' control over production.

We have now learned to make a concerted effort. The revolution that has just been accomplished is evidence of this. We possess the strength of mass organization, which will overcome everything and lead the proletariat to the world revolution.

We must now set about building a proletarian socialist state in Russia.

Long live the world socialist revolution! (Stormy applause.)

2. Resolution

The Petrograd Soviet of Workers' and Soldiers' Deputies hails the victorious revolution of the proletariat and the garrison of Petrograd. The Soviet particularly emphasizes the solidarity, organization, discipline and complete unanimity displayed by the masses in this unusually bloodless and unusually successful uprising.

It is the unshakable conviction of the Soviet that the workers' and peasants' government which will be created by the revolution, as a Soviet government, and which will ensure the urban proletariat the support of the whole mass of the poor peasantry, will firmly advance towards socialism, the only means of saving the country from the untold miseries and horrors of war. The new workers' and peasants' government will immediately propose a just and democratic peace to all belligerent nations.

It will immediately abolish landed proprietorship and hand over the land to the peasants. It will institute workers' control over the production and distribution of goods and establish national control over the banks, at the same time transforming them into a single state enterprise.

The Petrograd Soviet of Workers' and Soldiers' Deputies calls on all workers and all peasants to support the workers' and peasants' revolution devotedly and with all their energy. The Soviet expresses the conviction that the urban workers, in alliance with the poor peasants, will display strict, comradely discipline and establish the strictest revolutionary order, which is essential for the victory of socialism.

The Soviet is convinced that the proletariat of the West European countries will help us to achieve a complete and lasting victory for the cause of socialism.

V.I. Lenin, *Collected Works*, vol. 26, 4th English edition. Moscow: Progress Publishers, 1964.

Document 2: The Declaration of Rights of the Working and Exploited People

The following declaration was written by Lenin and Nikolai Bukharin to provide a framework for the future Bolshevik constitution. The All-Russia Central Executive Committee of the Bolshevik party adopted the Declaration on January 4, 1918. It was voted down by Bolshevik opponents in the Constituent Assembly the next day. After the Bolsheviks forcibly closed down the Assembly, it was approved by the Third All-Russia Congress of Soviets.

I.

1. Russia is hereby proclaimed a Republic of Soviets of Workers', Soldiers' and Peasants' Deputies. All power, centrally and locally, is vested in these Soviets.

2. The Russian Soviet Republic is established on the principle of a free union of free nations, as a federation of Soviet national republics.

II. Its fundamental aim being to abolish all exploitation of man by man, to completely eliminate the division of society into classes, to mercilessly crush the resistance of the exploiters, to establish a socialist organization of society and to achieve the victory of socialism in all countries, the Constituent Assembly further resolves:

1. Private ownership of land is hereby abolished. All land together with all buildings, farm implements and other appurtenances of agricultural production, is proclaimed the property of the entire working people.

2. The Soviet laws on workers' control and on the Supreme Economic Council are hereby confirmed for the purpose of guaranteeing the power of the working people over the exploiters and as a first step towards the complete conversion of the factories, mines, railways, and other means of production and transport into the property of the workers' and peasants' state.

3. The conversion of all banks into the property of the workers' and peasants' state is hereby confirmed as one of the conditions for the emancipation of the working people from the yoke of capital.

4. For the purpose of abolishing the parasitic sections of society, universal labour conscription is hereby instituted.

5. To ensure the sovereign power of the working people, and to eliminate all possibility of the restoration of the power of the exploiters, the arming of the working people, the creation of a socialist Red Army of workers and peasants and the complete disarming of the propertied classes are hereby decreed.

III.

1. Expressing its firm determination to wrest mankind from the clutches of finance capital and imperialism, which have in this most criminal of wars drenched the world in blood, the Constituent Assembly whole-heartedly endorses the policy pursued by Soviet power of denouncing the secret treaties, organizing most extensive fraternization with the workers and peasants of the armies in the war, and achieving at all costs, by revolutionary means, a democratic peace between the nations, without annexations and indemnities and on the basis of the free self-determination of nations.

2. With the same end in view, the Constituent Assembly insists on a complete break with the barbarous policy of bourgeois civilization, which has built the prosperity of the exploiters belonging to a few chosen nations on the enslavement of hundreds of millions of working people in Asia, in the colonies in general, and in the small countries. The Constituent Assembly welcomes the policy of the Council of People's Commissars in proclaiming the complete independence of Finland, commencing the evacuation of troops from Persia, and proclaiming freedom of self-determination for Armenia.

3. The Constituent Assembly regards the Soviet law on the cancellation of the loans contracted by the governments of the tsar, the landowners and the bourgeoisie as a first blow struck at international banking, finance capital, and expresses the conviction that Soviet power will firmly pursue this path until the international workers' uprising against the yoke of capital has completely triumphed.

IV. Having been elected on the basis of party lists drawn up prior to the October Revolution, when the people were not yet in a position to rise en masse against the exploiters, had not yet experienced the full strength of resistance of the latter in defense of their class privileges, and had not yet applied themselves in practice to the task of building socialist society, the Constituent Assembly considers that it would be fundamentally wrong, even formally, to put itself in opposition to Soviet power. In essence the Constituent Assembly considers that now, when the people are waging the last fight against their exploiters, there can be no place for exploiters in any government body. Power must be vested wholly and entirely in the working people and their authorised representatives—the Soviets of Workers', Soldiers' and Peasants' Deputies. Supporting Soviet power and the decrees of the Council of People's Commissars, the Constituent Assembly considers that its own task is confined to establishing the fundamental principles of the socialist reconstruction of society. At the same time, endeavoring to create a really free and voluntary, and therefore all the more firm and stable, union of the working classes of all the nations of Russia, the Constituent Assembly confines its own task to setting up the fundamental principles of a federation of Soviet Republics of Russia, while leaving it to the workers and peasants of each nation to decide independently at their own authoritative Congress of Soviets whether they wish to participate in the federal government and in the other federal Soviet institutions, and on what terms.

V.I. Lenin, *Collected Works*, vol. 26, 4th English edition. Moscow: Progress Publishers, 1964.

Document 3: Rallying the Army During the Civil War

Leon Trotsky, leader of the Red Guards, delivered the following speech in April 1919, as the Bolsheviks fought the Whites for control of Russia and while socialist revolutionaries were challenging the old regimes in central Europe.

The decisive weeks in the history of mankind have arrived. The wave of enthusiasm over the establishment of a Soviet Republic in Hungary had hardly passed when the proletariat of Bavaria got possession of power and extended the hand of brotherly unison to the Russian and Hungarian Republics. The workmen of Germany and Austria are hurrying in hundreds of thousands to Budapest, where they enter the ranks of the Red Army. The movement of the German proletariat, temporarily interrupted, again bursts forth with ever-increasing strength. Coal miners, metalworkers, and textile workers are sending brotherly greetings to the victorious Hungarian Republic and demand of the German Soviets a complete change of front, that is, a break with imperialists—their own, the English, French, and American—and the forming of a close union with Russia and Hungary. . . .

In Warsaw, which the Allied imperialists tried to make the center for the attack on Soviet Russia, the Polish proletariat rises in its full stature and through the Warsaw Soviet of Workmen's Deputies sends greetings to the Hungarian Soviet Republic.

The French Minister of Foreign Affairs, Pichon, the sworn enemy of the Russian Revolution, reports in Parliament on the sad state of affairs: "Odessa is being evacuated"; "the Bolsheviks are penetrating the Crimean Peninsula, the situation in the north is not favorable." Things are not going well. The Greek soldiers landed on the shores of Crimea, according to the reports of Allied diplomats and newspapermen, were mounted on Crimean donkeys, but the donkeys were not able to arrive in time at the Perekop Isthmus. Things are not going well. Evidently even donkeys have begun to shake off the imperialist harness.

Foreign consuls do not wish to leave the Ukraine and urge their governments to recognize the Ukrainian Republic. Wilson sent to Budapest not troops of occupation, to overthrow the Soviet Republic, but the honey-tongued General Smuts to negotiate with the Hungarian Council of People's Commissaries.

Wilson has definitely changed front and evidently has forced France to give up all hope of an armed crusade against Soviet Russia. War with Soviet Russia, which was demanded by the senseless French General, Foch, would take ten years in the opinion of the American statesman. Less than six months have passed since the decisive victory of the Allies over the central empires; six months ago it seemed that the power of the Anglo-French and American imperialism was without limits.

At that time all the Russian counterrevolutionists had no doubt that the days of the Soviet Republic were numbered; but events now move steadfastly along the Soviet road. The working masses of the whole world are joining the flag of the Soviet authority, and the world robbers of imperialism are being betrayed even by the Crimean donkeys. At the present moment one awaits from day to day the victory of the Soviet Republic in Austria and in Germany. It is not impossible that the proletariat of Italy, Poland, or France will violate the logical order and outstrip the working class in other countries. These spring months become the decisive months in the history of Europe. At the same time this spring will decide definitely the fate of the bourgeois and rich peasant, anti-Soviet Russia.

In the east, [General] Kolchak has mobilized all his [White army] forces, has thrown in all his reserves, for he knows definitely that if he does not win immediately, then he will never win. Spring has come, the spring that decides. Of course, the partial victories of Kolchak are insignificant in comparison with the general conquests of Soviet authority in Russia and in the whole world. . . .

Spring has come; the spring that decides; our strength is increased tenfold by the consciousness of the fact that the wireless stations of Moscow, Kiev, Budapest, and Munich not only exchange brotherly greetings but business agreements respecting common defensive struggle. But at home, on our own territory, we must direct the main portion of our increased strength against the most dangerous enemy—against the Kolchak bands. Our comrades of the Volga district are well aware of this. In the province of Samara all Soviet institutions have been put on a war footing, and the best forces have been diverted to support the army, to form reserve regiments to carry on agitation of an educational character in the ranks of the Red Army. Party, Soviet, and trade-union organizations in Syzran have unanimously responded to the appeal of the central authority to support the eastern front. A special shock regiment is being organized from the workmen and popular elements, which only recently were groaning under the heel of the White Guardist. The Volga district is becoming the center of attention of all Soviet Russia. To carry out our international duty we must first of all break up the bands of Kolchak in order to support the victorious workmen of Hungary and Bavaria. In order to assist the uprising of workmen in Poland, Germany, and all Europe, we must establish definitely and irrefutably the Soviet authority over the whole extent of Russia.

To the Urals: this is the slogan of the Red Army and of the whole Soviet country.

The Urals will be the last stage in this bitter struggle. Victory in the Urals not only will give grain to the famished country and cotton to the textile industries, but will secure finally the well-earned rest of our heroic Red Army.

Leon Trotsky, speech delivered in April 1919, from *A Treasury of the World's Greatest Speeches.* Ed. Houston Peterson. New York: Grolier, 1965.

Document 4: Defeating the Russian Church

Faced with the defiance of Pariah Tikhon, the head of the Russian Orthodox church, and a church-inspired rebellion in the town of Shuia, Lenin drew up the following plan of action against the church in a letter of March 19, 1922, to the members of the Politburo.

Top Secret For Members of the Politburo.

In regard to the occurrence at Shuia, which is already slated for discussion by the Politburo, it is necessary right now to make a firm decision about a general plan of action in the present course. Because I doubt that I will be able to attend the Politburo meeting on March 20th in person, I will set down my thoughts in writing.

The event at Shuia should be connected with the announcement that the Russian News Agency recently sent to the newspapers but that was not for publication, namely, the announcement that the Black Hundreds in Petrograd were preparing to defy the decree on the removal of property of value from the churches. If this fact is compared with what the papers report about the attitude of the clergy to the decree on the removal of church property in addition to what we know about the illegal proclamation of Patriarch Tikhon, then it becomes perfectly clear that the Black Hundreds clergy, headed by its leader, with full deliberation is carrying out a plan at this very moment to destroy us decisively.

It is obvious that the most influential group of the Black Hundreds clergy conceived this plan in secret meetings and that it was accepted with sufficient resolution. The events in Shuia is only one manifestation and actualization of this general plan.

I think that here our opponent is making a huge strategic error by attempting to draw us into a decisive struggle now when it is especially hopeless and especially disadvantageous to him. For us, on the other hand, precisely at the present moment we are presented with an exceptionally favorable, even unique, opportunity when we can in 99 out of 100 chances utterly defeat our enemy with complete success and guarantee for ourselves the position we require for decades.

Now and only now, when people are being eaten in famine-stricken areas, and hundreds, if not thousands, of corpses lie on the roads, we can (and therefore must) pursue the removal of church property with the most frenzied and ruthless energy and not hesitate to put down the least opposition. Now and only now, the vast majority of peasants will either be on our side, or at least will not be in a position to support to any decisive degree this handful of Black Hundreds clergy and reactionary urban petty bourgeoisie, who are willing and able to attempt to oppose this Soviet decree with a policy of force.

We must pursue the removal of church property by any means necessary in order to secure for ourselves a fund of several hundred million gold rubles. . . . In order to get our hands on this fund of several hundred million gold rubles (and perhaps even several hundred billion), we must do whatever is necessary. But to do this successfully is possible only now. All considerations indicate that later on we will fail to do this, for no other time, besides that of desperate famine, will give us such a mood among the general mass of peasants that would ensure us the sympathy of this group, or, at least, would ensure us the neutralization of this group in the sense that victory in the struggle for the removal of church property unquestionably and completely will be on our side.

One clever writer on statecraft correctly said that if it is necessary for the realization of a well-known political goal to perform a series of brutal actions then it is necessary to do them in the most energetic manner and in the shortest time, because masses of people will not tolerate the protracted use of brutality. This observation in particular is further strengthened because harsh measures against a reactionary clergy will be politically impractical, possibly even extremely dangerous as a result of the international situation in which we in Russia, in all probability, will find ourselves, or may find ourselves, after Genoa. Now victory over the reactionary clergy is assured us completely. . . .

V.I. Lenin from Library of Congress Internet exhibit "Revelations from the Russian Archives: Anti-Religious Campaigns," http://lcweb.loc.gov/exhibits/archives/anti.html.

Document 5: Lenin's Testament

In a secret letter dictated in late December 1922, Lenin gave instructions for the revolution's future as well as his blunt opinions of the Bolshevik leadership. It was kept secret by Lenin's widow, Krupskaya, until after Lenin's death and was not disclosed until the Thirteenth Party Congress in May 1924.

Our Party relies on two classes and therefore its instability would be possible and its downfall inevitable if there were no agreement between those two classes. In that event, this or that measure, and generally all talk about the stability of our C.C. [Central Committee of the Communist Party], would be futile. No measures of any kind could prevent a split in such a case. But I hope that this is too remote a future and too improbable an event to talk about.

I have in mind stability as a guarantee against a split in the immediate future, and I intend to deal here with a few ideas concerning personal qualities.

I think that from this standpoint, the prime factors in the question of stability are such members of the C.C. as Stalin and Trotsky. I think relations between them make up the greater part of the danger of a split, which could be avoided, and this purpose, in my opinion, would be served, among other things, by increasing the number of C.C. members to 50 or 100.

Comrade Stalin, having become Secretary-General, has unlimited authority concentrated in his hands, and I am not sure whether he will always be capable of using that authority with sufficient caution. Comrade Trotsky, on the other hand, as his struggles against the C.C. on the question of the Peoples Commissariat for Communications has already proved, is distinguished not only by outstanding ability. He is personally perhaps the most capable man in the present C.C., but he has displayed excessive self-assurance and shown excessive preoccupation with the purely administrative side of the work.

These two qualities of the two outstanding leaders of the present C.C. can inadvertently lead to a split, and if our Party does not take steps to avert this, the split may come unexpectedly.

I shall not give any further appraisals of the personal qualities of other members of the C.C. I shall just recall that the October episode with [Grigori] Zinoviev and [Lev] Kamenov was, of course, no accident, but neither can the blame for it be laid upon them personally, any more than non-Bolshevism can upon Trotsky.

Speaking of the young C.C. members, I wish to say a few words about [Nikolai] Bukharin and [Georgi] Pyatakov. They are, in my opinion, the most outstanding figures (among the younger ones), and the following must be borne in mind about them: Bukharin is not only a most valuable and major theorist of the Party; he is also rightly considered the favorite of the whole Party, but his theoretical views can be classified as fully Marxist only with the great reserve, for there is something scholastic about him (he has never made a study of dialectics, and, I think, never fully appreciated it).

December 25. As for Pyatakov, he is unquestionably a man of outstanding will and outstanding ability, but shows far too much zeal for administrating and the administrative side of the work to be relied upon in a serious political matter.

Both of these remarks, of course, are made only for the present, on the assumption that both these outstanding and devoted Party workers fail to find an occasion to enhance their knowledge and amend their one-sidedness.

Lenin, 24 December 1922.

Stalin is too rude and this defect, although quite tolerable in our midst and in dealing among us Communists, becomes intolerable in a Secretary-General. That is why I suggest the comrades think about a way of removing Stalin from that post and appointing another man in his stead who in all other respects differs from Comrade Stalin in having only one advantage, namely, that of being more tolerant, more loyal, more polite, and more considerate to the comrades, less capricious, etc. This circumstance may appear to be a negligible detail. But I think that from the standpoint of safeguards against a split, and from the standpoint of what I wrote above about the relationship between Stalin and Trotsky, it is not

a detail, or it is a detail which can assume decisive importance.
Lenin, 25 December 1922.

V.I. Lenin from Internet Modern History Sourcebook, www.fordham.edu/halsall/mod/lenin-testament.html.

Document 6: Terror and Famine in Communist Prisons

In the following letter to the Presidium of the Central Executive Committee of the Bolshevik party, written on December 14, 1926, three former prisoners describe the harsh conditions of a Soviet prison camp.

We appeal to you, asking you to pay a minimum of attention to our request.

We are prisoners who are returning from the Solovetsky concentration camp because of our poor health. We went there full of energy and good health, and now we are returning as invalids, broken and crippled emotionally and physically. We are asking you to draw your attention to the arbitrary use of power and the violence that reign at the Solovetsky concentration camp in Kemi and in all sections of the concentration camp. It is difficult for a human being even to imagine such terror, tyranny, violence, and lawlessness. When we went there, we could not conceive of such a horror, and now we, crippled ourselves, together with several thousands who are still there, appeal to the ruling center of the Soviet state to curb the terror that reigns there. As though it weren't enough that the Unified State Political Directorate [OGPU] without oversight and due process sends workers and peasants there who are by and large innocent (we are not talking about criminals who deserve to be punished), the former tsarist penal servitude system in comparison to Solovky had 99% more humanity, fairness, and legality. . . .

People die like flies, i.e., they die a slow and painful death; we repeat that all this torment and suffering is placed only on the shoulders of the proletariat without money, i.e., on workers who, we repeat, were unfortunate to find themselves in the period of hunger and destruction accompanying the events of the October Revolution, and who committed crimes only to save themselves and their families from death by starvation; they have already borne the punishment for these crimes, and the vast majority of them subsequently chose the path of honest labor. Now because of their past, for whose crime they have already paid, they are fired from their jobs. Yet, the main thing is that the entire weight of this scandalous abuse of power, brute violence, and lawlessness that reign at

Solovky and other sections of the OGPU concentration camp is placed on the shoulders of workers and peasants; others, such as counterrevolutionaries, profiteers and so on, have full wallets and have set themselves up and live in clover in the Soviet State, while next to them, in the literal meaning of the word, the penniless proletariat dies from hunger, cold, and back-breaking 14–16 hour days under the tyranny and lawlessness of inmates who are the agents and collaborators of the State Political Directorate [GPU].

If you complain or write anything ("Heaven forbid"), they will frame you for an attempted escape or for something else, and they will shoot you like a dog. They line us up naked and barefoot at 22 degrees below zero and keep us outside for up to an hour. . . .

We are sure and we hope that in the All-Union Communist Party there are people, as we have been told, who are humane and sympathetic; it is possible, that you might think that it is our imagination, but we swear to you all, by everything that is sacred to us, that this is only one small part of the nightmarish truth, because it makes no sense to make this up. We repeat, and will repeat 100 times, that yes, indeed there are some guilty people, but the majority suffer innocently, as is described above. The word law, according to the law of the GPU concentration camps, does not exist; what does exist is only the autocratic power of petty tyrants, i.e., collaborators, serving time, who have power over life and death. Everything described above is the truth and we, ourselves, who are close to the grave after 3 years in Solovky and Kemi and other sections, are asking you to improve the pathetic, tortured existence of those who are there who languish under the yoke of the OGPU's tyranny, violence, and complete lawlessness.

To this we subscribe: G. Zheleznov, Vinogradov, F. Belinskii.

From Library of Congress Internet exhibit "Revelations from the Russian Archives: The Gulag," http://lcweb.loc.gov/exhibits/archives/d2presid.html.

Document: 7: Platform of the Joint Opposition

Having lost the power struggle with Joseph Stalin, Trotsky and his allies published the "Platform of the Joint Opposition" in 1927. The book was intended as a rallying cry for Stalin's opponents, who claimed to conform to ideas and methods of Lenin.

We have frankly set forth our opinion of the serious mistakes committed by the majority of the Central Committee in all the fundamental spheres of foreign and domestic policy. We have shown how these mistakes of the Central Committee have weakened our party, which is the fundamental instrument of the revolution. We have shown that, in spite of it all, our party can correct its policy from within. But in order to correct the policy, it is necessary clearly and candidly to define the character of the mistakes committed by the party leadership.

The mistakes made have been opportunist mistakes. Opportunism in its developed form according to the classic definition of Lenin is a bloc formed by the upper strata of the working class with the bourgeoisie and directed against the majority of the working class. In the conditions now existing in the Soviet Union, opportunism in its completed form would be an aspiration of the upper strata of the working class towards compromise with the developing new bourgeoisie (kulaks and NEPmen) and with world capitalism, at the expense of the interests of the broad mass of the workers and the peasant poor. . . .

In their bureaucratic self-conceit, the Stalinists "facilitate" their maneuvers by cutting off the party, in the essence of the matter, from all participation in political decisions and thus avoiding its resistance. The Stalin officialdom decides and acts and then lets the party "digest" its decisions. But this process weakens, if it does not paralyze, those very forces which might be deployed in a good political maneuver, both necessary and timely or which might weaken and remove the bad consequences of maneuvers by the leaders which were obviously bad. Thus there is a cumulative result of the opportunist tendencies of the right wing of the Central Committee and the maneuvers of its centrist group, a result which in its sum total means: a weakening of the international position of the USSR, a weakening of the position of the proletariat in relation to other classes within the Union, a relative deterioration of its material conditions of life, a weakening of its bond with the peasant poor, threatening its alliance with the middle peasants, a weakening of its role in the state machine, a slowing down of the tempo of industrialization. . . . The Russian Communist party has been tempered in the fires of three revolutions. It has seized and held power against a world of enemies. It has organized the Third International. Its fate is the fate of the first victorious proletarian revolution. The revolution determines the tempo of its inner life. All intellectual processes within the party, taking place under high-class pressure, have a tendency to ripen and develop swiftly. Just for this reason it is necessary for us to have in our party a timely and decisive struggle against every tendency to depart from the Leninist line. . . .

We, the Opposition, unqualifiedly condemn every attempt whatsoever to create a second party. The slogan of two parties is the slogan of the Stalin group in its effort to crowd out of the All-Union Communist party the Leninist Opposition. Our task is not to create a new party, but to correct the course of the All-Union Communist party. The proletarian revolution in the Soviet Union can win through to the end only with a united Bolshevik party. We are struggling within the Communist party for our views, and we decisively condemn the slogan, "Two parties", as the slogan of adventurers. The slogan, "Two parties", expresses on the one hand the desire of certain elements in the party apparatus for a split, and on the other, a mood of despair and a failure to comprehend that the task of Leninists is to win the victory of Lenin's ideas within the party, notwithstanding all difficulties. Nobody who sincerely defends the line of Lenin can entertain the idea of "two parties" or play with the suggestion of a split. Only those who desire to replace Lenin's course with some other can advocate a split or a movement along the two-party road.

We will struggle with all our force against the formation of two parties, for the dictatorship of the proletariat demands as its very core a single proletarian party. It demands a single party. . . .

On the tenth anniversary of the October Revolution, we express our profound conviction that the working class did not make countless sacrifices and overthrow capitalism in order to prove unequal now to the task of correcting the mistakes of its leadership, carrying the proletarian revolution forward with a firm hand, and defending the Soviet Union, which is the center of the world revolution.

Against opportunism! Against a split! For the unity of the Leninist party!

Leon Trotsky, *Platform of the Joint Opposition*, 1927, from The Trotsky Internet Archive, http://csf.colorado.edu/mirrors/marxists.org/archive/trotsky/works/1927/opposition/ch12.htm.

Document 8: Dizzy with Success

His hold on power secure, Joseph Stalin published "Dizzy with Success" in Pravda *on March 2, 1930. The article was intended to calm the rising tensions surrounding the often-violent collectivization of farms. Stalin was concerned about the potential damage the Communists might suffer if collectivization led to splits and opposing factions within the party.*

The Soviet government's successes in the sphere of the collective-farm movement are now being spoken of by every one. Even our enemies are forced to admit that the successes are substantial. And they really are very great.

It is a fact that by February 20 of this year 50 per cent of the peasant farms throughout the U.S.S.R. had been collectivized. That means that by February 20, 1930, we had over-fulfilled the five-year plan of collectivization by more than 100 per cent.

It is a fact that on February 28 of this year the collective farms had already succeeded in stocking upwards of 36 million centners, i.e., about 220 million poods, of seed for the spring sowing, which is more than 90 per cent of the plan. It must be admitted that the accumulation of 220 million poods of seed by the collective farms alone—after the successful fulfilment of the grain-procurement plan—is a tremendous achievement.

What does all this show?

That a radical turn of the countryside towards socialism may be considered as already achieved.

There is no need to prove that these successes are of supreme importance for the fate of our country, for the whole working class, which is the leading force of our country, and, lastly, for the Party itself. To say nothing of the direct practical results, these successes are of immense value for the internal life of the Party itself, for the education of our Party. They imbue our Party with a spirit of cheerfulness and confidence in its strength. They arm the working class with confidence in the victory of our cause. They bring forward additional millions of reserves for our Party.

Hence the Party's task is: to consolidate the successes achieved and to utilize them systematically for our further advancement.

But successes have their seamy side, especially when they are attained with comparative "ease"—"unexpectedly," so to speak. Such successes sometimes induce a spirit of vanity and conceit: "We can achieve anything!", "There's nothing we can't do!" People not infrequently become intoxicated by such successes; they become dizzy with success, lose all sense of proportion and the capacity to understand realities; they show a tendency to overrate their own strength and to underrate the strength of the enemy; adventurist attempts are made to solve all questions of socialist construction "in a trice." In such a case, there is no room for concern to consolidate the successes achieved and to utilize them systematically for further advancement. Why should we consolidate the successes achieved when, as it is, we can dash to the full victory of socialism "in a trice": "We can achieve anything!", "There's nothing we can't do!"

Hence the Party's task is: to wage a determined struggle against these sentiments, which are dangerous and harmful to our cause, and to drive them out of the Party.

It cannot be said that these dangerous and harmful sentiments are at all widespread in the ranks of our Party. But they do exist in our Party, and there are no grounds for asserting that they will not become stronger. And if they should be allowed free scope, then there can be no doubt that the collective-farm movement will be considerably weakened and the danger of its breaking down may become a reality.

Hence the task of our press is: systematically to denounce these and similar anti-Leninist sentiments.

J.V. Stalin, "Dizzy with Success," from *Works*. Moscow: Foreign Languages Publishing House, 1955.

Document: 9: Article 58, Criminal Code of the Russian Soviet Federated Socialist Republic

The following section of the RSFSR criminal code, drawn up in 1934, formed the legal foundation for the Stalinist purges of the 1930s.

1. Counterrevolutionary Crimes

58-1. "Counterrevolutionary" is understood as any action directed toward the overthrow, subversion, or weakening of the power of worker-peasant councils or of their chosen (according to the Constitution of the USSR and constitutions of union republics) worker-peasant government of the USSR, union and autonomous republics, or toward the subversion or weakening of the external security of the USSR and the fundamental economic, political, and national gains of the proletarian revolution.

In consideration of the international solidarity of interests of all workers, acts are likewise considered "counterrevolutionary" when they are directed at any other workers' government, even if not part of the USSR.

58-1a. Treason to the motherland, i.e. acts done by citizens of the USSR in damage to the military power of the USSR, its national sovereignty, or the inviolability of its territory, such as: espionage, betrayal of military or state secrets, crossing to the side of the enemy, flight (by surface or air) abroad, shall be punishable by—

the supreme measure of criminal punishment—shooting with confiscation of all property, or with mitigating circumstances—deprivation of liberty for a term of 10 years with confiscation of all property.

58-1b. The same crimes, perpetrated by military personnel, are punishable by the supreme measure of criminal punishment—

shooting with confiscation of all property.

58-1v. In case of flight (by surface or air) across the border by a military member, the adult members of his family, if they in any way aided the preparation or carrying-out of treason, or only knew about it and failed to report it to authorities, shall be punishable by—

deprivation of liberty for a term of 5 to 10 years, with confiscation of all property.

Remaining adult members of the family of the traitor, living together with him or as his dependents at the moment of the perpetration of the crime, shall be deprived of voting rights and exiled to remote districts of Siberia for 5 years.

58-1. Failure by a military member to denounce preparations or the carrying-out of treason shall be punishable by—

deprivation of liberty for 10 years.

Such failure to denounce by other citizens (not military) shall be punished according to article 58-12. . . .

58-4. The offering of whatever kind of aid to that part of the international bourgeoisie, which, not recognizing the equal rights of a Communist system replacing a Capitalist system, exerts itself for its overthrow, and likewise to public groups and organizations, being under the influence of or directly organized by that bourgeoisie, in the carrying out of hostile activities toward the USSR, shall be punishable by—

deprivation of liberty for a term not less than three years with confiscation of all or part of one's property, with an increase, in especially aggravating circumstances, up to the supreme measure of social defense—shooting or declaration to be an enemy of the workers, with deprivation of citizenship of one's union republic, and, likewise, citizenship of the USSR and expulsion beyond the borders of the USSR forever, with confiscation of property. . . .

58-6. Espionage, i.e. the transmittal, seizure, or collection, with the purpose of transmittal, of information, being a specially kept state secret due to its content, to foreign governments, counter-revolutionary organizations, and private individuals, shall be punishable by—

deprivation of liberty for a term not less than three years, with confiscation of all or part of one's property, or in those cases where the espionage brought or could bring especially severe consequences for the interests of the USSR—the supreme measure of social defense—shooting or proclamation as an enemy of the workers with deprivation of citizenship of one's union republic and, likewise, of citizenship of the USSR and expulsion beyond the borders of the USSR forever with confiscation of property.

Transmittal, seizure, or collection for purpose of transmittal of economic information, not consisting by its content of specially preserved state secrets, but not subject to publication either due to direct legal prohibition, or due to the decision of the management of the department, institution, or enterprise, whether for a reward or for free, to organizations and persons listed above, shall be punishable by—

> deprivation of liberty for a term up to three years. . . .

58-14. Counterrevolutionary sabotage, i.e. conscious failure to perform some defined duties or intentionally negligent fulfillment of them, with the special purpose of weakening the authority of the government and functioning of the state apparatus, shall be punishable by—

> deprivation of liberty for a term not less than one year, with confiscation of all or part of one's property, with an increase, in especially aggravating circumstances, to the supreme measure of social defense—shooting, with confiscation of property.

Article 58, Criminal Code of the Russian Soviet Federated Socialist Republic, www.tiac.net/users/hcunn/rus/uk58-e.html.

Document 10: The Nazi-Soviet Pact

Concluded just before the invasion of Poland by Germany in September 1939, the Nazi-Soviet Non-Aggression Pact was intended by both sides as a means of buying time before the final clash between fascism and socialism. In a secret additional protocol, Hitler and Stalin agreed to zones of control in Poland, Finland, and the Baltic States for Nazi Germany and the Soviet Union.

The Government of the German Reich and The Government of the Union of Soviet Socialist Republics, directed by the wish to strengthen the cause of peace between Germany and the USSR . . . have reached the following agreement:

Article 1: The two contracting parties undertake to refrain from any act of violence, and aggressive action, or any attack against one another, whether individually or jointly with other powers.

Article 2: In case of the contracting parties should become the object of warlike acts on the part of a third party, the other contracting party will no longer support that third power in any form. . . .

Article 4: Neither of the two contracting parties will participate in any grouping of powers which is indirectly or directly aimed against the other party.

Article 5: Should disputes or conflicts arise between the contracting parties regarding questions of any kind whatsoever, the two parties would clear away these disputes or conflicts solely by means of friendly exchanges of views or if necessary by arbitrary commissions.

Secret Additional Protocol: On the occasion of the signature of the Non-Aggression Treaty between the German Reich and the Union of Soviet Socialist Republics, the undersigned . . . parties discussed in strictly confidential conversations the question of the delimitation of their respective spheres of interest in Eastern Europe. These conversations led to the following result:

In the event of a territorial and political transformation in the territories belonging to the Baltic States (Finland, Estonia, Latvia, Lithuania), the northern frontier of Lithuania shall represent the frontier of the spheres of interest both of Germany and the USSR. . . .

In the event of a territorial and political transformation of the territories belonging to the Polish State, the spheres of interest of both Germany and the USSR shall be bounded approximately by the line of the rivers Narev, Vistula, and San.

This Protocol will be treated by both parties as strictly secret.

The Nazi-Soviet Non-Aggression pact, www.pagesz.net/~stevek/europe/nazi_soviet.html.

Document 11: The German Invasion of the Soviet Union

Vyacheslav Molotov (1889–1986) was foreign minister of the Soviet Union at the time of the signing of the Nazi-Soviet Non-Aggression Pact, August 23, 1939. On the invasion of the Soviet Union by Germany in June 1941, he gave the following address to the Soviet Union.

Citizens of the Soviet Union:

The Soviet Government and its head, Comrade Stalin, have authorized me to make the following statement:

Today at 4 o'clock a.m., without any claims having been presented to the Soviet Union, without a declaration of war, German troops attacked our country, attacked our borders at many points and bombed from their airplanes our cities. Zhitomir, Kiev, Sevastopol, Kaunas and some others, killing and wounding over two hundred persons.

There were also enemy air raids and artillery shelling from Rumanian and Finnish territory.

This unheard of attack upon our country is perfidy unparalleled in the history of civilized nations. The attack on our country was perpetrated despite the fact that a treaty of non-aggression had been signed between the U.S.S.R. and Germany and that the Soviet Government most faithfully abided by all provisions of this treaty. The attack upon our country was perpetrated despite the fact that during the entire period of operation of this treaty, the German Government could not find grounds for a single complaint against the U.S.S.R. as regards observance of this treaty. Entire responsibility for this predatory attack upon the Soviet Union falls fully and completely upon the German Fascist rulers.

At 5:30 a.m.—that is, after the attack had already been perpetrated, Von der Schulenburg, the German Ambassador in Moscow, on behalf of his government made the statement to me as People's Commissar of Foreign Affairs to the effect that the German Government had decided to launch war against the U.S.S.R. in connection with the concentration of Red Army units near the eastern German frontier.

In reply to this I stated on behalf of the Soviet Government that, until the very last moment, the German Government had not presented any claims to the Soviet Government, that Germany attacked the U.S.S.R. despite the peaceable position of the Soviet Union, and that for this reason Fascist Germany is the aggressor. On instruction of the government of the Soviet Union I also stated that at no point had our troops or our air force committed a violation of the frontier and therefore the statement made this morning by the Rumanian radio to the effect that Soviet aircraft allegedly had fired on Rumanian airdromes is a sheer lie and provocation. Likewise a lie and provocation is the whole declaration made today by Hitler, who is trying belatedly to concoct accusations charging the Soviet Union with failure to observe the Soviet-German pact.

Now that the attack on the Soviet Union has already been committed, the Soviet Government has ordered our troops to repulse the predatory assault and to drive German troops from the territory of our country.

This war has been forced upon us, not by the German people, not by German workers, peasants and intellectuals, whose sufferings we well understand, but by the clique of bloodthirsty Fascist rulers of Germany who have enslaved Frenchmen, Czechs, Poles, Serbians, Norway, Belgium, Denmark, Holland, Greece and other nations.

The government of the Soviet Union expresses its unshakable confidence that our valiant army and navy and brave falcons of the Soviet Air Force will acquit themselves with honor in performing their duty to the fatherland and to the Soviet people, and will inflict a crushing blow upon the aggressor.

This is not the first time that our people have had to deal with an attack of an arrogant foe. At the time of Napoleon's invasion of Russia our people's reply was war for the fatherland, and Napoleon suffered defeat and met his doom.

It will be the same with Hitler, who in his arrogance has proclaimed a new crusade against our country. The Red Army and our whole people will again wage victorious war for the fatherland, for our country, for honor, for liberty.

The government of the Soviet Union expresses the firm conviction that the whole population of our country, all workers, peasants and intellectuals, men and women, will conscientiously perform their duties and do their work. Our entire people must now stand solid and united as never before.

Each one of us must demand of himself and of others discipline, organization and self-denial worthy of real Soviet patriots, in order to provide for all the needs of the Red Army, Navy and Air Force, to insure victory over the enemy.

The government calls upon you, citizens of the Soviet Union, to rally still more closely around our glorious Bolshevist party, around our Soviet Government, around our great leader and comrade, Stalin. Ours is a righteous cause. The enemy shall be defeated. Victory will be ours.

Vyacheslav Molotov, speech delivered in June 1941, www.historyplace.com/speeches/molotov.htm.

Document 12: The Warsaw Pact

To counter the North Atlantic Treaty Organization (NATO), the Soviet Union and its satellite states in central Europe signed the Warsaw Pact in 1955.

TREATY OF FRIENDSHIP, CO-OPERATION AND MUTUAL ASSISTANCE

Between the People's Republic of Albania, the People's Republic of Bulgaria, the Hungarian People's Republic, the German Democratic Republic, the Polish People's Republic, the Rumanian People's Republic, the Union of Soviet Socialist Republics, and the Czechoslovak Republic, May 1, 1955.

The contracting parties,

Reaffirming their desire for the organization of a system of collective security in Europe, with the participation of all the European states, irrespective of their social and state systems, which would make it possible to combine their efforts in the interests of securing peace in Europe,

Taking into consideration at the same time the situation obtaining in Europe as the result of ratification of the Paris agreements, which provide for the formation of a new military grouping in the shape of the "Western European Union" together with a remilitarized Western Germany, and for the integration of Western Germany in the North Atlantic bloc, which increases the threat of another war and creates a menace to the national security of the peaceloving states,

Convinced that, under these circumstances, the peaceloving states of Europe should take the necessary measures for safeguarding their security, and in the interests of maintaining peace in Europe,

Guided by the purposes and principles of the United Nations Charter,

In the interests of further strengthening and promoting friendship, co-operation and mutual assistance, in accordance with the principles of respect for the independence and sovereignty of states, and also with the principle of noninterference in their internal affairs,

Have resolved to conclude this Treaty of Friendship, Cooperation and Mutual Assistance. . . .

Article 1. The contracting parties undertake, in accordance with the Charter of the United Nations Organization, to refrain in their international relations from the threat or use of force, and to settle their international disputes by peaceful means so as not to endanger international peace and security.

Article 2. The contracting parties declare their readiness to take part, in the spirit of sincere co-operation, in all international undertakings intended to safeguard international peace and security and they shall use all their energies for the realization of these aims. Moreover, the contracting parties shall work for the adoption, in agreement with other states desiring to co-operate in this matter, of effective measures towards a general reduction of armaments and prohibition of atomic, hydrogen and other weapons of mass destruction.

Article 3. The contracting parties shall take council among themselves on all important international questions relating to their common interests, guided by the interests of strengthening international peace and security. They shall take council among themselves immediately, whenever, in the opinion of any of them, there has arisen the threat of an armed attack on one or several states that are signatories of the treaty, in the interests of organizing their joint defense and of upholding peace and security.

Article 4. In the event of an armed attack in Europe on one or several states that are signatories of the treaty by any state or group of states, each state that is a party to this treaty shall, in the exercise of the right to individual or collective self-defense in accordance with Article 51 of the Charter of the United Nations Organization, render the state or states so attacked immediate assistance, individually and in agreement with other states that are parties to this treaty, by all the means it may consider necessary, including the use of armed force. The states that are parties to this treaty shall immediately take council among themselves concerning the necessary joint measures to be adopted for the purpose of restoring and upholding international peace and security. . . .

Article 5. The contracting parties have agreed on the establishment of a joint command for their armed forces, which shall be placed, by agreement among these parties, under this command, which shall function on the basis of jointly defined principles. They shall also take other concerted measures necessary for strengthening their defense capacity, in order to safeguard the peaceful labour of their peoples, to guarantee the inviolability of their frontiers and territories and to provide safeguards against possible aggression. . . .

Article 9. The present treaty is open to be acceded to by other states—irrespective of their social and state systems—which may express their readiness to assist, through participation in the present treaty, in combining the efforts of the peaceloving states for the purpose of safeguarding the peace and security, of nations. This act of acceding to the treaty shall become effective, with the consent of the states that are parties to this treaty, after the instrument of accedence has been deposited with the government of the Polish People's Republic. . . .

Article 11. The present treaty shall remain in force for 20 years. For the contracting parties which will not have submitted to the government of the Polish People's Republic a statement denouncing the treaty a year before the expiration of its term, it shall remain in force throughout the following ten years.

In the event of the organization of a system of collective security in Europe and the conclusion of a general European treaty of collective security to that end, which the contracting parties shall unceasingly seek to bring about, the present treaty shall cease to be effective on the date the general European treaty comes into force.

The Warsaw Security Pact, May 14, 1955, www.yale.edu/lawweb/avalon/intdip/soviet/warsaw.htm.

Document 13: Khrushchev's Secret Speech (excerpts)

On February 24, 1956, Nikita Khrushchev delivered a scathing denunciation of Joseph Stalin at the Twentieth Congress of the Communist Party of the Soviet Union. The "secret speech," although it was given to a closed session, gradually leaked out to the Soviet people and to Communist parties around the world, stunning party loyalists who had looked to Stalin as a paragon of Communist thought and action.

We have to consider seriously and analyze correctly [the crimes of the Stalin era] in order that we may preclude any possibility of a repetition in any form whatever of what took place during the life of Stalin, who absolutely did not tolerate collegiality in leadership and in work, and who practiced brutal violence, not only toward everything which opposed him, but also toward that which seemed to his capricious and despotic character, contrary to his concepts.

Stalin acted not through persuasion, explanation, and patient cooperation with people, but by imposing his concepts and demanding absolute submission to his opinion. Whoever opposed this concept or tried to prove his viewpoint, and the correctness of his position, was doomed to removal from the leading collective and to subsequent moral and physical annihilation. This was especially true during the period following the XVIIth Party Congress (1934). . . .

Stalin originated the concept, enemy of the people. This term automatically rendered it unnecessary that the ideological errors of a man or men engaged in a controversy be proven; this term made possible the usage of the most cruel repression, violating all norms of revolutionary legality, against anyone who in any way disagreed with Stalin, against those who were only suspected of hostile intent, against those who had bad reputations. This concept, enemy of the people, actually eliminated the possibility of any kind of ideological fight or the making of one's views known on this or that issue, even those of a practical character. . . . The only proof of guilt used, against all norms of current legal science, was the confession of the accused himself; and, as subsequent probing proved, confessions were acquired through physical pressures against the accused.

This led to the glaring violations of revolutionary legality, and to the fact that many entirely innocent persons, who in the past had defended the Party line, became victims. . . .

The Commission [of Inquiry] has become acquainted with a large quantity of materials in the NKVD archives. It became apparent that many Party, Soviet and economic activists who were branded in 1937–1938 as enemies were actually never enemies, spies, wreckers, etc., but were always honest Communists; they were only so stigmatized, and often, no longer able to bear barbaric tortures, they charged themselves with all kinds of grave and unlikely crimes. . . .

Lenin used severe methods only in the most necessary cases, when the exploiting classes were still in existence and were vigorously opposing the revolution, when the struggle for survival was decidedly assuming the sharpest forms, even including a civil war.

Stalin, on the other hand, used extreme methods and mass repression at a time when the revolution was already victorious, when the Soviet state was strengthened, when the exploiting classes were already liquidated and Socialist relations were rooted solidly in all phases of national economy, when our Party was politically consolidated and had strengthened itself both numerically and ideologically. It is clear that here Stalin showed in a whole series of cases his intolerance, his brutality and his abuse of power. Instead of proving his political correctness and mobilizing the masses, he often chose the path of repression and physical annihilation, not only against actual enemies, but also against individuals who had not committed any crimes against the Party and the Soviet government.

Nikita Khrushchev, speech delivered on February 24, 1956, www.fordham.edu/halsall/mod/krushchev-secret.html.

Document 14: The Cuban Missile Crisis

Nikita Khrushchev sent the following letter to President John Kennedy on October 27, 1962, at the height of the Cuban Missile Crisis.

DEAR MR. PRESIDENT, I have studied with great satisfaction your reply to Mr. Thant concerning measures that should be taken to avoid contact between our vessels and thereby avoid irreparable and fatal consequences. This reasonable step on your part strengthens my belief that you are showing concern for the preservation of peace, which I note with satisfaction.

I have already said that our people, our Government, and I personally, as Chairman of the Council of Ministers, are concerned solely with having our country develop and occupy a worthy place among all peoples of the world in economic competition, in the development of culture and the arts, and in raising the living standard of the people. This is the most noble and necessary field for competition, and both the victor and the vanquished will derive only benefit from it, because it means peace and an increase in the means by which man lives and finds enjoyment. . . .

I understand your concern for the security of the United States, Mr. President, because this is the primary duty of a President. But we too are disturbed about these same questions; I bear these same obligations as Chairman of the Council of Ministers of the U.S.S.R. You have been alarmed by the fact that we have aided Cuba with weapons, in order to strengthen its defense capability—precisely defense capability—because whatever weapons it may possess, Cuba cannot be equated with you since the difference in magnitude is so great, particularly in view of modern means of destruction. Our aim has been and is to help Cuba, and no one can dispute the humanity of our motives, which are oriented toward enabling Cuba to live peacefully and develop in the way its people desire.

You wish to ensure the security of your country, and this is understandable. But Cuba, too, wants the same thing; all countries want to maintain their security. But how are we, the Soviet Union, our Government, to assess your actions which are expressed in the fact that you have surrounded the Soviet Union with military bases; surrounded our allies with military bases; placed military bases literally around our country; and stationed your missile armaments there? This is no secret. Responsible American personages openly declare that it is so. Your missiles are located in Britain, are located in Italy, and are aimed against us. . . .

I think it would be possible to end the controversy quickly and normalize the situation, and then the people could breathe more easily, considering that statesmen charged with responsibility are of sober mind and have an awareness of their responsibility combined with the ability to solve complex questions and not bring things to a military catastrophe.

I therefore make this proposal: We are willing to remove from Cuba the means which you regard as offensive. We are willing to carry this out and to make this pledge in the United Nations. Your representatives will make a declaration to the effect that the United States, for its part, considering the uneasiness and anxiety of the Soviet State, will remove its analogous means from Turkey. Let us reach agreement as to the period of time needed by you and by us to bring this about.

And, after that, persons entrusted by the United Nations Security Council could inspect on the spot the fulfillment of the pledges made. Of course, the permission of the Governments of Cuba and Turkey is necessary for the entry into those countries of these representatives and for the inspection of the fulfillment of the pledge made by each side. Of course it would be best if these representatives enjoyed the confidence of the Security Council as well as yours and mine—both the United States and the Soviet Union—and also that of Turkey and Cuba. I do not think it would be difficult to select people who would enjoy the trust and respect of all parties concerned. . . .

All of this could possibly serve as a good impetus toward the finding of mutually acceptable agreements on other controversial issues on which you and I have been exchanging views. These issues have so far not been resolved, but they are awaiting urgent solution, which would clear up the international atmosphere. We are prepared for this.

These are my proposals, Mr. President.

Respectfully yours,

N. Khrushchev

Nikita Khrushchev, letter to John F. Kennedy, October 27, 1962. www.state.gov/www/about_state/history/volume_vi/exchanges.html.

Document 15: The Brezhnev Doctrine

After the Soviet invasion of Czechoslovakia in August 1968, Leonid Brezhnev gave the following speech on the need for unity among socialist republics. The Brezhnev Doctrine meant, in practice, that no socialist ally of the Soviet Union would be allowed to alter its form of government— a theory that was put to its final test in Afghanistan a decade later.

In connection with the events in Czechoslovakia the question of the correlation and interdependence of the national interests of the socialist countries and their international duties acquire particular topical and acute importance.

The measures taken by the Soviet Union, jointly with other socialist countries, in defending the socialist gains of the Czechoslovak people are of great significance for strengthening the socialist community, which is the main achievement of the international working class.

We cannot ignore the assertions, held in some places, that the actions of the five socialist countries run counter to the Marxist Leninist principle of sovereignty and the rights of nations to self determination.

The groundlessness of such reasoning consists primarily in that it is based on an abstract, nonclass approach to the question of sovereignty and the rights of nations to self determination.

The peoples of the socialist countries and Communist parties certainly do have and should have freedom for determining the ways of advance of their respective countries.

However, none of their decisions should damage either socialism in their country or the fundamental interests of other socialist countries, and the whole working class movement, which is working for socialism.

This means that each Communist party is responsible not only to its own people, but also to all the socialist countries, to the entire Communist movement. Whoever forgets this, in stressing only the independence of the Communist party, becomes one sided. He deviates from his international duty.

Marxist dialectics are opposed to one sidedness. They demand that each phenomenon be examined concretely, in general connection with other phenomena, with other processes.

Just as, in Lenin's words, a man living in a society cannot be free from the society, one or another socialist state, staying in a system of other states composing the socialist community, cannot be free from the common interests of that community. . . .

The socialist states respect the democratic norms of international law. They have proved this more than once in practice, by coming out resolutely against the attempts of imperialism to violate the sovereignty and independence of nations. It is from these same positions that they reject the leftist, adventurist conception of "exporting revolution," of "bringing happiness" to other peoples.

However, from a Marxist point of view, the norms of law, including the norms of mutual relations of the socialist countries, cannot be interpreted narrowly, formally, and in isolation from the general context of class struggle in the modern world. The socialist countries resolutely come out against the exporting and importing of counterrevolution.

Each Communist party is free to apply the basic principles of Marxism Leninism and of socialism in its country, but it cannot depart from these principles (assuming, naturally, that it remains a Communist party).

Concretely, this means, first of all, that, in its activity, each Communist party cannot but take into account such a decisive fact of our time as the struggle between two opposing social systems—capitalism and socialism.

This is an objective struggle, a fact not depending on the will of the people, and stipulated by the world's being split into two opposite social systems. Lenin said: "Each man must choose between joining our side or the other side. Any attempt to avoid taking sides in this issue must end in fiasco."

It has got to be emphasized that when a socialist country seems to adopt a "nonaffiliated" stand, it retains its national independence, in effect, precisely because of the might of the socialist community, and above all the Soviet Union as a central force, which also includes the might of its armed forces. The weakening of any of the links in the world system of socialism directly affects all the socialist countries, which cannot look indifferently upon this.

The antisocialist elements in Czechoslovakia actually covered up the demand for so called neutrality and Czechoslovakia's withdrawal from the socialist community with talking about the right of nations to self determination.

However, the implementation of such "self determination," in other words, Czechoslovakia's detachment from the socialist community, would have come into conflict with its own vital interests and would have been detrimental to the other socialist states. . . .

Discharging their internationalist duty toward the fraternal peoples of Czechoslovakia and defending their own socialist gains, the U.S.S.R. and the other socialist states had to act decisively and they did act against the antisocialist forces in Czechoslovakia.

Leonid Brezhnev, speech delivered to Polish workers in November 1968, www.fordham.edu/halsall/mod/1968brezhnev.html.

Document 16: Perestroika

Mikhail Gorbachev gave the following speech on September 11, 1989, outlining his perestroika reforms, intended to open the Soviet economy to partial privatization, competition, and market forces.

Good evening, comrades, I am here to talk to you about our current affairs. The situation in the country is not simple. We all know and feel this. Everything has become entangled in a tight knot: scarcity on the consumer goods market, conflicts in ethnic relations, and difficult and sometimes painful processes in the public consciousness, resulting from the overcoming of distortions and from the renewal of socialism. People are trying to understand where we have found ourselves at the moment, evaluating the pluses and minuses of the path we have covered during the last four-plus years, the development of democracy and the pace of the economic and political reforms.

It is only natural that people want to know the real causes of our weaknesses and failures in carrying out specific programs for perestroika and in tackling urgent problems and to find out why the situation in some areas has deteriorated rather than improved.

In short, political life today is characterized by intense debate. But the main thing I want to emphasize is that the mass of people have become involved in this movement and they play an ever growing role in discussing and accomplishing social, economic, and political tasks. . . .

The Government of the U.S.S.R. is elaborating a program of extraordinary measures to improve the economy and, above all, to normalize the consumer market. The program is to be submitted to the Congress of People's Deputies. We believe that this program will give clear answers to the questions of how and when the most urgent social and economic problems will be solved. I think society will not accept it if the program does not determine clear and concrete measures, stages, and time limits as well as the responsibility of the republic and local bodies and labor collectives. I presume that this package may include unpopular, probably tough and even painful measures. This will be justified, however, only if they are prompted by the need to get out of the present situation. Shortages, which arouse the sharpest criticism and discontent of the people, are a special issue. The government is to give an explanation on this urgent social problem and come up with practical measures shortly. . . .

By restructuring itself, getting rid of all that hinders its activities, overcoming dogmatism and conservatism, mastering a new style and new methods of work, renewing its personnel, and working side by side with the working people, the Communist party of the Soviet Union will be able to fulfill its role of the political vanguard of society. The party will firmly pursue the policy of perestroika, heading the revolutionary transformation of society. We should realistically assess all processes and phenomena of the present-day situation, show restraint, see clearly where we are and not become confused. On this basis we should draw conclusions for our action at the given moment and in the future. We must act responsibly and prudently, without deviating from the course of perestroika in society.

Dear comrades, I wish you success in work, determination and firm spirit.

Mikhail Gorbachev, "Perestroika and the Socialist Renewal of Society," speech delivered on September 11, 1989.

Glossary

apparatchik: A member of a Communist Party organization, or "apparatus."

Bolsheviks: The radical wing of the Russian Social Democratic Party that split from the Menshevik faction in 1903. The Bolshevik ("majority") Party stood for a one-party state and for leadership by a revolutionary elite. After the Bolsheviks formed the Russian Communist Party in 1918, their members began calling themselves Communists.

bourgeoisie: The middle class of petty officials, shop owners, professionals, and property owners (as generally defined by Soviet communism) who are held up as enemies to the proletariat and to the Communist revolution.

cadre: A group of revolutionary leaders and activists, or a leader who holds a position of responsibility in the revolution.

Central Committee: The national organization of deputies representing local Communist parties from throughout the Soviet Union.

Cheka: The organization of secret police founded by the Bolsheviks after the revolution to enforce obedience through surveillance and terror, succeeded by the NKVD and then the KGB.

collectivization: The process of seizing private property, such as a farm, and gathering it into either a collective (cooperative) or state (government-operated) organization.

Comintern: "Communist International," the organization of international Communist parties founded by Lenin to carry out revolutions in foreign nations.

commissar: A Bolshevik official responsible for leading revolutionary activities in a certain region, town, or factory.

Congress of People's Deputies: An organization established by the Soviet Constitution to meet occasionally and make the most important policy decisions for the Soviet Union.

Duma: A council of advisers under the Russian czars, reconvened by Czar Nicholas II after the 1905 revolution.

glasnost: "Openness," a policy instituted by Mikhail Gorbachev and the Communist Party during the late 1980s that permitted more open debate and the freedom of the press to discuss problems within the party and the Soviet Union.

Gosplan: "State Planning Committee," the Soviet Union's economic planning organization that drew up annual and five-year plans and set production goals for Soviet industries.

Komsomol: "All-Union Lenin Communist Youth League," the Communist youth organization, which enlisted promising young party members from age fourteen and groomed them for future positions in the Soviet bureaucracy.

kulaks: Middle-class peasants subject to property confiscation, exile, prison terms, and execution during the Stalin-era collectivization of Soviet agriculture.

Mensheviks: The moderate wing of the Russian Social Democratic Party. In opposition to the more radical Bolsheviks, the Mensheviks sought the gradual achievement of socialism through parliamentary methods.

NEPmen: Term for traders, wholesalers, manufacturers, and a variety of private business owners who benefited from economic liberalization under the New Economic Policy of the 1920s.

New Economic Policy (NEP): An economic policy adopted by the Russian Communist Party from 1921 to 1928 that allowed private businesses to operate and peasants to sell their produce on an open market.

nomenklatura: The class of Communist Party officials who enjoyed material comforts and privileges that were denied to ordinary Soviet citizens.

perestroika: "Restructuring," a policy instituted by Mikhail Gorbachev and the Communist Party in the late 1980s that allowed partial privatization of Soviet industries and pay incentives for workers.

Politburo: "Political Bureau," the highest executive committee within the Communist Party.

proletarian: A member of the urban working class, occupying the vanguard of the ongoing socialist revolution according to Marxist and Leninist philosophy.

Social Revolutionaries (SR): The party of moderate socialists, at first accepted into the postrevolutionary government and then suppressed by the Bolsheviks.

Supreme Soviet: The national legislature of the Soviet Union, consisting of two houses representing, respectively, nationalities and administrative regions. The Supreme Soviet met twice a year and when called for emergency sessions. In effect, it served as a legislative rubber stamp for policies decided at the highest levels of the Communist Party. Each of the republics also elected their local Supreme Soviets.

War Communism: A policy of food requisitioning and forced labor and military service instituted by the Bolshevik Party during the Russian Civil War.

Whites: Colloquial term for those fighting against the Communist (Red) armies during the Russian Civil War.

Chronology

1903
The Social Democratic Party of Russian socialists breaks in to Bolshevik and Menshevik factions. Mensheviks favor open party membership and democratic elections, while Bolsheviks favor government by a revolutionary elite.

1905
Russia's defeat in the war with Japan leads to a violent public rebellion, which is crushed by the Russian military and czarist police. The czar agrees to allow an elected Duma, or assembly, to meet.

1914
In August, Russia joins the Allies of France and Great Britain at the outbreak of World War I. Fighting with Germany breaks out along Russia's western frontier.

1917
Bread rationing results in strikes and demonstrations in Petrograd, the renamed Russian capital. In March, Russian troops refuse to fire on demonstrators. On March 15, Czar Nicholas II abdicates, transferring power to a provisional government under Prince Georgi Lvov. Meanwhile, the Soviet of Workers' and Soldiers' Deputies, composed of Bolsheviks and other left-wing factions, meets in Petrograd and forms a shadow government. On April 16, the Bolshevik leader Vladimir Ilyich Ulyanov (Lenin) returns from political exile, arriving at the Finland Station in St. Petersburg. After an antigovernment uprising in July, Prince Lvov resigns and Aleksandr Kerensky becomes prime minister. In September, General Lavr Kornilov leads an unsuccessful attack on the capital. Leon Trotsky forms the Red Guards as the armed wing of the Bolshevik Party. On October 25, under Lenin's prompting, the Bolshevik uprising begins in Petrograd. Red Guards occupy railway stations, telephone exchanges, and public buildings. In November, elections for a Constituent Assembly are held. In December, the Bolshevik Party forms the Cheka, a secret police force. On December 20, the government begins armistice negotiations with Germany.

1918
In January, the Constituent Assembly meets one time and is closed down by the Red Guards. On March 3, the Bolshevik government

signs the Treaty of Brest-Litovsk, withdrawing from the war. Russia surrenders large territories to Germany, and Lenin moves the Russian capital from Petrograd to Moscow. On July 10, a new constitution, written by Lenin, establishing the Russian Federated Socialist Republic, is ratified. On July 17, Czar Nicholas and his family are murdered at Ykaterinburg in the Ural Mountains. In August, the Bolshevik government eliminates private ownership of land and inheritance. World War I ends on November 11, and the Bolsheviks repudiate the Treaty of Brest-Litovsk.

1919

The Russian Civil War continues; the Red (Bolshevik) armies under the leadership of Leon Trotsky fight the White armies, under former czarist generals, who oppose Lenin's government. The Bolsheviks establish the Comintern to carry out socialist revolutions abroad.

1920

The White armies, hampered by poor communication and coordination, gradually weaken, while the Red Army consolidates its hold on western Russia. In January, the Allies lift their blockade of Russia. In November, the last White army evacuates the Crimea, and the Russian Civil War ends.

1921

The Bolsheviks institute the New Economic Policy, allowing private firms to operate and peasants to sell some of their harvest in the open market. An uprising of sailors at the port of Kronstadt is put down by the Bolsheviks. The government signs the Treaty of Riga with Poland, establishing the frontier at the "Curzon Line" between Russia and Poland.

1922

In March, Lenin appoints Joseph Stalin as general secretary of the Central Committee of the Communist (formerly Bolshevik) Party. In April, the Communist Party declares the founding of the Union of Soviet Socialist Republics (USSR), which includes Russia, Ukraine, Belorussia, and the Transcaucasian Federation. Lenin suffers a stroke, and in December he begins writing his testament, in which he warns fellow Communists that Stalin is not fit to lead the party.

1923

In January, Lenin suffers a second stroke, leaving him unable to speak or to leave his house. Lenin's illness allows Stalin to gradually gain control of the Communist Party. Stalin forms an alliance with Lev Kamenev and Grigory Zinovyev to gradually force their rival Leon Trotsky out of the party leadership.

1924

On January 21, Lenin dies. Lenin's will is read aloud at a meeting of the Central Committee, embarrassing Stalin. Stalin offers to re-sign but is supported by Zinovyev. Stalin is then re-elected as general secretary. In honor of the Bolshevik leader, the city of Petrograd (formerly St. Petersburg) is renamed Leningrad. The constitution of the USSR is ratified, and Great Britain, France, and Italy formally recognize the union.

1925

Rivalries and infighting among the Bolshevik leadership at the Fourteenth Party Congress results in Trotsky's removal as war commissar. Stalin works behind the scenes to rid the Communist Party of his most powerful rivals.

1927

Trotsky attempts to organize public demonstrations against Stalin but fails. Stalin persuades the Central Committee to expel Trotsky from the party.

1928

The New Economic Policy ends, and the Soviet Union adopts its first Five-Year Plan, setting production targets for Soviet industry and agriculture. Stalin orders a program of industrialization and the building of new factories in order to make the Soviet Union self-sufficient in steel and other vital commodities.

1929

Leon Trotsky is deported from the Soviet Union. A crash program to collectivize farms begins, causing violence and famine in the countryside. Private farms are seized and gathered into state-owned collective farms, and the government diverts most grain to the cities.

1933

The United States recognizes the Soviet Union. The Soviet government draws up its second Five-Year Plan.

1934

Sergey Kirov, a high-ranking Communist Party official, is assassinated in Leningrad, an event that will bring about sweeping purges in the Soviet government and military. The Soviet Union joins the League of Nations, an organization founded by the Treaty of Versailles after World War I that was designed to prevent future world wars.

1935
The Stakhanovite campaign begins, encouraging Soviet workers to new feats of tireless work and surplus production. Workers suspected of opposition are accused of "wrecking" and sent to prison or executed as an example.

1936
Trials of Zinovyev, Kamenev, and others posing any challenge to Stalin's authority begin. The NKVD (formerly the Cheka) also begins rounding up military officers.

1938
The third Five-Year Plan takes effect.

1939
The Soviet Union signs a nonaggression pact with Nazi Germany. In September, World War II begins when Adolf Hitler orders the German invasion of Poland. Soviet armies advance from the east, occupying half of Poland. Soviet forces also occupy Latvia, Lithuania, and Estonia.

1940
The Soviet Union annexes the Baltic states of Latvia, Lithuania, and Estonia, as well as Bessarabia on the southwestern frontier. A Mexican named Ramon Mercador, perhaps working on Stalin's orders, murders Leon Trotsky in Mexico City.

1941
On June 22, Germany invades the Soviet Union. Taken by surprise, the Red Army is forced to retreat all along Russia's western front. Stalin takes personal command of the military.

1942
Soviet armies retreat to the outskirts of Moscow and Leningrad. A German army drives on Stalingrad, a city in southern Russia on the Volga River, but is encircled by the Soviets in bitterly cold winter weather.

1943
A German army surrenders after several months of fighting at Stalingrad. In the fall, the Germans are driven out of Kiev, the capital of Ukraine. At the Moscow Conference, the United States, Great Britain, the Soviet Union, and China agree to continue fighting for the unconditional surrender of the Axis powers (Germany and Japan).

1945

At the Yalta Conference in February and March, the Allies agree to the division of Europe after the war, with Britain, France, the United States, and the Soviet Union acquiring zones of influence in occupied Germany. On April 30, Hitler commits suicide in Berlin, the German capital. On May 7, Germany surrenders and the war in Europe ends. Soviet armies occupy Hungary, Poland, Czechoslovakia, Romania, Bulgaria, and the eastern sector of Germany. In August, Japan surrenders, and World War II ends. The Soviet Union occupies eastern Germany and the eastern sector of Berlin.

1948

The Soviet Union blockades Berlin, preventing supplies from moving into the city by land. The blockade is eventually broken by an airlift carried out by Great Britain and the United States.

1949

The Soviet Union successfully tests its first atomic bomb, based largely on the design of an explosive developed by the United States.

1950

The Soviet Union and Communist China sign a treaty of alliance.

1953

Stalin accuses Kremlin doctors of plotting against his life, threatening another widespread purge. On March 5, before the "Doctor's Plot" can take its effect, Stalin dies after suffering a stroke. Georgi Malenkov becomes premier, and Nikita Khrushchev becomes general secretary of the Communist Party.

1954

Khrushchev inaugurates the Virgin Lands program, designed to turn the arid plains of the Central Asian republics into a grain-producing region. The program is opposed by Malenkov but helps the USSR produce good harvests in the fall.

1955

Disgraced by his opposition to the Virgin Lands program, Malenkov resigns as premier and is replaced by Nikolai Bulganin. The Warsaw Pact is founded, establishing a military alliance among Soviet-bloc nations in Europe.

1956

In a "secret speech" to the Twentieth Party Congress, Khrushchev condemns the excesses and brutality of the Stalin era. The era of "destalinization" begins; the Communist Party purges members still showing loyalty to Stalin and his methods. Khrushchev's speech leads to anti-Communist demonstrations in Georgia, Poland, and Hungary. An anti-Communist uprising in Hungary is crushed by an invasion of Soviet military.

1957
Malenkov, Bulganin, and Vyacheslav Molotov vote to remove Khrushchev from his post. But the Central Committee votes in support of Khrushchev, and Malenkov and Molotov resign. On October 4, the Soviet Union launches *Sputnik*, the world's first orbital satellite, and tests its first intercontinental ballistic missile (ICBM).

1958
In March, Khrushchev replaces Bulganin as Soviet premier, giving him the two top positions in the Soviet Union. An English translation of Boris Pasternak's novel *Doctor Zhivago* appears in the United States. Pasternak is awarded the Nobel Prize for literature.

1961
Soviet cosmonaut Yuri Gagarin becomes the first human to fly into space. In October, the Berlin Wall is raised to prevent escape to western (non-Soviet) sectors of Berlin. Khrushchev again denounces Stalin at the Twenty-Second Party Congress.

1962
Aleksandr Solzhenitsyn's novel *One Day in the Life of Ivan Denisovich*, describing life in Soviet prison camps, is published. In October, a crisis over Soviet nuclear missiles in Cuba nearly leads to war between the United States and the Soviet Union.

1963
Food shortages, caused by drought and cool weather, and partially caused by Khrushchev's policy of planting unsuitable corn in Russian soil, force the Soviet Union to begin importing grain. The Soviet Union signs a test ban treaty, banning above-ground tests of nuclear weapons, with Great Britain and the United States.

1964
Angered by Khrushchev's foreign and domestic policies, party leaders oust Khrushchev as general secretary of the Communist Party and replace him with Leonid Brezhnev. Alexei Kosygin becomes premier of the Soviet government. Khrushchev retires.

1967
Joseph Stalin's daughter, Svetlana Aliluyeva, defects to the West.

Brezhnev appoints Yuri Andropov as head of the KGB, the Soviet state police organization.

1968
On August 20, the Soviet military invades Czechoslovakia to put an end to political reforms undertaken by the Czech government. On November 13, Brezhnev justifies the invasion in a speech to the Fifth Congress of the Polish United Workers' Party.

1970
The Soviet Union and the United States sign the Nuclear Nonproliferation Treaty, pledging to stop the spread of arms to nonnuclear nations. Aleksandr Solzhenitsyn wins the Nobel Prize for literature, and will be deported in the next year.

1972
U.S. president Richard Nixon arrives in the Soviet Union for a summit conference with Brezhnev. The first SALT treaty is signed; negotiations begin for SALT II.

1975
Physicist Andrei Sakharov wins the Nobel Prize but is denied permission to leave the Soviet Union to attend the award ceremony. The United States and Soviet Union undertake a joint space mission with the *Apollo* and *Soyuz* spacecraft.

1977
In November, a new Soviet constitution is ratified. A roundup of dissidents occurs.

1979
In June, the Soviet Union signs a second SALT treaty with the United States. In December, the Soviet Union invades Afghanistan to support a Marxist regime.

1980
To protest the invasion of Afghanistan, the United States imposes an embargo on grain exports to the Soviet Union and boycotts the 1980 Moscow Olympics. Physicist Andrei Sakharov is forced to go into exile in the town of Gorky. Popular poet and musician Vladimir Vysotsky dies, and fans gather at a massive funeral observance.

1982
On November 10, Leonid Brezhnev dies. Yuri Andropov is elected general secretary of the Communist Party.

1983

Andropov announces reforms designed to increase production through pay incentives, to punish laziness and drunkenness, and to cut down the size of the party bureaucracy. The United States and Soviet Union clash over the placement of U.S. nuclear missiles in Western Europe. On September 5, a Soviet fighter shoots down a Korean civilian airliner over Sakhalin Island, off the Pacific coast of Siberia. To counter U.S. missiles in Western Europe, the Soviet Union announces plans to deploy nuclear weapons in Eastern Europe.

1984

On February 10, Yuri Andropov dies and is succeeded by Konstantin Chernenko. Chernenko puts a stop to Andropov's reforms, allowing loyal party bureaucrats to keep their jobs.

1985

On March 10, Konstantin Chernenko dies. In March, the Politburo elects Mikhail Gorbachev as the new general secretary of the Communist Party. Gorbachev proposes perestroika, or restructuring of the Soviet economy to permit some private business initiatives and marketplace competition. The policy of glasnost will permit public criticism and open discussion of the Soviet system.

1986

On April 26, a meltdown occurs at the Chernobyl nuclear power station in northern Ukraine. The accident releases radioactivity over the western republics of the Soviet Union as well as northern Europe. Chernobyl brings further support for a reform of the Soviet economy and party bureaucracy. Opposition to Gorbachev's reforms grows among hardliners in the Communist Party. In December, Andrei Sakharov is released from his internal exile in Gorky.

1987

On May 28, a nineteen-year-old German pilot, Mathias Rust, lands a small plane in Moscow's Red Square, humiliating the Soviet military and lending support for Gorbachev's proposed reforms of the Red Army. The Central Committee votes to approve Gorbachev's economic reforms, which set 1991 as the date for the end of central planning. In October, Boris Yeltsin demands radical reforms in a speech to the Central Committee. Previously banned literature begins appearing in Soviet bookshops, including Yevfeny Zamyatin's *We*, Pasternak's *Doctor Zhivago*, and Anna Akhmatova's *Requiem*.

1988

Gorbachev becomes the Soviet president. Soviet forces begin leaving Afghanistan after a long stalemate. Demonstrations against Soviet government occur in the Baltic republics. Armenians and Azerbaijanis clash in the Transcaucasus region. At a party conference, the Communist Party resolves to elect its deputies by secret ballot and establishes a 2,250-member Congress of People's Deputies as the new legislative assembly. The party also establishes an elective presidency, in which future Soviet leaders will be limited to two five-year terms.

1989

Solzhenitsyn's *The Gulag Archipelago* is published for the first time within the Soviet Union. The Soviet military completely withdraws from Afghanistan. In April, Georgians demonstrate for independence in Tbilisi, the Georgian capital. Citizens of the Baltic states as well as Ukraine demand independence from the Soviet Union. In October, war erupts between Armenia and Azerbaijan. In November, the Berlin Wall is destroyed.

1990

Mikhail Gorbachev is awarded the Nobel Peace Prize. In March, Lithuania declares its independence. In June, censorship is ended by decree of the Supreme Soviet, the national legislature of the Soviet Union. On June 12, the Russian Congress of People's Deputies declares its sovereignty from the Soviet government. In September, new legislation establishes freedom of religious worship and association.

1991

In January, the Soviet military puts down demonstrations in the Baltic republics. On June 12, Boris Yeltsin is elected president of Russia. Gorbachev proposes a new union treaty that would grant greater autonomy to the Soviet republics. On August 19, Soviet military leaders declare a coup against the government and place Gorbachev under house arrest. On August 20, Yeltsin rallies crowds in Moscow; the coup falls apart. On August 21, Latvia declares its independence. On August 24, Gorbachev resigns as head of the Communist Party. On December 8, the presidents of Russia, Belarus, and Ukraine sign an agreement to abolish the USSR and establish the Commonwealth of Independent States. On December 25, Gorbachev resigns as president, and the Soviet Union comes to an end.

For Further Research

Books

Svetlana Alliluyeva, *Twenty Letters to a Friend*. New York: Harper & Row, 1967.

Robert Conquest, *Stalin: Breaker of Nations*. New York: Penguin Books, 1991.

———, *V.I. Lenin*. New York: Viking Press, 1972.

Edward Crankshaw, *Putting Up with the Russians: Commentary and Criticism, 1947–84*. New York: Penguin Books, 1985.

Robert V. Daniels, *Red October: The Bolshevik Revolution of 1917*. New York: Charles Scribner's Sons, 1967.

Dusko Doder, *Shadows and Whispers: Power Politics Inside the Kremlin from Brezhnev to Gorbachev*. New York: Random House, 1986.

Sheila Fitzpatrick, *The Russian Revolution*. New York: Oxford University Press, 1994.

Sheila Fitzpatrick, Alexander Rabinowitz and Richard Stites, eds., *Russia in the Era of NEP: Explorations in Soviet Society and Culture*. Bloomington: Indiana University Press, 1991.

James von Geldern and Richard Stites, *Mass Culture in Soviet Russia*. Bloomington: Indiana University Press, 1995.

Gabriel Gorodetsky, *Soviet Foreign Policy 1917–1991: A Retrospective*. London: Frank Cass, 1994.

Mikhail Heller and Aleksandr M. Nekrich, *Utopia in Power: The History of the Soviet Union from 1917 to the Present*. New York: Simon & Schuster, 1992.

Amy Knight, *Who Killed Kirov? The Kremlin's Greatest Mystery*. New York: Hill and Wang, 1999.

W. Bruce Lincoln, *Red Victory: A History of the Russian Civil War*. New York: Simon & Schuster, 1989.

Mary McAuley, *Soviet Politics 1917–1991*. New York: Oxford University Press, 1992.

Roy Medvedev, *Let History Judge: The Origins and Consequences of Stalinism*. New York: Columbia University Press, 1989.

G.D.G. Murrell, *Russia's Transition to Democracy: An Internal Political History, 1989–1996*. Brighton, England: Sussex Academic Press, 1997.

Thomas Naylor, *The Gorbachev Strategy: Opening the Closed Society*. Lexington, MA: Lexington Books, 1988.

Alexander Orlov, *The Secret History of Stalin's Crimes*. New York: Random House, 1953.

David Remnick, *Lenin's Tomb: The Last Days of the Soviet Empire*. New York: Random House, 1993.

Abraham Rothberg, *The Heirs of Stalin: Dissidence and the Soviet Regime, 1953–1970*. Ithaca, NY: Cornell University Press, 1972.

Andrei Sakharov, *Memoirs*. New York: Alfred A. Knopf, 1990.

Aleksandr Solzhenitsyn, *Letter to the Soviet Leaders*. New York: Harper & Row, 1974.

Dimitri Volkogonov, *Stalin: Triumph and Tragedy*. New York: Grove Weidenfeld, 1991.

Periodicals

Frederick Baker, "Stalin: Revolutionary, Dictator, Grandfather," *Independent*, May 28, 2001.

Jonathan J. Bean, "Nikolai Bukharin and the New Economic Policy: A Middle Way?" *Independent Review*, Summer 1997.

Graham Darby, "The October Revolution," *History Review*, September 1997.

Paul Dukes, "A Long View of the Cold War," *History Today*, January 2001.

John Erickson, "Barbarossa June 1941: Who Attacked Whom?" *History Today*, July 2001.

Peter Gatrell, "Lenin's New Economic Policy," *Modern History Review*, September 1993.

Amelia Gentleman, "Forgotten Ghosts of the Gulag," *Observer*, January 14, 2001.

David M. Glantz, "The Red Army at War, 1941–1945: Sources and Interpretations," *Journal of Military History*, July 1998.

Andrew Hannah, "Tsar Vladimir I?" *Modern History Review*, February 2001.

Christopher Hitchens, "The Children of '68." *Vanity Fair,* June 1998.

Adam Hochschild, "Notes from Former Underground: Encounters with Glasnost's Gonzos." *Mother Jones,* May 1989.

Peter Kenez, "The Common Folk in the Revolution," *Russian Review,* January 1998.

Nina Khrushchev, "The Case of Khrushchev's Shoe," *New Statesman,* October 2, 2000.

Sergei Khrushchev, "The Day We Shot Down the U-2," *American Heritage,* September 2000.

Valentina Kolesnikova, "All's Fair in Party Warfare," *Russian Life,* February/March 1999.

Valery Korotich, "The Ukraine Rising," *Foreign Policy,* Winter 1991.

Michael Lynch, "Trotsky: Angel of Enlightenment or Frustrated Dictator?" *History Review,* March 1999.

Stephen G. Rabe, "After the Missiles of October: John F. Kennedy and Cuba, November 1962 to November 1963," *Presidential Studies Quarterly,* December 2000.

Roger R. Reese, "Red Army Opposition to Forced Collectivization, 1929–1930: The Army Wavers," *Slavic Review,* Spring 1996.

Dmitri Shlapentokh, "Reconsidering Lenin," *World and I,* March 2001.

Vladimir Shlapentokh, "A Normal System? False and True Explanations for the Collapse of the U.S.S.R.," *Times* literary supplement, December 15, 2000.

Chris Ward, "The Road to Terror: Stalin and the Self-Destruction of the Bolsheviks, 1932–1939," *American Historical Review,* February 2001.

Albert L. Weeks, "Sixty Years After the Nazi-Soviet Pact," *Modern Age,* Summer 1999.

Index